Henry Blackburn

Artistic Travel in Normandy, Brittany, the Pyrenees, Spain and Algeria

Henry Blackburn

Artistic Travel in Normandy, Brittany, the Pyrenees, Spain and Algeria

ISBN/EAN: 9783337205171

Printed in Europe, USA, Canada, Australia, Japan

Cover: Foto ©Andreas Hilbeck / pixelio.de

More available books at **www.hansebooks.com**

Artistic Travel

A THOUSAND MILES TOWARDS THE SUN

JOAN OF ARC'S HOUSE AT ROUEN—BY THE LATE SAMUEL PROUT.

Frontispiece.

Artistic Travel

IN

NORMANDY, BRITTANY, THE PYRENEES, SPAIN AND ALGERIA.

BY

HENRY BLACKBURN,

EDITOR OF "ACADEMY NOTES," AUTHOR OF "MEMOIR OF RANDOLPH CALDECOTT," "ART IN THE MOUNTAINS," ETC.

WITH

ONE HUNDRED AND THIRTY ILLUSTRATIONS.

LONDON:
SAMPSON LOW, MARSTON AND COMPANY,
LIMITED,
St. Dunstan's House,
FETTER LANE, FLEET STREET, E.C.
1892.

All rights reserved.

LONDON:
PRINTED BY WILLIAM CLOWES AND SONS, Limited,
STAMFORD STREET AND CHARING CROSS.

PREFACE.

TRAVELLING in NORMANDY, BRITTANY, THE PYRENEES, SPAIN and ALGERIA, forms a splendid journey towards the Sun. It may be accomplished in one long autumn, or the visits may be extended (as the writer has extended them) over more than twenty years.

There are so many scenes and objects of interest on these journeys, which travellers in "trains de luxe" inevitably miss, that it has been thought desirable to collect in one volume a selection of notes made in various years; the point of view being always that of the artist in search of the picturesque.

The majority of these pages have already appeared in print, but some of the aspects of places and incidents of travel are so changed that the descriptions will have fresh interest in 1892.

There are some things which have not changed. The massive timbers of the houses in Normandy are still sound and strong, and the menhirs and dolmens of Brittany "rear their desolate heads" as of old. There are still bears in the Pyrenees and bull-fights in Spain, and the Kabyles are yet unconquered in Algeria.

The close juxtaposition in one volume of Normandy, Brittany and the Pyrenees—with illustrations by Sydney Hall, Randolph Caldecott, and Gustave Doré—present in curious contrast the characteristics of three provinces of France.

In the latter portion of the book we descend the southern side of the Pyrenees, and another contrast presents itself. The white caps and bright faces of the peasantry have disappeared; the black mantilla of Spain and the white haïk of North Africa, veil the faces (and, typically, the independence) of the women, as compared with their northern sisters who are the strength of France. But in Spain and Algeria the painter is more at home, revelling in colour and light.

The ILLUSTRATIONS, which to many readers will have a personal charm, are the result of an amount of labour and enthusiasm on the part of all concerned, which is becoming rarer every day. Here author, artists, and engravers have worked in complete *rapport*, without the aid of kodaks, or of any of the mechanical processes of illustration which, from an artistic point of view, disfigure so many modern books of travel.

H. B.

LONDON, *October*, 1892.

CONTENTS.

                                                                       PAGES

I. NORMANDY—

Pont Audemer — Lisieux — Caen — Granville — Avranches — The Valley of the Seine—The Watering Places of Normandy   1-60

II. BRITTANY—

The Western Wing—St. Malo—The Rance—Dinan—Guingamp — Lannion — Brest — Plougastel — Quimper—Douarnenéz—Quimperlé—St. Anne d'Auray—Vannes   61-128

III. THE PYRENEES—

Pau—Eaux Chaudes—Eaux Bonnes—Cauterets—Luz—Barèges—Bagnères—A Storm—Luchon—Port de Venasque   129-200

IV. SPAIN—

Burgos—Madrid—Two Bull Fights—Madrid to Cordova—Seville—Granada—The Alhambra   201-256

V. ALGERIA—

Algiers—Our Moorish Home—The Break of day—Arabs and Moors—Waiting—A clothes auction—The Arab quarter—Our Models—The Bouzareah—The Atlas Mountains—The Fort Napoleon—Conclusion   257-320

LIST OF ILLUSTRATIONS.

I. NORMANDY—

	PAGE
Joan of Arc's house at Rouen. (*S. Prout*)	*Frontispiece*
Map of Normandy	1
French dragoon	4
Old houses, Pont Audemer	8
Old wood-carving, Lisieux	16
A corner in Lisieux	19
Church of St. Pierre, Caen	*face* 21
Old woman of Caen	26
A Toiler of the Sea. (*Sydney P. Hall*)	35
Mont St. Michel from Avranches. (*H. B.*)	37
Tower at Vire. (*H.B.*)	40
Ancient Cross. (*H. B.*)	42
The Valley of the Seine. (*A. E. Browne*)	45
Market women, Lower Normandy. (*Sydney P. Hall*)	*face* 50
Modern seaside houses. (*H. B.*)	57

II. BRITTANY. (*By Randolph Caldecott.*)

Breton Farmer and his cattle	61
Map, Bay of St. Malo	64
The Rance	68
Under the ramparts, Dinan	72
A little mendicant	75
Achille and his horse	76
Cattle fair in Brittany	*face* 78
Old farm house	79
A licensed beggar	81
Sunday morning	*face* 82
The Ossuary at Guingamp	84
A quiet corner	*face* 87
"On loue et on échange de petits enfants"	89
Towers of St. Pol de Leon	*face* 92
Map, Bay of Brest	93
Going to a Pardon	*face* 95
The Gavotte	97

LIST OF ILLUSTRATIONS.

	PAGE
The Gavotte	99
Towers of Quimper	100
Cavaliers and Roundhead . . . *face*	102
Harvesting	104
Sardine fishing-boats, Douarnenéz . . . *face*	105
At the Hotel du Commerce, Douarnenéz	107
Near Pont Aven, Quimperlé	109
Augustine	110
Wayside Cross	113
At the Pardon, St. Anne d'Auray	115
,, ,,	117
,, ,,	119
,, ,,	120
,, ,,	122
Three hot men of Vannes	125
On the road	128

III. THE PYRENEES. (*By Gustave Doré.*)

The Pyrenees . . . *face*	129
"Les Landes" near Pau	129
Mountain tops	130
Pau . . . *face*	131
Chateau at Pau	132
"A wall of foliage"	133
Arms of Pau	135
Rustic dance	136
Environs of Eaux Chaudes . . . *face*	136
Near Gabas	138
Mountains near Eaux Bonnes	139
A Mountain village	141
The Pic de Ger	144
A mountaineer	145
Taking the waters	147
Cascade du Valentin	149
Waterfall	151
A mountaineer	152
Cauterets . . . *face*	153
Promenade horizontale	153
En route	154
Lac de Gaube	157
Performing bear	158
Cat (finial)	159
Fortified church, Luz	160
Ruin, near Luz . . . *face*	160
At Luz	161
Summer visitors	162
Winter visitors	163
"Une ascension"	165

	PAGE
Trees above Bagnères	169
Storm	171
A mountain storm . . . face	173
The battered pines	174
A mountain wreck	175
Sunset after the storm	177
Luchon	179
Environs of Luchon . . . face	180
The Woods near Luchon . . . face	183
Lac d'Oo . . . face	185
A visitor	188
A mountaineer	191
Path to Super-Bagneres	193
Route to the Port de Venasque	195
,, ,, ,,	196
The Maladetta . . . face	197
Port de Venasque from the South (H. B.)	198
,, from the North	199

IV. SPAIN—

A Balcony. (*John Phillip*)	201
Burgos Cathedral . . . face	207
Vespers. (*E. Lundgren*) . . . face	208
A sketch. (*John Phillip*) . . . face	214
"Loteria Nacionale." (*John Phillip*) . . . face	218
Dominguez the "Espada" . . . face	228
A Portrait. (*Walter Severn*)	233
"Caballeros" at Jaen, near Cordova. (*E. Lundgren*) . face	237
The Court of Oranges	239
La Giralda, Seville . . . face	243
Alhambra Towers by moonlight	247
The Alhambra, Granada . . . face	248
Patio de la Mesquita	253

V. ALGERIA—

View over the Bay, Algiers	257
The Great Mosque, Algiers . . . face	261
A Moorish home. (*H. B.*) . . . face	274
Camels	287
Our Model	291
A Portrait . . . face	295
A Ship of the Desert. (*H. B.*)	296
A palm stem	301
An aloe hedge . . . face	302
Storm at the Bouzareah. (*Arthur Severn*)	306
The Mountains of Kabylia. (*H. B.*)	313
A Warrior at Prayers	316
Zouave (finial)	320

ARTISTIC TRAVEL.

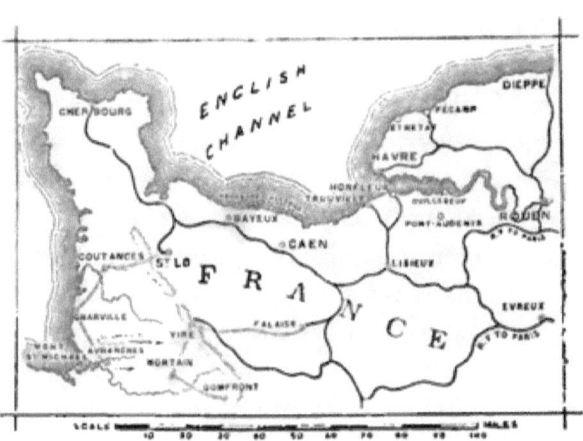

NORMANDY.

Pont Audemer.

About one hundred and fifty miles in a direct line south from London, sleeps the little town of Pont Audemer, with its quaint old gables, its tottering houses, its Gothic "bits," its projecting windows, carved oak galleries and streets of time-worn buildings,—centuries old. Old dwellings, old customs, old caps, old tanneries, set in a landscape of bright green hills.

"Old as the hills," and almost as unchanged in aspect

are the ways of the people of Pont Audemer, who dress and tan hides, and make merry as their fathers did before them. For several centuries they have devoted themselves to commerce and the arts of peace, and in the enthusiasm of their business have desecrated one or two churches into tanneries. But they are a conservative and primitive people, loving to do as their ancestors did, and to dwell where they dwelt; they build their houses to last for several generations, and take pride and interest in the "family mansion," a thing unknown and almost impossible in the middle classes of most communities.

Pont Audemer was once warlike; it had its castle in feudal times (destroyed in the 14th century), and the legend exists that cannon was here first used in warfare. It has its history of wars in the time of the Norman dukes, but its aspect is now quiet and peaceful, and its people appear happy and contented; the little river Rille winds about it, and spreads its streamlets like branches through the streets, and sparkles in the evening light. Like Venice, it has its "silent highways"; like Venice, also, on a small and humble scale, it has its old façades and lintels drooping to the water's edge; like Venice, too, it has its odours here and there—odours not always proceeding from the tanneries.

There are few monuments or churches to examine, and when we have seen the stained-glass windows in the fine old church of St. Ouen, and walked by the banks of the Rille to the ruins of a castle of the 12th century at Montfort, we shall have seen the "chief objects of interest" in what Murray laconically describes as "a prettily situated town of 6,000 inhabitants, famed for its tanneries." In the chief place of the *arrondissement*, and in a rapidly increasing town, with a reputation for healthiness and cheapness of living, and with a railway from Paris, we must naturally look for changes and modern ways; but Pont Audemer is still essentially old.

If we take up our quarters at the old-fashioned inn called the *Pot d'Étain*, we shall find much to remind us of the 15th century. If we take a walk by the beautiful banks of the Rille on a summer's evening, or in the fields where the peasants are at work, we shall find the aspect curiously English, and in the intonation of the voices the resemblance is sometimes startling; we seem hardly amongst foreigners—both in features and in voice there is a strong family likeness. There is a close tie of blood relationship, no doubt, of ancient habits and natural tastes; but, in spite of railways and steamboats, the two peoples know very little of each other.

That young girl with the plain white cap fitting close to her hair, who tends the flocks on the hillside, and puts all her power and energy into the little matter of knitting a stocking, is a Norman maiden—a lineal descendant, it may be, of some ancient house, whose arms we may find in our own heraldic albums. She is of noble birth, and has the advantage over her coroneted cousins in being permitted to wear a white cap out of doors, and a short costume of simple stuff; in the fact of her limbs being braced by a life spent in the open air, and her head not being plagued with the proprieties of cities. She is pretty; but, what is of more importance, she knows how to cook, and she has a little store of money in the bank. She has been taught enough for her station, and has few wishes beyond it; and some day she will marry Jean, and happy will be Jean if he proves sober and true.

The stalwart warrior whom we have sketched overleaf sunning himself outside his barrack door, having just clapped his helmet on the head of a little boy in a patched blouse and sabots, is surely a near relation to our guardsman; he is certainly brave, he is full of fun and intelligence, he very seldom takes more wine than is good for him, and a game at dominoes delights his soul.

But it is in the market-place of Pont Audemer that we shall obtain the best idea of the place and of the people. On market mornings and on fête days, when the *Place* is crowded with old and young,—when all the old caps of every variety of shape, from the "helmet" to the *bonnet rouge*, and all the old brown coats with short tails, are collected together,—we have a picture the like of which we may have seen in paintings, but seldom realize in life. Of the tumult of voices on these busy mornings, of the harsh, discordant sounds that sometimes fill the air, we must not say much, remembering their continual likeness to our own; but, viewed picturesquely, it is a sight not to be forgotten.

Here the artist will find plenty of congenial occupation,

and opportunities (so difficult to meet with in these days) of sketching both architecture and people of a picturesque type—groups in the market-place, groups down by the river fishing under the trees, groups at windows of old hostelries and seated at inn doors; horses in clumsy wooden harness; calves and pigs, goats and sheep; women at fruit-stalls, under tents and coloured umbrellas; piles upon piles of baskets, a wealth of green things, and a bright fringe of fruit and flowers, arranged with all the fanciful grace of *les dames des Halles*, in Paris.

All this and much more the artist finds to his hand; and what does the architect discover? First of all, that if he had only come here before, he might have saved himself some thought and trouble, for he would have found such suggestions for ornament in wood carving, for panels, doorways, and the like, of so good a pattern, and so old, that they are new to the world of to-day; he would have found houses built out over the rivers, looking like pieces of old furniture, ranged side by side—rich in colour and wonderfully preserved, with their wooden gables, carved in oak of the 15th century, supported by massive timbers, sound and strong, of even older date. He would see many of these houses with windows full of flowers, and creepers twining round the old eaves; and long drying-poles stretched out horizontally, with gay-coloured clothes upon them, flapping in the wind, and contrasting vividly with the dark buildings.

But he would also find some houses on the verge of ruin. If he explored far enough in the dark, narrow streets, where the rivers flow under the windows of empty dwellings, he might see them tottering, and threatening downfall upon each other—leaning over and casting shadows, black and mysterious, upon the water—no line perpendicular, no line horizontal, the very beau-ideal of picturesque decay. In short, he would find Pont Audemer (and the neighbouring town of Lisieux) treasure-houses of old mysterious "bits," suggestive of simple domestic usage in one building and princely grandeur in another—strength and simplicity, grace and beauty of design—all speaking to him of a past age with the eloquence of history.

Let us look well at these old buildings, many of them reared and dwelt in by men of humble birth and moderate means—(men who lived happily and died easily without amassing a fortune); let us, if we can, without too much envy, think for a moment of the circumstances under which these houses were built. To us, to many of us, who pay dearly for the privilege of living between four square walls—so slight and thin sometimes that our neighbours are separated from us by sight, but scarcely by sound—walls that we hire for shelter, from necessity, and leave generally without reluctance, partitions that we are prone to cover with paper in the likeness of oak and marble to hide their meanness—these curious, odd-shaped interiors, with massive walls and solid oak timbers, should be especially attractive. How few modern rooms, for instance, have such niches in them, such seats in windows and snug corners, that of all things make a house comfortable! Some of these rooms are twenty feet high, and are lighted from windows of the oddest shapes and in surprising places. What more charming than this variety, to the eye jaded with monotony; what more suggestive than the apparently accidental application of Gothic architecture to the wants and requirements of the age?

We will not venture to say that these old buildings are altogether admirable from an architect's point of view, but to us they are delightful, because they were designed and inhabited by people who had time to be quaint, and could not help being picturesque. If they are wanting (as many are wanting) in the appliances and fittings which modern habits have rendered necessary, it was assuredly no fault of the 15th-century architect. They display, both in design and construction, the elements of common-sense in meeting the requirements of their own day, which is, as has been well remarked, "the one thing wanting to give life to modern architecture"; and they have a character and individuality about them which renders almost every building unique. Like furniture of rare design, they bear the direct impress of their maker. They were built in an age of comparative leisure, when men gave their hearts to the meanest, as well as to the mightiest, works of their hands; in a simple, industrious age when love, hope, and a worthy emulation moved them, as it does not seem to move men now; in an age when an approving notice in the columns of a newspaper was not a high aspiration.

But in nothing is the attraction greater, to us who are accustomed to the monotonous perspective of modern streets, than the irregularity of the *exteriors*, arising from their independent method of construction; for, by varying the depth and height and pattern of each façade, the builders obtained to almost every house what architects term the "return" to their cornices and mouldings, *i.e.* the corner-finish and completeness to the most important projecting lines. And yet these houses are built with relation to each other; they generally harmonize, and set off, and uphold each other, just as forest-trees form themselves naturally into groups for support and protection.

All this we may see at a glance, looking down the varied perspective of these streets of clustering dwellings; and the closer we examine them the more we find to interest, if not to admire. If we gain little in architectural knowledge, we at least gain pleasure; we learn *the value*

OLD HOUSES—PONT AUDEMER.

of variety in its simplest forms, and notice how easy it would be to relieve the monotony of modern streets; we realise the artistic value of high-pitched roofs, of contrasts in colour,—if it be only of dark beams against plaster,—and of *meaning* in every line of construction.

These and many more such sheaves we gather from our Norman harvest, but we must haste and bind them, for the winds of time are scattering fast. Pont Audemer is being modernized, and many an interesting old building is doomed to destruction; whilst cotton-mills and steam-engines, and little white villas amongst the trees, black coats and Parisian bonnets, all tend to blot out the memories of mediæval days. Let us make the most of the place whilst there is time,—and let us, before we pass on to Lisieux, add one picture of Pont Audemer in the early morning,—a picture which every year will seem less real.

Early Morning at Pont Audemer.

That there is "nothing new under the sun" may perhaps be true of its rising; nevertheless, a new sensation awaits most of us, if we choose to see it under various phases. The early morning at Pont Audemer is the same early morning that breaks upon the unconscious inhabitants of a great city; but the conditions are more delightful, and very much more picturesque; and we may be excused for presenting the picture on the ground that it treats of certain hours out of the twenty-four of which most of us know nothing, and in which (such are the exigencies of modern civilization) most of us do nothing.

A storm passed over the town one night in August, which shook the great rafters of the old houses, and made the timbers strain; the water flowed from them as from the sides of a ship,—one minute they were illuminated, the next they were in blackest gloom. In two or three hours it has all passed away, and as we go out into the silent town, and cross the street where it forms a bridge over the Rille (from which the sketch on p. 8, is taken), a faint gleam of light appears upon the water, and upon the wet beams of one or two projecting gables. The darkness and the silence are soon to be disturbed—one or two birds fly out from the black eaves, a rat crosses the street, some distant chimes come upon the wind, and a faint clatter of sabots on the wet stones; the town-clock strikes half-past four, and the watchman puts out his lantern, and goes to sleep.

The morning is breaking on Pont Audemer, and it is the time for surprises—for the sudden appearance of a gable-end, which just now was shadow; for the more gradual, but not less curious formation of a street in what seemed to be space; for the sudden creation of windows in dead walls; for the turning of fantastic shadows into palpable carts, baskets, piles of wood, and the like; and for the discovery of a number of coiled-up dogs (and one or two coiled-up men) who had weathered the night in sheltered places.

But the grey light is turning fast to gold, warmer tints begin to prevail, the streets leading eastward are gleaming, and the hills are glistening in their bright, fresh green. The sweet morning air welcomes us as we leave the streets and its five thousand sleepers, and pass over another bridge and out by the banks of the Rille, where the fish are stirring in the swollen stream, and the lilies are dancing on the water. The wind blows freshly through the trees, and scatters the raindrops thickly; the clouds, the last remnant of the night's storm, career through a pale blue space, the birds are everywhere on the wing, cattle make their appearance in the landscape, and peasants are already to be seen on the roads leading to the town. Suddenly—with gleams of gold, with a rushing chorus of insect life, and a thousand voices in the long grass on the river's bank—the day begins.

It is market-morning, and we go a little way up the hill to watch the arrivals—a hill from which there is a view over town and valley, the beauty of which it would be difficult to picture in words. Listen! for there is a cavalcade coming down the hill; we can see it at intervals through the trees, and hear men's voices, the laughter of women, the bleating of calves, and the crushing sound of wheels upon the road. It is a peaceful army, though the names of its leaders (if we heard them) might stir up warlike memories; there are Howards and Percys amongst them, but there is no clash of arms, they come of a brave lineage, their ancestors fought well under the walls of Pont Audemer, but they have laid down their arms for centuries—their end is commerce and peace.

Let us stand aside under the lime-trees, and see them pass. But they are making a halt, their horses go straight to the water-trough, and the whole cavalcade comes to a stand in the road; the old women in the carts (wearing starched caps a foot high), with baskets of eggs, butter, cheeses, and piles of merchandise, sit patiently until the time comes to start again; and the drivers, in blouses and wooden sabots, lounge about and smoke, or sit down to rest. The young women who accompany the expedition, and who will soon take their places in the market, now set to work systematically to perform their toilets, commencing by washing their feet in a stream, hard by, and putting on the shoes and stockings which they had carried in a basket during their wet march; then more ablutions, with much fun, and laughter, and tying up of tresses, and producing from baskets the wonderful caps which have been sketched so often—*soufflés* of most fantastic shape and startling dimensions. This is the crowning work; the picture is now complete. Bright, fresh morning faces glowing under white caps; neat gray or dark blue stuff dresses, with white bodices or coloured handkerchiefs; dark grey woollen stockings, shoes with buckles, and perhaps a silver cross, a rosary, or a flower. And we must not forget the younger men (with coats, not blouses), who plume themselves in a rough way, and wear felt hats with wonderful brims; nor, above all, a peep through the trees far away down the valley, at the gables and turrets of Pont Audemer, glistening through a cloud of haze. This is all; a word more would spoil the picture: like one of Edouard Frère's paintings, the charm and pathos of the scene lie in its simplicity and harmony with Nature.

If we choose to stay until the day advances, we may see more market-people come crowding in, and white caps will crop up in the distance through the trees, till the green meadows blossom with them and sparkle like a lawn of daisies; we may hear the ringing laughter of the girls to whom market-day seems an occasion of great rejoicing, and be somewhat distracted with the steady droning patois of the old women; but we come to see rather than to hear, and, returning to the town, take our station at the corner of the market-place, to sketch a group of Norman maidens who are alone worth coming out to see.

LISIEUX.

"O the pleasant days, when men built houses after their own minds, and wrote their own devices on the walls, and none laughed at them; when little wooden knights and saints peeped out from the angles of gable-ended houses, and every street displayed a store of imaginative wealth."—*La Belle France.*

WE now pass on to the neighbouring town of LISIEUX, which is even more interesting than Pont Audemer in examples of domestic architecture of the Middle Ages—resisting with difficulty a passing visit to Pont l'Évêque, another quaint old town a few miles distant. "Who does not know Pont l'Évêque," asks an enthusiastic Frenchman,—"that clean little smiling town, seated in the midst of adorable scenery, with its little black, white, rose-colour, and blue houses? One sighs, and says, 'It would be good to live here,' and then one passes on and goes to amuse oneself"—at Trouville-sur-mer!

If we approach Lisieux by the road from Pont Audemer (a distance of about twenty-six miles), we shall get a better impression of the town than if riding upon the whirlwind of an express-train, the approach to Lisieux from the railway station being singularly uninteresting. By road we pass through a prettily wooded country, studded with villas and comfortable-looking houses, surrounded by pleasant fruit and flower gardens, the modern abodes of wealthy manufacturers from neighbouring towns, and of a few English families. We ought to come quietly through the suburbs of Lisieux, if only to see how its 13,000 inhabitants are busied in their woollen and cloth factories; how they have turned the old timber-framed houses of feudal times into warehouses, how the banners and signs of chivalry are desecrated into trade-marks, and how its inhabitants are devoting themselves heart and soul to the arts of peace. We should then approach the town by picturesque wooden bridges over the rivers which have brought the town its prosperity, and see some isolated examples of carved wood-work in the suburbs, in houses surrounded by gardens, which would have been missed by any other road.

The churches at Lisieux are scarcely as remarkable as its domestic architecture ; but we must not neglect to examine the pointed Gothic of the 13th century in the cathedral of St. Pierre. The door of the south transept, and one of the doors under the western towers (the one on the right hand), is very beautiful, and quite mauresque in the delicacy of its design. The interior is of fine proportions, but it is disfigured with a coat of yellow paint, whilst common wooden seats (of church-warden pattern) and wainscoting have been built up against its pillars, the stone-work having been cut away to accommodate the painted wood ! There are some good memorial windows ; one of Henry II. being married to Eleanor (1152), and another of Thomas à Becket visiting Lisieux when exiled in 1169.

The church of St. Jacques with its fine stained-glass, the interior of which is much plainer than St. Pierre, will not detain us long ; it is rather to such streets as the celebrated *Rue aux Fèvres* that we are attracted by the decoration of the houses, and their curious construction. There is one wooden house in this street, the entire front of which is covered with grotesquely carved figures, intricate patterns, and graceful pillars. The exterior wood-work is blackened with age, and the whole building threatens to fall upon its present tenant,—the keeper of a café. The beams which support the roof inside are also richly decorated.

To give the reader any idea of the variety of the wooden houses at Lisieux would require a series of drawings or photographs: we can do little more in these pages than point out these charming corners of the world where something is still left of the work of the Middle Ages.

The general character of the houses is better than at Pont Audemer, and the style is altogether more varied. Stone as well as wood is used in their construction, and the rooms are more commodious and more elaborately decorated. But the exterior carving and the curious signs engraved on the time-stained wood are the most distinctive features. Here we may notice, in odd corners, names and legends carved on the panels, harmonizing curiously with the decoration: just as the names of the owners (in German characters) are carved on Swiss chalets; and the words "God is great," and the like, form appropriate ornaments (in Arabic) over the door of a mosque. Here upon heraldic shields, or amidst groups of clustering leaves, we may trace the names of the founders, often the architects, of the houses in which several generations have lived and died.

The strange familiarity of some of these crests and devices (lions, tigers, dragons, griffins, and other emblems of ferocity), the English character of many of the names, and the Latin mottoes, identical with some in common use in England, may give us a confused and not very dignified idea respecting their almost universal use by the middle classes in England. M. Taine, the well-known French writer, remarks that "c'est loin du monde que nous pouvons jugez sainement des illusions dont ils nous environnent," and perhaps it is from Lisieux that we may best see ourselves wearing "coats of arms."

It is considered by many an unmeaning and unjust phrase to call the 19th century "an age of shams," but it seems appropriate enough when we read in newspapers of "arms found" and "crests designed"; and when we consider the extent of the practice of assuming them, we cannot think much of the fashion.

It was assuredly a good time when men's lives and actions were handed down, so to speak, from father to son, and the poor man had his *locum tenens* as well as the rich;

and how he loved his dwelling, how he decked it with ornament according to his taste or his means, how he watched over it and preserved it from decay, how, in short, his pride was in his own hearth and home,—these old buildings tell us. The influence of all this on character, its tendency to contentment and self-respect, are subjects suggestive enough, but on which we must not dwell. It flourished during the 13th and 14th centuries, and it declined when men commenced crowding into cities, and were no longer content to do without what they could not produce. Without entering into a genealogical discussion, we have plenty of evidence that after the Conquest the arms of the Normans were spread over England ; but not in any measure to the extent to which they are used amongst us. In these days nearly every one has a "crest" or a "coat of arms." Such things did not, and could not exist in mediæval times, in the days when every one had his place, from the noble to the vassal, when every man's name was known, and his title to property, if he had any, clearly defined. A "title" in those days meant a title to land, and an acceptance of its responsibilities. How many "titled" people in these days possess the one or accept the other? It would seem reserved for the 19th century to create a state of society when the question "Who is he?" has to be perpetually asked and not always easily answered.[1]

Let us stay quietly at Lisieux, if we have time, and *see* the place, for we shall find nothing in all Normandy to exceed it in interest; and the way to see it best, and to remember it, is, undoubtedly, to *sketch*. Let us make out all these curious "bits," these signs and emblems in wood and stone—twigs and moss, and birds with delicate wings, a spray of leaves, the serene head of a Madonna, the rampant heraldic griffin ; let us copy, if we can, their colour and marks of age. We may sketch them, and we may dwell upon them, here, with the enthusiasm of an artist who returns to his favourite picture again and again ; for we have seen the sun scorching the panels and burning the gilded shields, and have seen snow-flakes fall

---

[1] The contrast between the present and former states of society might be typified by the general substitution of the screw for the nail in building ; both answering the purpose of the modern builder, but the former preferred, because *removable* at pleasure. It is a restless age, in which advertisements of " FAMILIES REMOVED " are pasted on the walls of a man's house without appearing to excite his indignation.

upon these sculptured eaves, silently, softly, thickly—like the dust upon the bronze figures of Ghiberti's gates at Florence—so thickly fall, so soon disperse, leaving dark outlines sharp and clear against the sky; the wood almost as indestructible as the bronze. The historian is nowhere so eloquent as when he points to such examples as these.

It is evident enough that in those old times, when men were very ignorant, easily led, impulsive (childlike we might almost call them), everything they undertook like the building of a house was a serious matter, a labour of love, and the work of many years; to be an architect and a builder was the aspiration of boyhood, the natural growth of artistic instinct, guided by so much right as they could glean from their elders. With few books or rules, they worked out their designs for themselves, irrespective, it would seem, of time or cost. And why should they consider either the one or the other, when time was of no "marketable" value, when the buildings were to last for ages, and when there were no such things as builders' estimates? Like the Moors in Spain, they did much as they pleased, and, like them also, they had a great advantage over architects of our own day—they had little to *unlearn*. They knew their materials, and had not to endeavour, after a laborious and expensive education in one school, to modify and alter their method of treatment to meet the exigencies of another. They were not cramped for space, nor for money; they were not tied for time; and they had not to fight against, and make compromises with, the two great enemies of modern architects—Economy and Iron.

At Lisieux, as at Pont Audemer, we cannot help being struck with the extreme simplicity of the method of building, and with the *possibilities* of Gothic for domestic purposes. We see it here, in its pure and natural development, as opposed to the rather unnatural adoption of mediæval art in England, in the latter half of the 19th century.

The quiet contemplation of the old buildings in such towns as Pont Audemer, Lisieux, and Bayeux must, we should think, convince the most enthusiastic admirers of the archaic school that the mere isolated reproduction of such houses in the midst of modern streets is of little use, and is, in fact, beginning at the wrong end. It might occur to them, when examining the details of these buildings, and picturing to themselves the lives of the inhabitants in the 13th or 14th century, that the forcing system is a mistake; that art never flourished as an exotic and assuredly never will; that, before we live again in mediæval houses, and realize the true meaning of what is " Gothic," and appropriate, in architecture, we

must begin at the beginning, our lives must be simpler, our costumes more graceful and appropriate, and the education of our children more in harmony with a true feeling for art.

CAEN.

"Large, strong, full of draperies, and all sorts of merchandise; rich citizens, noble dames, damsels, and fine churches."

THE ancient city of Caen, which was thus described by Froissart in the middle of the 14th century (when the English sacked the town and carried away its riches), might be described in the 19th in almost the same words; when a goodly company of English people have again taken possession of it—for its cheapness.

The chief town of the department of Calvados, with a population numbering about 50,000—the centre of the commerce of lower Normandy, and of the district for the production of black lace—Caen has a busy and thriving aspect. The river Orne, on which it is built, is laden with produce; with corn, wine, oil, and cider; with timber, and with ship-loads of the celebrated Caen stone. On every side are the signs of productiveness and plenty, and consequent cheapness of many of the necessaries of life. Calvados, like the rest of lower Normandy, has earned for itself the name of the "food-producing land" of France, from whence both London and Paris, and all great centres, are supplied. The variety and cheapness of manufactures testify to the industry and enterprise of the people; there is probably no city in Normandy where purchases of clothing, hardware, &c., can be more advantageously made.

There is commercial activity at Caen, and little sympathy with idlers. If we take up a position in the *Place Royale*, adorned with a statue of Louis XIV., or, better, in the *Place St. Pierre* near the church-tower, we shall see a mixed and industrious population; and hear several dif-

CHURCH OF ST. PIERRE, CAEN.

ferent accents of Norman patois. We shall also see a number of modern-looking shops, and warehouses filled with Paris goods, and even find smooth pavements to walk upon.

We are treading in the "footsteps of the Conqueror" at Caen, but its busy inhabitants have little time for historic memories; they will jostle us in the market-place, and in the principal streets they will be seen rushing about as if "on change," or hurrying "to catch the train for Paris," like the rest of the world. A few only have eyes of love and admiration for the noble spire of the church of St. Pierre, which rises above the old houses and the market-place with a grand effect. "St. Pierre, St. Pierre," are the first and last words we heard of Caen: the first time, when, approaching it one summer's morning from Dives, by the banks of the Orne, the driver of our calèche pointed to its summit (with the pride of a Savoy peasant, showing the traveller the highest peak of Monte Rosa), and the last, when Caen was *en fête*, and "all the world" flocked to hear a great preacher from Paris, and the best singers in Calvados.

Built in the 13th and 14th centuries, in the best period of Gothic art in Normandy, its beautiful proportions and grace of line (especially when seen from the north side) have been the admiration of ages of architects, and the occasion of many a special pilgrimage in our own day. Pugin has sketched its western façade and its "lancet windows"; and Prout has given us drawings of the spire, "*percée au jour*,"—perforated with such accuracy at different points, that, as we approach the tower, there are always one or more openings in view; as one star disappears, another shines out, as in many cathedrals in Italy and Spain. In the interior, the nave is chiefly remarkable for its fine proportions, but the choir is richly ornamented in the style of the renaissance. The church of St. Pierre has been restored at different periods, but, as usual in France, the interior has been coloured or whitewashed, so that it is difficult to detect old work from new. The sculptured pendants and the decorations of the aisles will attract us by their boldness and originality, and the curious legends in stone on the capitals of the pillars, of "Alexander and his Mistress," of "Launcelot crossing the Sea on his Sword," and of "St. Paul being lowered in a Basket," may take away attention a little too much from the carving in the chapels; but when we have examined them all, we shall probably remember St. Pierre best as Prout and Pugin have shown it to us, and care for it most (as do the inhabitants of Caen) for its beautiful exterior.[1]

The most interesting and characteristic buildings in Caen, its historical monuments, in fact, are the two royal abbeys of William the Conqueror—*St. Étienne*, called the "Abbaye aux Hommes," and *la Ste. Trinité*, the "Abbaye aux Dames,"—both founded and built in the 11th century; the first (containing the tomb of the Conqueror) with two plain, massive towers, with spires; and an interior remarkable for its strength and solidity—"a perfect example of Norman Romanesque"; adorned, it must be added, with twenty-four 19th-century chandeliers with glass lustres suspended by cords from the roof, and with gas brackets of a cheap modern pattern. The massive grandeur, and the "newness," if we may use the word, of the interior of St. Etienne, are its most remarkable features; the plain marble slab in the chancel, marking the spot where William the Conqueror was buried and disinterred (with three mats placed in front of it for prayer), is shown with much ceremony by the custodian of the place.

[1] It is remarkable that with all their care for this building, the authorities permit apple-stalls and wooden sheds to be built up against the tower.

The Abbaye aux Dames is built on high ground at the opposite side of the town, and is surrounded by conventual buildings of modern date. It resembles the Abbaye aux Hommes in point of style, but the carving is more elaborate, and the transepts are much grander in design; the beautiful key-pattern borders, and the grotesque carving on the capitals of some of the pillars, strike the eye at once; but what is most remarkable is the extraordinary care with which the building has been restored, and the whole interior so scraped and chiselled afresh that it has the appearance of a building of to-day. The eastern end and the chancel are partitioned off for the use of the nuns attached to the Hôtel Dieu; the sister who conducts us round this part of the building softly raises a curtain, stretched across the chancel-screen, and shows us twenty or thirty of the nuns at prayer. Visitors can see the hospital wards in the cloisters, and, if they desire it, ascend the eastern tower, and obtain a view over a vast extent of country, with the town of Caen set in the midst of gardens and green meadows, and the river winding far away to the sea.

"These two royal abbeys," writes Dawson Turner, "which have fortunately escaped the storm of the Revolution, are still an ornament to the town, an honour to the sovereign who caused them to be erected, and to the artist who produced them." Both edifices rose at the same time and from the same motive. William the Conqueror, by his union with Matilda, had contracted a marriage proscribed by the decrees of consanguinity. The clergy, and especially the Archbishop of Rouen, inveighed against the union; and the Pope issued an injunction, that the royal pair should erect two monasteries by way of penance, one for monks, the other for nuns; as well as that the Duke should found four hospices, each for one hundred poor persons. In obedience to this command, William founded the Church of St. Stephen, and Matilda the Church of the Holy Trinity.

At Caen we are in an atmosphere of heroes and kings, we pass from one historical site to another until the mind becomes half confused; we are shown (by the same valet-de-place) the tomb of the Conqueror and the house where Beau Brummel died. We see the ruins of a castle on the heights where "le jeune et beau Dunois" performed historical prodigies of valour; and the chapel where he "allait prier Marie, bénir ses exploits." But the modern military aspect of things is, we are bound to confess, prosaic to a degree; we find the Dunois of the period occupied in more peaceful pursuits—mending shoes, tending little children and carrying wood for winter fires.

There are many other buildings and churches at Caen which we should examine, especially the exterior carving of "*St. Etienne-le-vieux*," which is now used as a warehouse. The cathedrals and monuments are generally, as we have said, in wonderful preservation, but they are desecrated without remorse; on every side of them, and indeed, upon them, are staring advertisements of "magazines," dedicated "*au bon diable*," "*au petit diable*," or to some other presiding genius; of "*magasins les plus vastes du monde*," and of "*loteries nationales de France*"; whichever way we turn there are these staring affiches; in the "footsteps of the Conqueror" the bill-sticker is master of the situation.

SUNDAY IN CAEN.—It is early on a Sunday morning in August, and Caen is *en fête*. We have reason to know it by the clamour of church-bells which attends the sun's rising. There is terrible energy, not to say harshness, in thus ushering in the day. There seems no method in the madness of these sturdy Catholics, for they make the tower of St. Pierre vibrate to most uncertain sounds; the bells ring out all at once with a burst, tumbling over one another (hopelessly involved) *en masse;* a combination terribly dissonant to musical ears. Then comes the military *réveille* and the deafening "rataplan" of regimental drums, and the town is soon alive with people arriving and departing by the early trains; whilst others collect in the market-place in holiday attire with baskets of flowers, and commence the erection of an altar to the Virgin in the middle of the square. Then women bring their children dressed in white, with bouquets of flowers and white favours, and a procession is formed with a priest at the head, and marshalled through the principal streets and back again to where the altar to "Our Lady" stands, now decorated with a profusion of flowers and an effigy of the Virgin.

The bells continue to ring at intervals, and omnibuses loaded with holiday people rattle past through the rough paved streets with much shouting and cracking of whips. Everybody seems to be out this morning; the old fashion and the new become mingled and confused, old white caps and Parisian bonnets, old ceremonies and modern ways; the Norman peasant and the English school-girl walk side by side in the crowd, whilst the western door of the church of St. Pierre, to which a crowd is tending, bears in flaming characters the name of a vendor of "*modes parisiennes.*" Men, women, and children, all in Sunday attire, fill the streets and quite outnumber those of the peasant class, the black coat and hat predominating everywhere. A play-bill is thrust into our hands, announcing the performance of an opera in the evening, and we are requested frequently to partake of coffee, syrup and bonbons as we make our way through the Rue St. Pierre and across the crowded square.

Stay here for a moment and witness a little episode—another accidental collision between the old world and the new. An undergraduate, just arrived from England on the "grand tour," gets into a wrangle with an old woman in the market-place; an old woman of nearly eighty years, with a cap as old and ideas as primitive as her dress, but with a sense of humour and natural combativeness that enables her to hold her own in lively sallies and smart repartees against her youthful antagonist.[1] It is a curious contrast, the wrinkled old woman of Caen and the English lad—the one full of the realities and cares of life, born in revolutionary days, and remembering in her childhood Charlotte Corday going down this very street on her terrible mission to Paris; her daughters married, her only son killed in war, her life now (it never was much else) an uneventful round of market-days, eating and sleeping, knitting and prayers: the other—young, careless, fresh to the world, his head stored with heathen mythology, the loves of the gods, and problems of Euclid—taking a light for his pipe from the old woman, and airing his French in a discussion upon a variety of topics, from the price of apples to the cost of a dispensation; the conversation merging finally into a religious discussion, in which the disputants are more abroad than ever—a religion outwardly repre-

[1] This old woman was well known at Caen, and her encounter with the "*garçon anglais*" is matter of history amongst her friends in the town.

sented, in the one case by so many chapels, in the other by so many beads.

It is a "*grande fête*" to-day, according to a notice pasted upon a pillar of the church, "*avec Indulgence plénière.*"

> "GRAND MESSE à 10 a.m.,
> LES VÊPRES à 3 p.m.,
> SALUT ET BÉNÉDICTION DU SACREMENT,
> SERMON, &c."

Let us now follow the crowd into the church of St. Pierre, which is already overflowing with people coming and going, pushing past each other through the baize door, dropping sous into the "*tronc pour les pauvres,*" and receiving, with bowed head and crossed breast, the holy water, administered with a brush.

We pay two sous for a chair and take our places, under a fire of glances from our neighbours, who pray the while and tell their beads; and we have scarcely time to notice the beautiful proportions of the nave, the carving in the side chapels, or the grotesque figures, when the service commences, and we can just discern in the distance the priests at the high altar (looking in their bright stiff robes, and with their backs to the people, like golden beetles under a microscope). We cannot hear the Latin service distinctly, for the moving of the crowd, the creaking of chairs, and the whispering of many voices; but we can see incense rising, children in white robes swinging silver chains, and the cocked hat of the tall "Suisse" moving to and fro.

Presently the congregation sits down, the organ peals forth, and a choir of sweet voices chants the "Agnus Dei." Again the congregation kneels to the sound of a silver bell; the smoke of incense curls through the aisles, and the golden beetles move up and down. Then there is much scraping of chairs, and shuffling of feet, and a general movement towards the pulpit, the men standing in groups round it with their hats in their hands; then a pause, and for the first time so deep a silence that we can hear the movement of the crowd outside, and the distant rattle of drums.

All eyes are now turned to the preacher; a man of about forty, of an austere but ordinary and rather low type of face, closely shaven, with an ivory crucifix hanging at his girdle and a small black book in his hand.

His voice was powerful (almost too loud sometimes) and most persuasive; he was eloquent and impassioned, but he used little gesture or any artifices to arrest attention. He commenced with a rhapsody—startling in the sudden flow of its eloquence, thrilling in its higher notes, tender and compassionate (almost to tears) in its lower passages —a rhapsody to the Virgin—

"O sweet head of my mother; sacred eyes!"

. . . . .

and then an appeal—an appeal for all true Catholics to "the Queen of Heaven, the beautiful, the adorable." He seemed to elevate our hearts with his moving voice, almost to a frenzy of adoration; he taught us how the true believer, "clad in hope," would one day (if he leaned upon Mary his mother in all the weary stages of the "Passage of the Cross"), be crowned with fruition. He lingered with almost idolatrous emphasis on the charms of Mary, and, with his eyes fixed upon her image, his hands outstretched and a thousand upturned faces listening to his words—the aisles echoed to the theme—

"With my lips I kneel, and with my heart
I fall about thy feet and worship thee."

* * *

A stream of eloquence followed—studied or spontaneous

it mattered not—the congregation held their breath and listened to a story for the thousandth time repeated.

The preacher paused for a moment, and then, with another burst of eloquence, he brought his hearers to the verge of a passion which was (as it seemed to us) dangerously akin to human love and the worship of material beauty. Then he lowered our understandings by the enumeration of "works and miracles," and ended with words of earnest exhortation, the burden of which might be shortly translated: "Pray earnestly, and always, to Mary our mother, for all souls in purgatory; confess your sins unto us your high-priests; give, give to the Church and to the poor, strive to lead better lives, look forward ever to the end; and bow down, O, bow down, before the golden images [manufactured for us in the next street] which our Holy Mother the Church has set up."

With a transition almost as startling as the first, the book is closed, the preacher has left the pulpit, the congregation (excepting a few in the side chapels) have dispersed; and Caen keeps holiday after the manner of all good Catholics, putting on its best attire, and disporting itself in somewhat rampant fashion.

The streets are crowded all day with holiday people, and somewhat obstructed by the fashion of the inhabitants taking their meals in the street. We also, in the evening, dine at an open café with a marble table and a pebble floor, amidst a wonderful clamour and confusion of voices. But we are in good company: three tall mugs of cider are on the next table to our own; a dark stout figure, with shaven crown, is seated with his back to us—it is the preacher of the morning, who with two lay friends for companions, also keeps the feast.

GRANVILLE.

THE town of GRANVILLE by the sea, with its dark granite houses, its harbour and fishing-boats, presents a scene of bustle and activity in great contrast to the Cathedral towns. There is an upper and lower Granville —a town on the rocks, with its old church with five gilt statues, built almost out at sea, and another town on the shore. The streets of the old town are narrow and badly paved, but there is great commercial activity, and a general sign of prosperity amongst its seafaring population. The approach to the town on the shore, is very striking; we emerge suddenly through a fissure in the cliffs, into the very heart and life of the place—into the midst of a bustling community of fishermen and women. There is fish everywhere, both in the sea and on the land, and the flavour of it is in the air; there are baskets, bales, and nets, and there is, it must be added, a familiar ring of Billingsgate in the loud voices that we hear around us.

Granville is the great western seaport of France, from which Paris is constantly supplied; and, in spite of inadequate railway communication, it keeps up constant trade with the inland towns. All through the fruitful land that we have passed, we could not help being struck with the inadequate means of transport for goods and provisions; at Coutances, for instance, and at Granville (the great centre of the oyster fisheries of the west) they have not completed connections with the principal centres, and we may still see long lines of carts and wagons, laden with perishable commodities, being carried no faster than in the days of the first Napoleon. But we, who are in search of the picturesque, should be the last to lament the fact, and we may even join in the sentiment of the Maire of Granville, and be "thankful" that the great highways of France are under the control of a careful government; and that her valleys are not (as in England) strewn with the wrecks of abandoned railways—ruins which, by some strange fatality, never look picturesque.

Granville is a favourite place of residence, and a great resort for bathing in the summer; although the "Établissement" is second-rate, and the accommodation is not equal to that of many smaller watering-places of France. It is, however, a pleasant and favourable spot in which to study the manners and customs of a seafaring population. For besides the active human creatures which surround us, those who settle down for a season and spend their time on the sands and on the dark rocks which guard this iron-bound coast, soon become conscious of the presence of another active, striving, but more silent community, digging and delving, sporting and swimming, preying upon each other, and enjoying intensely the luxury of living.

If we, *nous autres*, who dwell upon the land and prey upon each other according to our opportunities, will go down to the shore when the tide is out and ramble about in the

"Rosy gardens revealed by low tides,"

we may make acquaintance with a vast Lilliput community; we may learn some surprising lessons in natural history, and read sermons in shells. There is no better place for exploration of this kind than Granville.

But, amidst this most interesting and curious congregation of fishes—a concourse of crabs, lobsters, eels in holes, limpets on rocks, and a hundred other inhabitants of the sea, in every form of activity around us—we must not forget the treacherous tides on this coast, and the great

Atlantic waves that will suddenly overwhelm the flat shore, and cut off retreat from those who are fishing on the rocks.

This happens so often, and is so full of danger to those unacquainted with the coast, that we may do good service by relating again an adventure which happened to the late Campbell of Islay and a friend, who were nearly drowned near Granville. They had been absorbed in examining the rocks at some distance from the shore, and in collecting the numerous marine plants which abound in their crevices, when suddenly one of the party called out—

"Mercy on us! I forgot the tide, and here it comes."

Turning towards the shore, they saw a stream of water running at a rapid pace between them and the sands. They quickly descended the rocks, but before they could reach the ground "the sand was in stripes, and the water in sheets." They then ran for the shore, but before they had proceeded far they were met by one of the fisher-girls, who had seen their danger from the shore, and hastened to turn them back, calling to them—

"The wave! the wave! it is coming—turn! turn and run for the rock—or you are lost!"

They did turn, and saw far out to sea a large wave rolling towards the shore. The girl led the way, and the two friends strained every nerve to keep pace with her. As they neared the rock the wave began to roll in and for the last ten steps they were up to their knees in water—but they were on the rock.

"Quick! quick!" said the girl, pointing upward; "*there* is the passage to the Cross at the top; but if the second wave comes we shall be too late."

She scrambled on for a hundred yards till she came to a fissure in the rock, six or seven feet wide, along which the water was rushing like a mill sluice. With some difficulty they reach the upper rocks. Here they rest a moment—when another great wave rolls in, and the water runs along the little platform where they are sitting; they all rise, and mounting the rocky points (which the little Granvillaise assures them are never quite covered with water), cluster together for support. In a few moments the suspense is over, the girl points to the shore, where they can hear the distant sound of a cheer, and see people waving their handkerchiefs.

"They think the tide has turned," says the girl, "and they are shouting to cheer us."

She was right, the tide had turned. Another wave came and wetted their feet, but when it had passed the water had fallen, and in five minutes the platform was again dry!

The fisherwomen of Granville are famed for their beauty, industry, and courage; they seem to do everything—the "boatmen" are women, and the "fishermen" young girls.

We may well admire some of these handsome Granvillaises, living their free life by the sea, earning less in the day, generally, than Staffordshire pit girls, but living much more enviable lives. Here they are by hundreds, scattered over the beach in the early morning, and afterwards crowding into the market-place, driving hard bargains for the produce of their sea-farms, and—with rather shrill and unpronounceable ejaculations and many most winning smiles—displaying their shining wares. It is all for the Paris market they will tell you, and they may also tell you (if you win their confidence) that they, too, are one day for Paris.

Let us leave the old women to do the best bargaining, and picture to the reader a bright figure that we once saw upon this shining shore, a Norman maiden, about eighteen years of age, without shoes or stockings; a picture of health and beauty bronzed by the sun. This young creature, who had spent her life by the sea and amongst her own people, could not strictly be called handsome, and she might be considered very ignorant; but she bloomed with freshness, she knew neither ill health nor *ennui*, and happiness was a part of her nature.

This charming "aphrodite piscatrix" is stalwart and strong (she can swim a mile with ease), she has carried her basket and nets since sunrise, and now at eight o'clock on this summer's morning sits down on the rocks, makes a quick breakfast of *potage*, plumes herself a little, and commences knitting. She does not stay long on the beach, but before leaving makes a slight acquaintance with two strangers, and evinces a curious desire to hear anything they may have to tell her about the great world. It is too bright a picture to last; she too, it would seem, has day-dreams of cities; she would give up her freedom, she would join the crowd and enter the "great city," she would have a stall at "*les Halles*," and see the world. Day-dreams but too often fulfilled—the old story of centralisation doing its work. Look at the map of Normandy, and see how the great western railway from Paris is putting forth its arms, which, like the devil-fish in Victor Hugo's "*Travailleurs de la Mer*," will one day draw irresistibly to itself our fair "Toiler of the sea."

"What does Monsieur think?" (for we are favoured with a little confidence from our young friend,) and what can we say? Could we draw a tempting picture of life in cities—could we, if we had the heart, draw a favourable contrast between *her* life, as we see it, and the lives of girls of her own age who live in towns, who seldom see the breaking of a spring morning, or know the beauty of a summer's night? Could we picture to her, if we would, the gloom that shrouds the dwellings of many of her Northern sisters? and could she but see the veil that hangs

A "TOILER OF THE SEA."

over cities on almost any morning in the year, she might well be reconciled to her present life!

Is it nothing, we are inclined to ask her, to feel the first rays of the sun at his rising, to be fanned with fresh breezes, to rejoice in the wind, to brave the storm; to have learned from childhood to welcome as familiar friends the changes of the elements, and, in short, to have realized in a healthful life the "mens sana in corpore sano"? Would she be willing to repeat the follies of her ancestors in the days of the *Trianon* and Louis XIV.? Would she complete the fall which began when knights and nobles turned courtiers and roués? Let us read history to her and remind her what centralisation did for old France; let us whisper to her, whilst there is time, what Paris is like in our own day.

AVRANCHES.

HERE are some places in Europe which English people seem, with one consent, to have made their own; they take possession of them, peacefully enough it is true, but with a determination that the inhabitants find it impossible to resist. Thus it is that Avranches—owing principally, it may be, to its healthiness and cheapness of living, and to the extreme beauty of its situation—has become an English country town, with many of its peculiarities, and a few, it must be added, of its rather unenviable characteristics.

The buildings at Avranches are not very remarkable. The cathedral has been destroyed, and the houses are of the familiar French pattern; some charmingly situated in pleasant gardens commanding the view over the bay. The situation seems perfect. Built upon the extreme western promontory of the long line of hills which extend from Domfront and the forest of Audaine, with a view unsurpassed in extent towards the sea, with environs of undulating hills and fruitful landscape, with woods and streams (such as the traveller who has only passed through Central France could hardly imagine), we can scarcely picture to the reader a more favoured spot.

"No district in Normandy," a resident assures us, "affords a more agreeable resting-place than the hills of Avranches, excepting, perhaps, the smiling environs of Mortain and Vire. Mortain is within easy distance, as well as Mont St. Michael (which we have sketched from the terrace at Avranches,) and Granville. To the extreme south is seen the Bay of Cancale in Brittany, and the promontory of St. Malo; to the north, the variegated landscape of the Cotentin—'hills, valleys, woods, villages, churches, châteaux smiling in the sunshine, the air melodious with the song of the lark and innumerable nightingales.'"

True as is this picture of the natural beauty of the position of Avranches, we will add one or two facts, gathered lately on the spot, which may be useful to newcomers. Within the last few years house-rent, though still cheap, has greatly increased; and the prices of provisions, which used to be so abundant from Granville and St. Malo, have risen, as they have, indeed, all over France. The railway from Granville to Paris makes matters worse, and the resident sees the butter, eggs, and fowls, which used to throng the market of Avranches, packed away in baskets for Paris and London. The salmon and trout in the rivers are already netted and sold by the pound, and larks are very seldom heard in the sky. Thus, like Dinan, Tours, and Pau, Avranches feels the effects of rapid communication with the capital, and will in a few years be anything but a cheap place of residence. A few years ago a good ten-roomed, unfurnished house, with garden ground, could be obtained for 1,000 francs a year, but in 1890 it cost 2,000 francs. However, from information gathered only yesterday, we learn that "house-rent bears favourable comparison with many English provincial towns; that servants' wages are not high, and that provisions are comparatively cheap"; also that the climate is "very cold sometimes in winter."

An amusing book might be written about English society in French towns; no one indeed knows, who has not tried it, with what little society-props such coteries as those at Avranches are kept up. But what we might say of Avranches would apply to nearly every little English colony abroad. There are two sides to the picture, and there is of course a good, pleasant side to the English society in most French towns; there is also great necessity to be "particular," however much we may laugh. English people who come to reside abroad are not, as a rule, very good representatives of their nation: neither they nor their children seem to flourish on a foreign soil; they differ in their character as much as transplanted trees, and in a few years seem to have more affinity with the poplars and elms of France than with the sturdy oaks of England.

Let us not be thought to disparage Avranches; if it is our lot to live here, we may enjoy life well; and if we are not deterred by the dull and "weedy" aspect of some of the old châteaux, we may also make some pleasant friends amongst the French families in the neighbourhood. In summer time we may almost live out of doors, and ramble about in the fields and sketch, as we should do in England; the air is fresh and bracing, and the sea-breeze comes gratefully on the west-wind. We may stroll through shady lanes and between hedge-rows, and hear the familiar sound of church bells; but here the similarity to England ceases, for we may enter these buildings at any hour and find peasant women at prayers.

And we may see sometimes a party of English girls from

TOWER AT VIRE, NEAR AVRANCHES.

a French school, with their drawing-master, sketching from nature and making minute studies of the branches of trees. They are seated on a hillside, and there is a charming pastoral scene before them—wood and water, pasture-land and cattle-grazing, women with white caps, and little white houses peeping through the trees.

But the trees that they are studying are small and characterless compared with our own; they are scattered about the landscape, or set in trim lines along the roads: our fair artists had better be in England for this work. There is none of the mass and grandeur here that we see in our forest-trees, none of the suggestive groups with which we are so familiar, even in the parks of London, planted "by accident" as we are apt to call it, but standing together with clear purpose of protection and support—the strong-limbed facing the north and stretching out their protecting arms, the weaker towering above them in the centre of the square, whilst those to the south spread a deep shade almost to the ground. French trees are under an Imperial necessity to form into line; the groves at Fontainbleau are as straight as the Fifth Avenue at New York. There are no studies of trees in all Normandy like the royal oaks of Windsor; there is nothing to compare in grandeur with the stems of the Burnham beeches, set in a carpet of ferns; and nothing equal in effect to the massing of the blue pines, with their bronzed stems against an evening sky, in Woburn Park in Bedfordshire. We may bring some pretty studies from Avranches and from the country round, but we should not come to France to draw trees. There are, however, some studies which we may make near Avranches of scenes which are full of interest. If we descend the hill and walk a few miles in the direction of Granville, we may see by the roadside the remnants of several wayside "stations" of very early date.

Let us sit down by the roadside to sketch one of these (A.D. 1066), and depict for the reader, almost with the accuracy of a photograph, its grotesque proportions. It stands on a bank, in a prominent position, by the road-

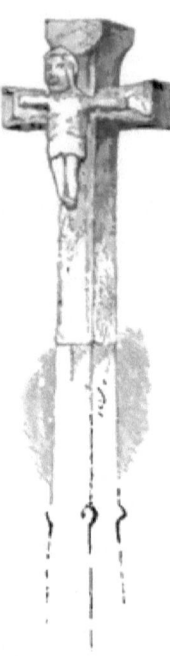

side, a rude contrast to the surrounding scenery. Presently there comes up an old cantonnier in a blouse and heavy sabots, who has just returned from mending the roads; he takes off his cap, crosses himself devoutly, and kneels down to pray. The sun shines upon the cross and upon the kneeling figure; the soft wind plays about them, the bank is lovely with wild-flowers; there are purple hills beyond, and a company of white clouds careering through space. But the old man sees nothing but the cross; he has no eyes for the beauty of landscape, no ear for the music of the birds or the voices of nature; he sees nothing but the hideous image of his Saviour; he kneels as he knelt in childhood before the cross; he clasps his worn hands, and prays, with many repetitions, words which evidently bring comfort to his soul. In a few minutes the old man rises and puts on his cap, with a brass plate on it with the number of his canton, produces a little can of soup and bread, and sits down on the bank to breakfast; ending by unrolling a morsel of tobacco from a crumpled paper, putting it into his mouth, and going fast asleep.

Many more such scenes we could record, but they are more fitted for the pencil than the pen; the artist can fill his sketch-book without going far from Avranches.

But as autumn advances our thoughts are naturally turned more towards "le sport"; and if we are fortunate enough to be on visiting terms with the owners of the neighbouring châteaux, we may be present at some interesting scenes that will remind us of pictures in the galleries at Versailles.

"With good books, a good rod, and a double gun, one could never weary of a residence at Avranches," says an enthusiastic settler who has found out the best corners in the trout-streams, and possibly the denizens of the neighbouring woods. The truth, however, is that in spite of the beautifully wooded country and the rivers that wind so picturesquely beneath us, Avranches is scarcely the spot for a sportsman to select for a residence. In the season there are numerous shooting-parties, and occasionally a very fair bag may be made; but, game not being preserved systematically, the supply is variable, and accounts of sport naturally differ very widely. We can only say that it is poor work after English covers, and that we know some residents at Avranches who prefer making excursions into Brittany for a week's shooting. Trout may be caught in tolerable abundance, and salmon of good weight are still to be found in the rivers; but they are diminishing fast, being, as we said, netted at night for the Paris market. There is one drawback to the pleasures of sport in France, which should be mentioned here, namely, the heavy octroi duty which a successful shot has to pay upon every head of game which he brings home.

It was in the shooting season of the year, when game had been unusually scarce for the sportsman and provokingly plentiful to behold in the market-place at Granville—when the last accounts we had of the success of a party (who had been out for a week) was that they had bagged "only a few woodcocks, three partridges, and a hare or two,"—that the following clever sketch appeared in the newspapers.

An enthusiastic French marquis offered a friend whom he met in Paris a few days' shooting on his estate. He accepted, and went the next day; the journey was seven hours by railway, but to the true sportsman this was nothing. The morning after his arrival he was attended by the marquis's keeper, who, in answer to the inquiries of the visitor, thus mapped out the day's sport:—

"Pour commencer, monsieur, nous chasserons dans les vignes de M. le Marquis, où à cette saison nous trouverons certainement des grives [thrushes]." "Et après?" says the visitor. "Eh bien! après, nous passerons une petite heure sur la grande plaine, où, sans doute, nous trouverons une masse d'alouettes [larks]. Ensuite je montrerai à monsieur certaines poules d'eau [moor-hens] que je connais; fichtre! nous les attraperons. Il y a là-bas aussi, dans le marais, un petit lac où, l'année passée, j'ai vu un canard, mais un canard sauvage! Nous le chercherons; peut-être il y sera."

"But have you no partridges?" "Des perdreaux! mais oui! je le crois bien! (il demande si nous avons des perdreaux!) il y en a, mais ils sont difficiles. Nous en avions *quatre*, mais, le mois passé, M. le Marquis en a tué un et sérieusement blessé un second. La pauvre bête n'est pas encore guérie. Cela ne nous laisse que deux. Nous les chasserons sans doute si monsieur le veut; *mais que ferons-nous l'année prochaine?* Si monsieur veut bien achever cette pauvre bête blessée, ça peut s'arranger."

"Well, but have you no covert shooting,—no hares?"

"Les lièvres? mais certainement, nous avons des lièvres. Nous irons dans la forêt, je prendrai mes chiens, et je vous montrerai de belles lièvres. J'en ai trois,—*Josephine, Alphonse*, et le vieux *Adolphe*. Pour le moment Josephine est sacrée,—elle est mère. Le petit Alphonse s'est marié avec elle, comme ça il est un peu père de famille; nous l'épargnerons, n'est-ce-pas, monsieur? Mais le vieux Adolphe, nous le tuerons; c'est déjà temps; voilà cinq ans que je le chasse!"

The Valley of the Seine.

N the fruitful hills that border the river Seine, and form part of the great watershed of Lower Normandy, Nature has poured forth her blessings; and her daughters, who are here lightly sketched, dispense her bounties.

It is a pleasant thing to pass homeward through this food-producing land—to go leisurely from town to town, and see something more of country life in Normandy—to see the laden orchards, the cattle upon the hills, and the sloping fields of corn. It is yet early in the autumn, but the variety of colour spread over the landscape is delightful to the eye; the rich brown of the buckwheat, the bright yellow mustard, the green pastures by rivers, and the poppies in the golden corn; the fields, divided by high hedges, and interspersed with mellowed trees; the orchards raining fruit that glitters in the sunshine as it falls; the purple heath, the luxuriant ferns. There is "*une récolte magnifique*" this year, and the people have but one thought, "the gathering in"; the country presents to us a picture—not like Watteau's "*fêtes galantes*," but rather that of an English harvest-home.

We are in the midst of the cornfields near Villers-sur-mer, and the hill-side is glorious; it is covered to the very summit with riches—the heavily laden corn-stems wave their crests against a blue horizon, whilst, in a cleft of the hill, a long line of poppies winds downwards in one scarlet stream. They are set thickly in some places, and form a blaze of colour, inconceivably, painfully brilliant—a concentration of light far beyond the power of imitation by the pencil. We could not paint it if we would, but we might see in it an allegory of plenty and of peace—of the peace which the peasantry of France so urgently desire. We see her blood-red banner of war laid down to garland the hillside with its crimson folds, and her children laying their offerings at the feet of Ceres and forgetting Mars altogether. The national anthem becomes no longer a natural refrain—anything would sound more appropriate than "partant pour la Syrie" (there is no time for *that* work)—to our little friend in fluttering blouse, who sits in the grass and "minds" fifty head of cattle by moral force alone; we should rather sing—

> "Little boy blue, come blow me your horn,
> The orchards are laden, the cow's in the corn!"

We should not leave this pastoral scene, at least until the evening; when the sun goes down behind the sea, leaving a glow upon the hillside and upon the crowd of gleaners who have just come up, and casts long shadows across the stubble and on the sheaves of corn; when the harvest moon shines out, and the picture is completed—the corn-sheaves lighted on one side by the western glow, on the other by the moon; like the famous shield over which knights did battle—one side silver, the other gold.

All this time we are within sight, and nearly within sound, of the "happy hunting-grounds" of Trouville and Deauville, two famous watering-places on the coast; but the country people are singularly unaffected by the proximity of these towns invented by Dumas and peopled by his following. It is true that on the walls of a little village inn there is something paraded about a "Trouville Association, Limited," and a share list exhibited by the host, who is an agent; but these things do not seem to find much favour amongst the thrifty peasantry. They have, in their time, been tempted to unearth their treasures, and to invest in bubble companies like the rest of the world; but there is a reaction here—the Normans evidently thinking, like the old Colonnæ, that a hole in the bottom of the garden is about the safest place after all. And they have, it is true, some other temptations, which come to them with a cheap press, under the titles of "*La Sûreté financière*," "*Le Moniteur des tirages financiers*," "*Le petit Moniteur financier*," etc.—newspapers whose special business it is to teach the people how to dispose of their savings; and there are many other things in these halfpenny French newspapers which find their way into remote corners of France, which must make the curé sometimes regret that he had taught his flock to read.

In these rich and prosperous provinces the people, revolutionary and excitable as their ancestors were, certainly appear happy and contented; the most un-educated of them are quick-witted and ready in reply;

they are not boorish or sullen; they have more readiness, at least in manner, than the Teutonic races, and are, as a rule, full of gaiety and humour. These people do not want war: they hate the conscription which takes away the flower of the flock; they regard with anything but pleasure the rather dictatorial "*Moniteur*" that comes to them by post sometimes, whether they ask for it or not, and would much rather be let alone.

It is worthy of note that the people in this part of Normandy are becoming less political and more conservative every day—a conservatism which, in their case, may be taken as a sign of prosperity, and of a certain unwillingness to be disturbed in their business; they are content with a paternal government—at a distance; they wish for peace and order, and have no objection to be taken care of. They are so willing to be led, that, as a Frenchman expressed it to us, "they would prefer, if they could, to have an omnipotent Postmaster-General to inspect all letters, and see whether they were creditable to the sender and fitting to be received!"

Such is a picture of Lower Normandy, the land of plenty where we wander with so much pleasure in the summer months, putting up at wayside inns (where the hostess makes her "note" on a slate and finds it hard work to make the amount come to more than five francs, for the night, for board and lodging for "monsieur") and at farm-houses sometimes; chatting with the people in their rather troublesome patois, and making excursions with the local antiquary or curé to some spot celebrated in history. They are pleasant days, when, if we will put up with a few inconveniences, and live principally out of doors, we may see and hear much that a railway traveller misses altogether. We shall not admire the system of farming, as a rule (each farmer holding only a few acres), and we shall find some of the cottages of the labourers very primitive, badly built, and unhealthy, although generally neat; we shall notice that the people are rather cruel and careless of the sufferings of animals, and that no farm-servant knows how to groom a horse; we shall see them clever in making cider, and prone to drink it; we shall see plenty of fine, strong, rather idle men, and women, in the fields carrying tremendous burdens, but *hardly any children:* they are almost as rare in the country as a lady or a gentleman. Indeed, in all our country wanderings the "gentry" make little figure, and appear much less frequently on the scene than would be supposed. There are, of course, *propriétaires* in this part of Normandy, who spend both their time and money in the country, and are spoken of with respect and affection by the people; but they are *raræ aves*, men of mark, like the founder of the Protestant colony at Beuzeval on the sea.

Nearly every Sunday after harvest-time there will be a village wedding, where we may see the bride and bridegroom coming to take the first sacrament, seated in a prominent place in front of the altar, and receiving the elements before the rest of the congregation—the bride placing a white favour on the basket which contains the consecrated bread, and afterwards coming from the church, the bride with a cap nearly a foot high, the bridegroom wearing a dress-coat, with a tremendous bouquet, and a wedding-ring on his forefinger; and if we stand near the church porch, we may be deafened with a salute fired by the villagers in honour of the occasion, and overwhelmed by the eloquence of the "best man," who takes this opportunity of delivering a speech; and finally, the bells will ring out with such familiar tone that we can hardly realize that we are in France.

These people are of the labouring class, but they have

some money to commence life with: the poorest girls seldom marry without a portion; indeed, so important is this considered amongst them that there are societies for providing portions for the unendowed, and they are, with few exceptions, provident and happy in married life. They are so in the country at least, in spite of all that has been said and written to the contrary. A lady who has had five-and-twenty years' acquaintance with French society assures us that "the stereotyped literary and dramatic view of French married life is wickedly false." The corruption of morals, she says, which so generally prevails in Paris, and which was so systematically aggravated by the luxury and extravagance of the second Empire, has "emboldened writers to foist these false pictures of married life on the world."

Of one more ceremony we must speak, differing in character, but equally characteristic and curious. We are in the country again, spending our days in sketching, or wandering amongst the hills; enjoying the "perfect weather," as we call it, and a little careless, perhaps, of the fact that the land is parched with thirst, that the springs are dried up, and that the peasants are beginning to despair of rain.

We see in the landscape at our feet a little white smoke curling through the branches of trees, and hear in faint, uncertain cadence the voices of men and children singing. Presently there comes up a pathway, between two lines of poplars, a long procession, headed by a priest, holding high in the air a glittering cross; there are old men with bowed heads, young men erect, with shaven crowns, and boys in scarlet and white robes, carrying silver censers; there is a clanking of silver chains, a tinkling of little bells, and an undertone of oft-repeated prayer. The effect is startling and brilliant; the sunlight glances upon the white

MARKET WOMEN, LOWER NORMANDY.

Face p. 50.

robes of the men, in alternate stripes of soft shadow and dazzling brightness; the wind plays round their feet as they march heavily along, in a whirl of dust which robs the leaves of their morning freshness; whilst the scarlet robes of the children light up the grove as with a furnace, and the rush of voices disturbs the air. On they come through the quiet country fields, hot and dusty with their long march—the foremost priest holding his head high, and doing his routine work manfully, never wearying of repeating the same words, or of opening and shutting the dark-bound volume in his hand; and the children, not yet tired of singing and of swinging incense-burners, keeping close together two and two in line; the people following being less regular, less apparently enthusiastic, but walking close together in a long winding stream up the hill.

What does it all mean? Why, that these simple people want rain on the land, and that they have collected from all parts of the country to offer their prayers, and their money, to propitiate the Deity.

But we are in a land where we are taught, not only to pray for our wants, but to pay for their expression; so let us not question the motive of the procession, but follow it again, in the evening, into the town, where it becomes lost in the crowded streets—so crowded that we cannot see more than the heads of the people; but the line is marked above them by a stream of sunset, which turns the dust-particles above their heads into a golden fringe. They make a halt in the square and sing the "Angelus," and then enter the cathedral.

Such scenes may still be witnessed in Normandy (although, of course, becoming less primitive and characteristic every year) by those who are not compelled to hurry through the land. And the best way to travel is by diligence. The seat on the *banquette* on a fine summer's day is one of the most enjoyable places in life; it is cheap, and certainly not too rapid, five or six miles an hour. The roof is overloaded with goods and passengers, which gives a pleasant swaying motion to the vehicle; but the road is so smooth and even that "nobody cares"—the rocking to and fro is soothing, and sends the driver to sleep, the pieces of string that keep the harness together will hold for another hour or two, and the crazy machine will last our journey at least. In this beautiful country we should always either drive or walk, if we have time; the diligence is the most amusing and sometimes the slowest method of progress. Nobody hurries, although we carry "the mails," and have a letter-box in the side of the conveyance, where letters are posted as we go along. It is scarcely like travelling; the free and easy way in which people come and go on the journey is more like "receiving visitors" than taking up passengers. As we jog along, to the jingling of bells and the creaking of rusty iron, the people that we overtake on the road keep accumulating on our vehicle one by one, until we become incrusted with human things like a rock covered with limpets. There is no shaking them off; the driver does not care, and they certainly do not all pay. It is a pleasant family affair which we should all be sorry to see disturbed; and the roads are so good and even, that it does not matter much about the load. The neglect and cruelty to the horses, which we are obliged to witness, is certainly one drawback, and the dust and crowding on market days are not always pleasant; but we can think of no other objections in fine weather to this quiet method of seeing the country.

THE WATERING-PLACES OF NORMANDY.

"Trouville est une double extrait de Paris,—la vie est une fête, et le costume une mascarade."

THE principal bathing-places on the north coast are the following, commencing from the east—DIEPPE, FÉCAMP, ÉTRETAT, TROUVILLE, and DEAUVILLE, VILLERS-SUR-MER, HOULGATE, CABOURG, and CHERBOURG. We will say a few words about Trouville and Étretat.

Life at Trouville is the gayest of the gay. It is not so much to bathe that we come here, as because on this fine sandy shore near the mouth of the Seine, the world of fashion and delight has made its summer home; because here we can combine the refinements, pleasures and "distractions" of Paris with northern breezes, and indulge without restraint in those rampant follies that only a Frenchman or a Frenchwoman understands. It is a pretty, graceful and rational idea, no doubt, to combine the ball-room with the sanatorium, and the opera with any amount of ozone; and we may well be thankful to Dumas for inventing a seaside resort at once so pleasant and so gay. Of the daily life at Trouville and Deauville there is literally nothing new to be told; they are the best, the most fashionable, and the most extravagant of French watering-places; and there is the usual round of bathing in the early morning, breakfast at half-past ten, donkey-riding, bicycle racing, and driving in the country until the afternoon, promenade concerts and indoor games at four, dinner at six or seven (table-d'hôte, if you please, where new-comers are stared at with that solid, stony stare, of which only the politest nation in the world is capable), casino afterwards, with pleasant, mixed society, concert again and "*la danse.*"

Of the fashion and extravagance at Trouville a moralist might feel inclined to say much; but we are here for a summer holiday, and we *must* be gay both in manner and attire. *Dress* is the one thing needful at Trouville—in the water or on the sands. Look at that old French gentleman, with the decoration of the Legion of Honour on his breast; he is neat and clean, his dress is, in all respects, perfection; and it is difficult to say whether it is the make of his boots, the fit of his gloves, or his hat, which is most on his mind —they furnish him with food for much thought, and sometimes trouble him not a little. Of the ladies' attire what shall we say? It is all described in the last number of "*Le Follet,*" and we will not attempt to compete with that authority; we will rather quote two lines from the letter of an English girl who thus writes home to quiet friends: "We are all delighted with Trouville; we have to make *five toilettes daily*, the gentlemen are so particular."

Of the bathing at Trouville, a book might be written on costume alone—on the suits of motley, the harlequins, the mephistopheles, the spiders, the "grasshoppers green," and the other eccentric *costumes de bain*—culminating in a lady's dress trimmed with death's heads, and a gentleman's, of an indescribable colour, after the pattern of a trail of seaweed. Strange, costly creatures—popping in and out of little wooden houses, seated, solitary, on artificial rocks, or pacing up and down within the limits prescribed by the keeper of the show—tell us, " Monsieur l'administrateur," something about their habits; stick some labels into the sand with their Latin names; tell us how they manage to feather their nests, whether they "ruminate" over their food—and we shall have added to our store of knowledge at the seaside!

It is all admirably managed ("administered" is the word), as everything of the kind is in France. In order to bathe, as the French understand it, you must study costume; and to make a good appearance in the water you must move about with the dexterity and grace required in a ball-room; you must remember that you are present at a *bal de mer*, and that you are not in a tub. There are water velocipedes, canoes for ladies, and floats for the unskilful; then a lounge across the sands and through the "Établissement," before an admiring crowd, in costumes more scanty than those of Neapolitan fish-girls!

Yes, youth and beauty come to Trouville-by-the-sea; French beauty of the Dresden china pattern side by side and hand in hand with the young English girl of the heavy Clapham type (which elderly Frenchmen adore)—all in the water together, in the prettiest dresses, sweetly trimmed and daintily conceived; all joining hands, men and women having a "merry-go-round" in the water—some swimming, some diving, shouting and "playing fantastic tricks before high heaven," to the admiration of a crowded beach!

"*Honi soit qui mal y pense*," when English ladies join the party, and write home that "it is delightful, that there is a refreshing disregard for what people may think, at French watering-places, and a charming absence of self-consciousness that disarms criticism"!

But the system of bathing in France is so sensible and good compared with that in England; the facilities for learning to swim, the accommodation for bathers, and the accessories, are so superior to anything we know of in Europe, that we hardly like to hint at any drawbacks. We need not all go to Trouville (some of us cannot afford it), but we may live at most of these bathing-places at less cost, and with more comfort and amusement than at home.

The aspect of Trouville is thus described by the late Blanchard Jerrold, who knew the district better than most Englishmen : " Even the shore has been subdued to comfortable human uses ; rocks have been picked out of the sand, until a carpet as smooth as Paris asphalte has been obtained for the fastidious feet of noble dames, who are the finishing bits of life and colour in the exquisite scene. Even the ribbed sand is not smooth enough ; a boarded way has been fixed from the casino to the mussel-banks, whither the dandy resorts to play at mussel gathering, in a nautical dress that costs a sailor's income. The great and rich have planted their Louis XIII. châteaux, their 'maisons mauresques' and 'pavillons à la renaissance,' so closely over the available slopes, round about the immense and gaudily appointed casino and the Hotel of the Black Rocks, that it has been found necessary to protect them with masonry of more than Roman strength. From these works of startling force and boldness of design, the view is a glorious one indeed. To the right stretches the white line of Havre, pointed with its electric *phare;* to the left, the shore swells and dimples, and the hills, in gentle curves, rise beyond. Deauville is below and beyond—a flat, formal place of fashion, where ladies exhibit the genius of Worth to one another and to the astonished fisherwomen.

"Imagine a splendid court playing at seaside life; imagine such a place as Watteau could have designed, with inhabitants as elegantly rustic as his, and you imagine a Trouville. It is the village of the millionnaire— the stage whereon the duchess plays the hoyden, and the princess seeks the exquisite relief of being natural for an hour or two. No wonder every inch of the rock is

MODERN SEASIDE HOUSES IN NORMANDY.

disputed; there are so many now in the world who have sipped all the pleasures the city has to give. Masters of the art of entering a drawing-room—the Parisians crowd seaward to get the sure foot of the mussel-gatherer upon the slimy granite of a bluff Norman headland; they bring their taste with them, and they get heartiness in the bracing air. The *salon* of the casino, at the height of the season, is said to show at once the most animated and diverting assemblies of Somebodies to be seen in the world."

DEAUVILLE, separated by the river Touques, is a place of greater pretension even than Trouville, but the death of the Duc de Morny stopped its growth—large tracts of land, in what should be the town, still lying waste. It is quiet compared with Trouville, select, "aristocratic," and boasts "the handsomest casino in France;" it is built for the most part upon a sandy plain, but the houses are so tastefully designed, and so much has been made of the site, that from some points of view it presents, with its background of hills, a singularly picturesque appearance.

No matter how small or uninteresting the locality, if it is to be fashionable, *il n'y aura point de difficulté*. If there are no natural attractions, the ingenious and enterprising speculator will provide them; if there are no trees, he will bring them; no rocks, he will manufacture them—no river, he will cut a winding canal—no town, he will build one— no casino, he will erect a wooden shed on the sands!

But of all the bathing-places on the north coast of Normandy the little fishing-village of ÉTRETAT will commend itself to most people, for its bold coast and bracing air. Situated about seventeen miles north-east of Havre, shut in on either side by rocks which form a natural arch over the sea, the little bay of Étretat, with its brilliant summer crowd of idlers and its little group of fishermen who stand by it in all weathers, is one of the quaintest of the nooks and corners of France. There is a homelike snugness and retirement about the position of Étretat, and a mystery about the caves and caverns—extending for long distances under its cliffs—which form an attraction that we shall find nowhere else. Since Paris has found it out, and taken it by storm as it were, the little fishermen's village has been turned into a gay parterre; its shingly beach is lined with chairs, and its shores are smoothed and levelled for delicate feet. The *Casino* and *Établissement* are all that can be desired, whilst pretty chalets and villas are scattered upon the hills that surround the town. There is scarcely any "town" to speak of; a small straggling village, with the remains of a Norman church, formerly close to the sea (built on the spot where the people once watched the great flotilla of William the Conqueror drift eastward to St. Valery), and on the shore, old worn-out boats, thatched and turned into fishermen's huts and bathing retreats.

Étretat has its peculiar customs; the old fisherwomen, who assume the more profitable occupation of washer-women during the summer, go down to the shore as the tide is ebbing, and catch the spring water on its way to the sea, scooping out the shingle, and making natural washing-tubs of fresh water close to the sea,—a work of ten minutes or so, which is all washed away by the next tide. At Étretat almost everybody swims and wears a costume of blue serge, trimmed with scarlet or other bright colour; and everybody sits in the afternoon in the gay little bay, purchases shell ornaments and useless souvenirs, sips coffee or ices, and listens to the band.

The show is nearly over for the season, at Étretat, by the time we leave it; the puppets are being packed up for

Paris, and even the boxes that contain them will soon be carted away to more sheltered places. It is late in September, and the last few bathers are making the most of their time, and wandering about on the shore in brilliant attire. But their time is nearly over; Étretat will soon be given up to the fishermen again; like the bears in the high Pyrenees, that wait at the street corners of the mountain towns, and scramble for the best places after the visitors have left, the natives of Étretat are already preparing to return to their winter quarters.

It is the finest weather of the year, and the setting sun is brilliant upon the shore; a fishing-boat glides into the bay, and a little fisher-boy steps out upon the sand. He comes down towards us, facing the western sun, with such a glory of light about his head, such a halo of fresh youth and health, as we have not seen once this summer in the "great world." His feet are bare, and leave their tiny impress on the sand, a thousand times more expressive than any Parisian boot; his little bronzed hands are crystallized with the salt air, his dark-brown curls are flecked with sea-foam, and flutter in the evening breeze; his face is radiant—a reflection of the sun, a mystery of life and beauty half revealed.

After all we have seen and heard around us, it is like turning from the contemplation of some tricky effect of colour to a painting by Titian or Velasquez; it is, in an artistic sense, a transition from darkness to light—from the glare of the lamp to the glory of the true day.

BRITTANY.

"THE WESTERN WING."

IN an old-fashioned country-house there is often to be found a room built out from the rest of the structure, forming, as it were, the extreme western wing. It has windows looking to the west, its door of communication with the great house, and, in summer-time, a southern exterior wall laden with fruit and fragrant with clematis, honeysuckle, or jasmine. The interior differs from the rest of the mansion both in its furnishing and in the habits of its occupants. It is a room in which there is an absence of bright colours, where everything is quiet in tone and more or less harmonious in aspect; where solid woodwork takes the place of veneer and gilding, where furniture is made simply and solidly, for use and ease, where decoration is *the work of the hand*—holding a needle, a chisel, or a hammer. The prevailing colours in this quaint old room, which give a sense of repose on coming from more highly decorated saloons, are blue, grey and green—the blue of old china, the grey of a landscape by Millet or Corot, the green that we see in the works of Paul Veronese.

This "western wing" is haunted, and full of mysteries and legends ; its furniture is antique, and has seldom been dusted or put in order. Nearly every object is a curiosity in some way, and was designed in a past age ; on the high wooden shelves over the open fireplace there are objects in wrought metal work, antique-shaped pots and jars. About the room are fragments of Druidical monuments, menhirs and dolmens of almost fabulous antiquity, ancient stone crosses, calvaries and carvings, piled together in disorderly fashion with odd-shaped pipes, snuff-boxes, fishing-rods, guns, and the like ; on the walls are little oil paintings of mediæval saints in roughly carved gilt frames, and a few low-toned landscapes by painters of France ; on shelves and in niches are large brown volumes with antique clasps, and perhaps a model in clay of an old woman in a high cap, a priest, or a child in sabots.

The room is a snuggery, well furnished with pipes and tobacco, and hitherto evidently not much visited by ladies ; but the door is open wide to the rest of the mansion, through which the strains of Meyerbeer's opera of *Dinorah* may sometimes be heard. The lady visitor is welcome to this out-of-the-way corner, but she must not be surprised to find herself greeted on entering in a language which, with all her knowledge of French, she can scarcely understand ; to be asked, perhaps, to take a pinch of snuff, and to conform in other homely ways to the habits of the inhabitants.

Such a quiet, unobtrusive corner—pleasant with its open windows to the summer air, but much blown and rained upon by winter storms—is Brittany, the "western wing" of France, holding much the same position geographically and socially to the rest of the country, as the room we have pictured in a great house, to the rest of the mansion.

Brittany is essentially the land of the painter. It would be strange indeed if a country sprinkled with white caps, and set thickly in summer with the brightest blossoms of the fields, should not attract artists in search of picturesque costume and scenes of pastoral life. Rougher and wilder than Normandy, more thinly populated, and less visited by tourists, Brittany offers better opportunities for outdoor study, and more suggestive scenes for the painter. Nowhere in France are there finer peasantry; nowhere do we see more dignity of aspect in field labour, more nobility of feature amongst men and women; nowhere more picturesque ruins; nowhere such primitive habitations and, it must be added, such dirt. Brittany is still behindhand in civilisation; the land is only half cultivated and divided into small holdings and the fields are strewn with Druidical stones. From the dark recesses of the Montagnes Noires the streams come down between deep ravines as wild and bare of cultivation as the moors of Scotland, but the hillsides are clothed thickly in summer with ferns, broom and heather. Follow one of these streams in its windings towards the sea, where the troubled waters rest in the shade of overhanging trees, by pastures and cultivated lands, and we may see the Breton peasants on their farms, reaping and carrying their small harvest of corn and rye, oats and buckwheat; the women with white caps and wide collars, short dark skirts, and heavy wooden sabots, the men in white woollen jackets, breeks (*bragous bras*), and black gaiters, broad-brimmed hats and long hair streaming in the wind—leading oxen yoked to heavy carts painted blue. Here we are reminded at once of the French painters of pastoral life, of Jules Breton, Millet, Troyon, and Rosa Bonheur; and as we see the dark brown harvest fields, with the white clouds lying low on the horizon, and the strong erect figures and grand faces of the peasants lighted by the evening sun, we understand why Brittany is a chosen land for the painter of *paysages*. Low in tone as the landscape is, sombre as are the costumes of the people, cloudy and fitful in light and shade as is all this wind-blown land, there is often a clearness in the atmosphere which brings out the features of the country with great distinctness, and impresses them upon the mind.

ST. MALO—DINAN.

ON a bright summer's morning in July the *ballon captif*, which we may use in imagination in these pages—our French friends having taught us its use in peace as well as in war—floats over the blue water-gate of Brittany like a

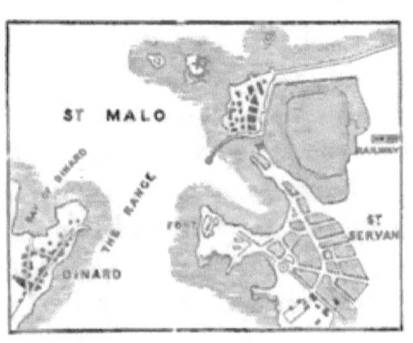

golden ball. The sun is high, and the tide is flowing fast round the dark rock islands that lie at our feet, pouring into the harbour of ST. MALO, floating the vessels and fishing-boats innumerable that line the quays inside the narrow neck of land called Le Sillon, which connects the city with the mainland, and driving gay parties of bathers up the sands of the beautiful Baie d'Écluse at Dinard.

On the little map we can see at a glance the relative positions of St. Malo, St. Servan, and Dinard, also the mouth of the river Rance which flows southward, wide and strong, into innumerable bays, until it winds under the walls and towers of Dinan. Looking down upon the city, now alive with the life which the rising tide gives to every sea-port, seeing the strength of its position seaward, and the protection from without to the little forests of masts, whose leaves are the bright trade banners of many nations, it is easy to understand how centuries ago St. Malo, and St. Servan were chosen as military strongholds, and how in these later times St. Malo has a maritime importance apparently out of proportion to its trade, and to its population of not more than 15,000 inhabitants.

From a bird's-eye point of view we may obtain a clearer idea of St. Malo and of its neighbourhood than many who have actually visited these places, and can judge for ourselves of its probable attractions for a summer visit. It seems unusually bright and pleasant this morning, for the light west wind has cleared the air, and carried the odours of St. Malo landward. There is to be a regatta in the afternoon, the principal course being across, and across, the mouth of the Rance, between St. Malo and Dinard, and already little white sails may be seen spread in various directions, darting in and out between the rock islands outside the bay. On one of these islands, Grand Bé, (marked with a cross on the map), is the tomb of the illustrious Chateaubriand, a plain granite slab, surmounted by a cross, and railed in with a very ordinary-looking iron railing. This gravestone, which stands upon an eminence, and is conspicuous rather than solitary, is described by a French writer as a romantic resting-place for the departed diplomatist, characteristic and sublime—"ni arbres, ni fleurs, ni inscription—le roc, la mer et l'immensité!" but as a matter of fact it is anything but solitary in summer-time, and it is more visited by tourists than by sea-gulls. The waves are beating round it now, but at low water there will be a line of pedestrians crossing the sands; some to bathe and some to place *immortelles* on the tomb.

F

The sands of Le Sillon are covered with bathers and everywhere there is life and movement; the narrow, winding streets of St. Malo pour out their contents on the seashore; little steamers pass to and from Dinard continually, fishing and pilot boats come and go, and yachts are fluttering their white sails far out at sea. Everything looks gay, for the sun is bright, and it is the day of the regatta.

Looking landward, the eye ranges over a district of flat, marshy land, that once was sea, and we may discern in the direction of Dol an island rock in the midst of a marshy plain, at least three miles from the sea. On the summit of this rock is a chapel to Notre Dame de l'Espérance, and near it, standing alone on the plain, is a column of grey granite nearly thirty feet high, one of the "menhirs" or "Druid stones" that we shall see often in Britanny. Eastward there is the beautiful bay of Cancale, famous for its oyster-fisheries; the village built on the heights is glistening in the sunlight, and the blue bay stretches away east and north as far as Granvillle.

The Bretons, both in St. Malo and the suburb of St. Servan, are a little demoralised in summer, and wish to be "fine." To-day being a fête day, they are *en grande toilette*, and the white caps worn by some of the women are trimmed with real old lace. In the shops and on the promenades the majority of people are dressed as in Paris; the country people and the fishing and poorer class of Malouins, only, wearing any distinctive costume. The fishermen of Cancale make money and save it, and send their children to school by train to Rennes, and the fisherman's daughter comes back in a costume that makes her neighbours envious. Every year more white caps are thrown aside, for Mathilde will not be outdone by Louise; and so the change goes on, and each year the markets of St. Malo and St. Servan have less individuality of costume.

We have come to Brittany to sketch and to note what is most characteristic and picturesque. So far, on the threshold, as it were, what have we seen? Coming from England, and sailing southward into its blue bay on a summer morning, there was an impression of brightness and colour unusual to our own shores. In St. Malo itself three pictures remain upon the memory. The first is the sunset between the islands and across the sands, near the bathing-place of Le Sillon; the second the moonlight view of its cathedral tower at the end of a narrow street, filling it and towering above it with a grandeur of effect almost equal to that of St. Stephen's at Vienna; the third picture is in the old courtyard of the Hôtel de France. This house, or part of it, belonged to the family of the Vicomte de Chateaubriand, and it was here, in a room facing the sea, that the celebrated author and diplomatist was born. On the hotel the family arms (the peacock's plume) are emblazoned, and just outside its gates, in the little dusty square called "La Place de Chateaubriand," a new bronze statue, bright and shining, has lately been erected to his memory. Travellers imprisoned between the narrow streets and dingy walls of St. Malo, fortified and barricaded against the fresh breezes of the sea, may perchance seek the cool courtyard of the Hôtel de France as a place of refuge during the heat of the day, and, if not quite tired of hearing of Chateaubriand, may dwell in imagination upon the historic associations of this house. In a corner of the courtyard, now used as a café, there is an old stone staircase leading to the first *étage*, such as we may see in many a French château, and upon it there lingers this afternoon an English girl in the graceful costume of to-day. She wears a rich, dark, close-fitting dress in simple folds, spreading where it trails upon the rough granite steps with the stealthy grandeur of a peacock's tail upon a ruined wall. As she turns her head and leans over between the pillars of the covered balcony, her " Rubens hat " and fair hair are framed in antique carved stone. The effect is accidental, but the harmonious combination of costume and architecture brings out suddenly the beauties of each, and gives us a glimpse, not to be forgotten, of the graces of a past age.

THE RANCE.

THE tide is now flowing fast up the Rance, filling its numerous bays and inlets, floating odd-shaped little boats and rafts that are moored off the villages on its banks, running up here and there inland between rocks and trees and forming miniature lakes, which will disappear as the tide goes down. The little steamer for Dinan starts from the Quai Napoléon, and goes up on the flood in about three hours, having just time to reach Dinan and return to St. Malo before the water has subsided. The fore-deck is crowded with market-women and small merchandise, and on the after-deck, which is but a few yards square, there are some French and English tourists under a canvas awning, which is useful alike for shelter from sun, rain, and cinders. Steering south-east by south, we steam gently up the Rance (getting a fine view of St. Servan in passing), a river that, near its mouth, seems to have no boundaries or banks, that flows in and out amongst cultivated fields, then suddenly through narrow defiles of rocks and under the shadow of forest trees that might be in Switzerland. Once or twice we sail, as it were, in an inland lake, or, as the French call it, "une petite Méditerranée"; we can neither see where we entered nor any outlet on our route. There are fishing and market boats, lying in quiet corners, and one or two pleasure yachts with flags flying, moored in the prettiest spots near modern summer châlets, the slate roofs of which appear above the trees. We pass one considerable village, St. Suliac, on the east bank, behind which is the ancient fort of Châteauneuf; and, on the west, the grey walls of more than one old château are visible. The water is blue and tidal until we arrive at a lock a few miles farther, when the little steamer ploughs through a narrow canal-like stream, and sends the water flowing over the banks, washing the stems of the poplar trees, and smothering their leaves in clouds of smoke.

We are entering Brittany now, and are far out of hearing of the waves that beat upon St. Malo, and of the band of the casino on its sands. On either side the valleys are rich with verdure and with orchards of fruit. There are farmhouses and villas dotted about, and peasants at work in the fields. We pass close to the banks during the last mile, and are shut in by rocks and trees; but all at once the view enlarges, and there rises before us a scene so grand and, at the same time, so familiar that we feel delighted and rewarded at having approached DINAN by water. The prevailing tone of landscape during the last few miles has been sombre, and the valleys in shadow with their dark granite rocks and gloom of firs have contrasted picturesquely with the sunshine on distant fields.

As we reach Dinan in the afternoon, the valley of the Rance is in shadow, whilst above and before us, crowning a hill, are the old roofs, towers, and spires of Dinan shining in the sun. The sides of the valley here are almost precipitous, and across it, high above our heads, is a plain modern viaduct, reaching to the suburb of Lanvallay. Dinan is on the left bank of the Rance; and near the bridge where we land the steep streets of the old town reach to the water's edge. Above our heads are feudal towers, and parts of old walls and the grey roofs of houses between the trees, and away southward the valley of the Rance winding out of sight. We said it was a familiar picture for the approach to Dinan by water, and the view from the hills on the opposite bank of the Rance, seen under summer suns, have been perpetuated on canvas by many an English artist. It is well to see Dinan thus, *en couleur de rose*, for on a nearer and longer acquaintance our impressions may change.

Dinan—situated on the summit and slopes of wooded hills, their dark granite sides appearing here and there through the trees; with its mediæval towers and terraces, its old grey houses with pointed roofs, and its handsome white modern houses—forms a background to the market-women, with their stalls of fruit and vegetables, peasants in blue blouses, and the usual summer crowd, including Parisians in suits of white, with broad straw hats and blue umbrellas, thronging on the quay waiting for our little steamer.

As we climb up a steep, dirty street, leading from the quay, called the Rue de Jersual, and under a Gothic gateway—past old houses, with high-pitched roofs and leaning timbers, rising one above another in irregular steps—we hear the sound of the loom in the darkness on either side, and the inhabitants come out to stare as usual; shining red faces, under white caps, lean out from little latticed windows and from doorways, and in the gutters many a little pair of sabots stuffed with hay, is rattling on the stones. It is a ladder of cobblestones and dirt, cool and slippery, sheltered by projecting eaves from the afternoon sun, the principal approach from the river a century ago, up which a stream of modern pilgrims now files into the upper town. They pause to take breath at the top (300 feet), and then disperse on the *Place*, where, in front of dusty rows of trees, the omnibuses and carts, which have come round by the broad, circuitous road, are setting down travellers. We have ascended at least 300 feet to the *Place*, and take up our quarters in the wide open square, looking as dusty and uncared for as usual in French provincial towns, and commanding, as usual also, no view of the country round. Nurses, in white caps, sit knitting under the shadows of stunted trees, while the children play in the dust; cavalry officers of all grades play at cards and drink absinthe at little tables half hidden by trees planted in boxes at the hotel doors; ladies and children, a priest, a workman in blue blouse dragging a load of stones, a woman coming from market, and an Englishman or two, on pleasure intent, with draggled beards and grey knickerbockers much too wide for them, as is the fashion of the time. Above the trees, the houses across the square rise in irregular lines, their steep roofs, old and sun-stained, are full of variety and colour; behind them tree tops wave, and great masses of white clouds drive northward to the sea.

Dinan is full of interest both for the artist and the antiquary, and the environs are full of variety and beauty; on every side will be found charming wooded walks and valleys, from which we can see Dinan, set high on green hills, the sky-line a fringe of trees and towers. The walks on the ramparts, with their lines of poplars and the views across the deep fosse below will give an idea of the military architecture of the middle ages, and especially of the natural strength and importance of Dinan as a fortified city when besieged by the Duke of Lancaster in 1359 and defended by the brave Du Guesclin. In St. Malo, Chateaubriand was the hero; in Dinan it is Du Guesclin, constable of France in the fourteenth century. Whichever

way we turn we find some new view and point of interest, and the inhabitants are so accustomed to the incursion of strangers, and reap so many benefits by their coming, that we are allowed to sketch almost undisturbed.

The ramparts are comparatively deserted by day, and form a promenade by moonlight worth coming far to see. If ever there was a spot on earth prepared for lovers, it is the broad walk on the southern ramparts of Dinan, where the moon shines upon the path between tall waving poplars and silvers the distant trees, where there is scarcely a sound to break the stillness, where there is room for every Romeo out of hearing of his neighbour, and where the sounds of the city are hushed behind granite walls. It is naturally romantic and beautiful, and, with the associations which cling around its towers, has a charm which is almost unique; but let us tell the truth. There are clusters of white roses clinging to the old masonry above, which have scattered their full-blown leaves at our feet, and below, in the deep dell which formed the ancient fosse, there is honeysuckle in the straggling garden; but the odours that rise on the evening air are not of roses nor of honeysuckle, nor from the broad champaign around. There surely was never a beautiful spot so defiled. As a picture, the general aspect of Dinan will remain in memory —a picture not to be effaced by the erection of large new barracks, or by the railway now constructing in the valley —stately Dinan with its ancient groves and terraces, its hanging gardens, and sylvan views.

We must not linger in such a well-known part of Brittany, but we must take one walk, leaving the town by the ramparts towards the north. Here in the midst of a tangle of briars and bushes, hemmed in on every side, run over with ivy and every variety of creeper, shut off entirely from some points of view by an orchard laden to the ground with fruit and by a garden of flowers, is the one tower left of the famous château of La GARAYE. The grey octagonal turret, with its crumbling Renaissance ornament, stands high above the surrounding trees, and catches the evening sunlight long after the avenues of beeches by which it is approached is in gloom. The place is as solemn and quiet, at the end of a long avenue, as any poet could desire; but as we approach the gate of the château of "the lady with the liberal hand," whom Mrs. Norton has immortalised in her poem, there are the usual signs of demoralisation. There are pigs about, and tourists; and the show is charged for in the usual way. We pay our money and take away some souvenir of the place. Americans who have read (and recited often in their own homes) "The Lady of La Garaye" sometimes make Dinan the extreme western point of their tour in Europe, and have trodden the ground into a hard track to the château with their pilgrim feet; but the position is inconvenient for American tourists who have much to see, and so, it is understood, they are going to buy the turret and take it home. The idea is not as absurd as it may sound; it is a very pretty ruin, but it will fall soon if not cared for, and the low wall on either side of the turret will disappear behind the fruitful orchard. The old hospital is now used as a farm-shed, but wants repairing to be habitable; and the ancient cider-press, with its massive wooden beams, lies rotting in the sun. The farm children are gathering blackberries from the bushes which grow between the hearthstones of the old banquet-hall, poultry swarm in my lady's boudoir, and there is a hum of bees and insects about the ruin.

As we leave Dinan by diligence with much cracking of whips and jingling of bells through a long straggling suburb, the peasants stare at us from their dark dwellings; we stop at wayside inns—unnecessarily, it would seem—and are surrounded by beggars of all ages and sizes. Here a little child comes suddenly to earth at the sound of wheels and peers from the darkness of her home underground with the brightness and vivacity of a weasel; her black eyes glisten with astonishment and with the instinct of animal nature scenting food; she transforms herself in an instant from buoyant youth and almost cherub-like beauty, to a cringing, whining mendicant. "Quelque chose, quelque chose pour l'amour de Dieu," in good, clear French, nearly all the words that her parents would have her learn, in the intervals of playing and road-scraping — the latter her only serious business in life. But the school-master is abroad in Brittany; the edict has gone forth that every child of France shall henceforth learn the French tongue; and this little creature will be taught and tamed, and civilised into ways that her parents never knew.

One more picture on the road, an incident common enough, but characteristic and worth recording. It is a sultry afternoon, with a deep blue sky and a burning sun. So fierce is the heat that it has silenced for a time the barking of dogs and the arguments of some of our passengers. Just outside a village the straight road, unsheltered even by poplars, is fringed with low brushwood and long grasses withering under a curtain of dust. There is nothing stirring but a little yellowhammer and a magpie on the road, a *cantonnière* in wide straw hat, chipping at a heap of stones, and the lumbering diligence in which we travel; no shelter but in a wood hard by.

Presently we come to a halt in a narrow part of the road, where M. Achille Dufaure's empty wood cart stops the way. It is a suggestive picture, which we may call "The Hour of Repose." In the foreground, in the burning road is a tall white horse, encumbered, now in his old age, with a great wooden collar and clumsy harness, chained to a dark blue cart with dirt-encrusted wheels, half-smothered on this summer's day with a blue woolsack over his shoulders, foaming at the mouth, and streaming with the wounds of flies and other injuries, but pricking his ears as of old at the sound of approaching wheels. In the background, but a few yards off, is a cool wood of beech and elm, dark in its shadows, green in its depth with ivy and fern, and fringed against the sky with tops of waving poplars. This

broad mass of green, which comes between the brightness of sky and the burning road, with its foreground of dry grasses, is relieved on one spot by a cool ripple of blue—it is Achille lying on his face asleep, his blouse just lifted by a breeze; he will repose for two or three hours, whilst his horse stands in the sun, and the hot shadows lengthen from his heels. No amount of shouting on the part of our driver will waken the sleeper; blessings and curses, cracking of whips and blowing of horns, are all tried in vain, and the monotony of our journey is relieved by the diligence being dragged (as it might have been at first) over the field at the roadside and we resume our way.

As we travel westward, the aspect of the land becomes suddenly changed; it is clouded over and rained upon, and is a sombre contrast to the former brightness. After the glare of the sun the senses are grateful for quiet tones; but the sight is strange, almost mournful. The district is only a few miles from busy towns and sea-ports and on the main line of railway from Paris to Brest, but it is out of the world, and seems, under its cloudy aspect, farther than ever removed from civilisation; we pass substantial-looking farmhouses, but the dwellings of the peasants are generally hovels, with tumble-down mud walls and immovable windows; in their gardens are dungheaps and stagnant pools of water. We see women at work in the fields, girls tending cattle, and the men, generally, looking on. Everything we pass on the road looks comparatively untidy, rough, and poor, with the poverty of ignorance and neglect rather than of means, for the soil is rich, and yields well. The country is really fruitful, but an acre of land is often divided into twenty different lots, in each of which there are separate crops of hemp, buckwheat, or potatoes, or they are filled with gorse for winter fodder for cattle. The high hedges are made of mud-banks, gorse, and ferns, and the gates between them are formed of felled trees, the stem forming the bar, the roots being left as a counterpoise to lift the gate on its rough, wooden latch.

The rain ceases as we approach Lamballe; the air is fresh with the wind coming from the bay of St. Brieuc, and as the sky clears, we obtain, at intervals on the undulating road, views over finely wooded valleys, with high hedgerows, banked up and planted with elms and oaks. The chestnut trees, wet with the rain, are rich in colour, and the fields of buckwheat lighten the landscape again.

Another turn in the road, and we are in evening light, there is open pasture land, and the cattle are winding home; at another, a farmer is meditating on his stock in the corner of a field. Thus we pass from one picture to another, quaint and idyllic, the last reminding us more of Troyon than of Rosa Bonheur.

In ST. BRIEUC we find ourselves in a busy city of 15,000 inhabitants, apparently too much occupied with trade and agriculture to think about beautifying their houses and streets. There are many narrow, irregular streets, in which the old houses have been replaced by others generally modern and mean; "une vraie ville de rentiers qui aurait besoin d'être 'hausmannisée.'" There is a large square *Place* for the military, and a market-place near the cathedral, where the old women congregate. St. Brieuc is the principal town in the department; it carries on a large export trade in the produce of the country, especially in butter and vegetables, for the English and European markets. Cattle are exported largely from Légué, the actual port, about two miles off, in the centre of the bay of Brieuc, hidden from the town by intervening hills.

In the country round and on the hills overlooking the sea, there are men and women at work in the fields, girls carrying milk on their heads from the neighbouring farms, and others busy in the farmyards. The buckwheat harvest has commenced, and the fields are being robbed of their rich colour; but the scene is bright with fresh green and yellow mustard, and rich here and there with clover. The sombre figures are the peasantry with their dark costumes. Here we feel inclined, for the first time, to stay and sketch, wandering along the coast to the fishing villages on the western shore of the wide-spreading bay of St. Brieuc, visiting the farms and homesteads, and making studies.

CATTLE FAIR IN BRITTANY.

Face p. 78.

It is at a village on the cliff near Fort Rosalier that we first see a number of men and women winnowing, their arms extended in the breeze, a bright and characteristic scene; a picture soon to vanish before patent winnowing-machines and other improvements.

About midway between St. Brieuc and Guingamp, on the north side of the railway, is the quiet little town of Châtelaudren. It is washed and watered by the Leff, the "river of tears," which, coming from the mountains that we see to the south, winds its way through rich valleys, seaward. In its course, and in its time, the Leff has done much havoc in this peaceful valley, inundating and destroying Châtelaudren in 1773, and still occasionally overflowing its banks. To-day it is to the angler a capital trout stream, if he will follow its course southward to the mountains; to the artistic eye it is a sparkling river of light, set in a landscape of green and grey. The land is thickly cultivated, and well grown with crops almost down to the sea; and on every side in this autumn time there are signs of industry. From the fields we hear voices of women at work; in the farmyards there is the dull thud of the flail and the burr of the winnowing machine. Across the sloping fields from the sea come sounds of singing and laughter, disconnected and weird sometimes, from being caught up by the wind, then dropped and taken up again.

GUINGAMP.

EIGHT miles from Châtelaudren, in a green valley watered by the river Trieux, is the quiet old town of Guingamp. Its past history, like that of nearly every town in Brittany, has been so eventful that its present normal state may well be calm; but once a year its inhabitants neither work nor repose. In the month of September they hold their annual Fête de St. Loup, and pilgrims come from all parts of Brittany by excursion trains to the famous "Pardon" of Guingamp.

Guingamp is a town of not more than 8000 inhabitants, with one principal street, which winds irregularly down like a stream, spreading and overflowing its banks at one point, in triangular fashion, in what is called the marketplace, then narrowing again, and working its way through a suburb of small houses into the great high-road to Morlaix. It has two monuments—the church of Notre Dame, and a bronze fountain in the market-place. The timbered houses are old, and many of their gables lean; the cobblestones in the streets are rough, and the public promenade of dust, with withering trees, built on the old ramparts, looks as dreary as any we shall see on our travels. But it is surrounded by green landscape, and the view from the walks on the ramparts, seen through the tops of poplars, is of a green valley with trees and grey rooftops between which winds the river Trieux, slowly turning waterwheels.

The church was built between the fourteenth and sixteenth centuries, and represents several styles of architecture—Romanesque, Gothic, and Renaissance. It was originally founded as a castle chapel, and part of the structure is as early as the thirteenth century. It has three towers, the centre one having a spire.

Brittany is a land of lasting monuments; and of its buildings it has been well said, "ce que la Normandie modelait dans le tuf, la Basse-Bretagne le ciselait en granit"; but remembering the magnificent churches to be seen in Normandy, we need not detain the reader long in Guingamp. If we were asked by tourists if the church of Notre Dame at Guingamp was worth going very far to see, we should answer, No. It is only as a picture that it attracts us much. We shall see finer buildings in other parts of Brittany, but nowhere a more characteristic assembly. The most curious feature is a chapel forming the north porch, which is open and close to the street, lighted at night for services, and separated only from the

G

road by a grille. This *portail*, as it is called, forms the chapel of Notre Dame de Halgoet, and is the sacred shrine to which all come at the fête of Guingamp. It is ornamented by rich stone carving and grotesque gurgoyles. The people of Guingamp love the chapel of Notre Dame de Halgoet; it is a retreat for them by day and by night, a place of meeting for old and young, with a perpetual beggars' mart at the door. This north porch with its open grille is a house of call for rich and poor of both sexes, and placed as it is in the centre of the town, abutting upon the principal street, it forms part of their everyday life to go in and out as they pass by. It is one of the many welcome retreats in France; in a land of perpetual noises and glare, of shrill, uncouth voices and latchless doors, the church gives peace and shade.

In the centre of Guingamp is its market-place, and in the centre of the market-place is a fountain, consisting of a circular granite basin with a wrought-iron railing. There is a second basin of bronze, supported by four sea-horses with conventional wings, and a third by four naiads; the central figure is the Virgin, her feet resting on a crescent. This fountain was constructed by an Italian artist, and its waters played for the first time on the night of the annual Pardon, in 1745.[1]

A few yards from the cathedral, on the opposite side of the street, is the old Hôtel de l'Ouest, where travellers are entertained in rather rough but bountiful fashion.

"Take a little trout or salmon, caught this morning in the Trieux, a little beef, a little mutton, a little veal, some tongue, some omelettes, some pheasant, some fish salad, some sweets, some coffee, and then—stir gently," is the prescription for travellers who stay at the Hôtel de l'Ouest.

---

[1] The religious aspect of these Pardons, and the gathering of the pilgrims, is described at page 113.

SUNDAY MORNING.

Face p. 82.

As this is a good inn, it may be worth while to state that the total charge for *three* English travellers, who spent a night and part of a day there, was 12 fr. 80 c.

Excepting at the time of fêtes, Guingamp is almost as quiet and primitive in its ways as in the days of the Black Prince; but on one summer's morning we hear an unusual sound from the great bell of Notre Dame, and find a procession of priests and choristers winding up the principal street, followed by hundreds of the inhabitants. What is the occasion? "The mother of the Maire is dead," is the answer; "she was a bountiful lady, beloved by all, and we are to bury her this morning." And so the inhabitants turn out *en masse*, and march with slow steps, for about half a mile, to the cemetery. It is a dark, silent stream of people, filling the street and carrying everything slowly before it; the only sounds being the chanting of the choir, and the repetition of prayers. We follow to the cemetery, which is crowded with graves, each headed by little iron or wooden crosses, hung with immortelles. The procession divides and disperses down the narrow paths, a few only of the friends of the deceased standing near the grave.

At one corner of the cemetery is a shabby little wooden building, like a gardener's tool-house, which seems to excite much interest. A girl, with shining bronzed face, in a snow-white cap, holding a little child by the hand, is coming out of the door; we venture to ask the reason of her visit. "Just to see my father for a minute," is the ready answer.

In a little wooden box, about the size of a small dog kennel, is her father's skull, or *chef* as it is called; he is tumbling over with his neighbours in other boxes as in the sketch overleaf, which, rough as it is, has the grim merit of accuracy. The sight is a common one in Brittany, but it is startling and takes us by surprise at first, to see at least fifty of these shabby boxes, some on shelves in rows, but generally piled up in disorder and neglect. The lady who is being buried so solemnly this morning will some day be unearthed, and her *chef*, in a box duly labelled and decorated with immortelles, will take its place in the ossuary of Guingamp.

Looking round over the thickly-wooded but rather sombre landscape, and on the old grey roofs of the town, one is a little at a loss to account for the rapturous descriptions which nearly all travellers give of Guingamp. On a fine summer's morning the landscape is seen to perfection; but to tell the truth, the scene is not very striking either for beauty or for colour. Guingamp has been described as "a diamond set in emeralds," and we read of its landscape *riant*, and so on. "Guingamp m'a pris le cœur," says another traveller; but their interest is in the past, they people it with memories.

The artist and the angler may linger in its valleys, and make it headquarters for many an excursion. If we might suggest one more, we should say—go and see the ruins of the abbey of Ste. Croix, in a south-easterly direction, following the course of the river Trieux. Turn round to the right hand, just by a wayside cross, and enter a large farmyard. The women are busy winnowing, not with hands upraised in the wind, as we may see them at St. Brieuc, but twirling by hand a new patent blue-painted rotatory winnowing-machine with a burring sound, in a cloud of choking dust. They are storing their harvest in a large barn, the remains of an ancient Gothic church, the abbey of Ste. Croix, with its choir window piled up with straw. The garden reaches to the river, where ancient and historic trout disregard the angler of to-day. The farm and its surroundings are as picturesque as any painter could desire.

The inhabitants of this suburb have a real grievance; they had lived for generations in familiar sight and sound of the cathedral of Guingamp; they saw its spire and towers at evening, standing out sharp and clear against the western sky, and were in feeling living almost in the town itself, when suddenly the engineers of the "Chemin de Fer de l'Ouest" threw up a mountain of earth in their midst, and shut out the town and the sunset light from them, and from their children, for evermore.

Twelve miles north-east of Guingamp is Lanleff—"the land of tears," celebrated for one of the most curious architectural monuments in Brittany, the circular temple of Lanleff. Leaving Guingamp, we pass through a solitary wooded country, the undulating road soon rising high above the valley of the Trieux. The air is fresh and invigorating, and the views from the summits of the hills extend over a wide range of land. At Gommenech we enter the valley of the Leff that we passed at Châtelaudren. There is no prettier river, or one that should more truly delight an artist's eye, than the Leff in its long, winding journey from the mountains to the sea.

Sheltered by woods, shut in here and there by granite walls, with ruins crowning the heights, between green banks and through sloping fields, it is one of those picturesque rivers which are peculiar to Brittany of which we seldom hear mention, but which many an English angler knows well.

Continuing northward, we soon arrive at the summit of a hill overlooking the bay of Paimpol and the thickly wooded country round; we have passed good country-houses on the route, with flower-gardens skirted by hanging woods; and as we approach Paimpol, there are houses scattered in sheltered bays, with fishing and pleasure boats aground; an old church surrounded closely by houses, a little *Place*, a custom-house, a quay, boatmen, and fisherwomen; but—where is the water? It has retreated for more than a mile, and the long bay or estuary and the port of Paimpol are a desolate waste of mud. Paimpol is a small but busy fishing village, much frequented in the summer by the French for bathing. It is not fashionable, but the inns are comfortable, and the country is full of attractions for the summer visitor. The houses on the *Place* and in the narrow streets are old and weather-worn; some are dark and mysterious-looking, and have that peculiar smuggling aspect with which we soon become familiar on this coast.

In a corner of the quiet churchyard of Paimpol there reposes at full length, in stone, "L'Abbé Jean Vincent Moy," many years *curé* of this place and honorary canon of St. Brieuc; and round about him, placed thickly in rows, the former inhabitants of Paimpol rest under black wooden crosses. The *curé* is carved in dark green stone, from which time has taken the sharpness of the chiselling; but the expression is life-like, representing him in the popular act of blessing. There is a cup of holy water at his feet, supplied by an old woman who kneels before the tomb on the damp ground. It is her pious office to guard

A QUIET CORNER.

Face p. 87.

the tomb of her pastor, and brush off the autumn leaves which fall thickly from a grove of elms. They move slowly and die leisurely at Paimpol; this old woman's time is not yet, for she "has only eighty years." In four newly made graves there repose Eugénie, Marie, Mathilde, and Hortense, and their respective ages are eighty-two, eighty-four, eighty-eight, and eighty-nine!

At Paimpol in summer every one seems to take life easily, the French visitors driving about, bathing, boating, and living perpetually in the fresh, pure air; the native inhabitants getting up boat-races, and dancing the "gavotte" at night, in streets lighted by paper lanterns in old Breton fashion.

There is unusual brightness on this sombre, storm-washed shore; there is the dazzle of a crimson pennant, and the flashing of a snow-white sail; there are green banks, in contrast to water of the deepest blue, for in these little inlets of the sea the summer sun clothes everything with brightness in a moment. Perhaps we have seen Paimpol *en couleur de rose*, for there has been blue sky overhead nearly every day for a fortnight, and the sun is so hot at midday that the market-women put up their red umbrellas, and the men descend into cool cellars for shelter and refreshment.

It is a shaded walk of about a mile and a half from Paimpol to the abbey of BEAUPORT. The road and the by-paths are shut in by high banks, so that we come upon it rather suddenly, looking down upon the ruins, through the bare windows of which we can see the sea. The Gothic chapel is a complete ruin, but part of the abbey building is in good preservation, and inhabited. One room is turned into a school-house, and a great roofless hall, once the refectory, is used as a threshing-floor. The romantic aspect of the ruins of Beauport, with its surrounding scenery, has been described in every book on Brittany, and the view of it by moonlight over the bay of Paimpol is as famous as that of "fair Melrose." To this ancient abbey come pilgrims of the nineteenth century to study and wonder at the art of life shown by the monks of the thirteenth. Here the fruitful land meets the bountiful sea, and there is no arid line of demarcation; the corn waves at the water's edge, and the flowers bloom and shed their leaves into the water. The soil is rich, and the air is soft, and in this autumn time the harvest seems everywhere ready to man's hand—a harvest of fruit and grain on land, and of fish and rich seaweed upon the shore.

The abbey of Beauport is considered by M. Merrimée to be "the most perfect example of the monastic architecture of the thirteenth century"—in fact, the most important and beautiful ruin in Brittany.

> "It lies
> Deep-meadow'd, happy, fair with orchard-lawns
> And bowery hollows, crown'd with summer sea."

As we wander round the gardens and through the avenues of trees that line the raised walks on the breakwater, or under the shadow of high brick walls, laden with old fruit-trees, it is easy to realise in our minds the lives of its former occupants. The picturesqueness of Beauport, especially the view, from the eastern side, of the chapter-house and other dwellings, should attract artists. This afternoon there is one large white umbrella planted firmly in the gravel of its deserted walks, and one canvas spread with a green landscape in which old, grey, mullioned windows, and the stems of weather-beaten trees, form prominent features.

From Paimpol to the town of Lannion is twenty miles by the road, crossing the river Trieux by a lofty suspension bridge at Lézardrieux, and halting at the ancient cathedral town of Tréguier by the way.

It is near Lannion that we make the discovery of a watering-place, called Perros-Guirec, where we can live in the summer season for five francs a day, and where

"On loue et on échange de petits enfants;
On coupe des orielles et la queue aux chiens d'après la dernière mode."

it is difficult to spend more. The bay of Perros-Guirec is just sufficiently off the track of tourists to make it delightful in summer. There are two small inns on the shore, one at either extremity; but the actual village of Perros-Guirec is situated amongst the trees which crown the northern promontory of the bay; there are a few summer-houses and gardens, an old church, and near it a convent. It seems hard to break up the peace of this retreat by printing a description, but here, we are bound to record, is a spot where we can spend our summer days with the greatest delight. We can live as we like, dress as we like, bathe in the water at our feet, sit and sketch in the shade of woods, through the branches of which we see the shining sea. The air, so fresh and bracing, sweet with the breath of pines, is more grateful in the hot summer months than at Dinard or Trouville, and the sights and sounds are certainly more healthful and restful.

It is evening as we return from a walk by the sea north of Perros-Guirec; before us is a wide and beautiful bay, extending for nearly half a mile in a noble curve of shore; it is shut off from the land by sloping hills, and bounded at either extremity by rocks. The tide is nearly out, and the sand is as pure, smooth, and untrodden, as on Robinson Crusoe's island. There are no projecting rocks or stones on this wide plain; nothing to be seen on its surface but our long dark shadows and two little crabs, behind their time, making hard for the retreating water. We cross the bay leisurely, treading lightly on the carpet of sand, and watching the sunset light on the rocks and on the little islands which make this coast such a terror to navigators. They are smiling this evening in that roseate hue which storm-washed red granite rocks put forth on gala days, and their purple reflections in the water are as deep and glowing as from the steep walls of the Lago di Gardo under an October sun.

The two crabs soon disappear in the water, but as we cross the bay, two other little spots appear at some distance on the sand. The sight is so unusual here that the thought of Crusoe on his island occurs again, and we approach cautiously. The objects are larger and farther off than at first appeared, in fact nearly a quarter of a mile; they consist of two little neat bundles of clothing, one of which appears to be a silk dress surmounted by a white straw hat! There is nothing near them but sand, no sign of human creature; but, presently looking seaward, the mystery is explained by two heads appearing suddenly on the surface of the sea, one with long hair floating from it. We beat a retreat and learn afterwards that an evening walk in "ce pays ici" is often supplemented by an evening bath. Thus Monsieur and Madame, strolling together on the sands, make a diversion without ceremony or "machines," and without the slightest "mauvaise honte."

A little to the north of Perros-Guirec is the village of Ploumanach, almost built out into the sea. It is a place to be visited above all others on this coast for its wildness, and to see the hardy fishing population, living amongst a loose mass of rocks, nearly surrounded by water. Looking northward, on a clear day, we may see a group of islands, one of which, the abode of innumerable wild-fowl, is said, (with doubtful authority) to be the Island of Avalon, or Avilion, where King Arthur was buried.

LANNION, at the time of writing, may be said to be one of the outposts of French tourist civilisation in the Côtes-du-Nord. Hither come in summer time a few Parisians, and families from the interior, for the bathing; driving to and from Perros-Guirec and other places on the coast daily, but seldom actually staying on the seashore. In their train come the latest fashions, both in manners and in dress, and it is here we may notice, especially on Sundays and fêtes, the strange contrasts in costume between the Bretons and "the French," as the natives persist in calling their visitors.

It is on their way down to the Jardin Anglais one Sunday morning that a gay Parisian and his wife walk through the market-place and down one of the old steep streets;

behind them come nurse and *bébé* all " en grande toilette de l'été." The lady wears a white dress, which trails over the cobblestones; the gentleman is in brown holland, with white shoes, white tie, and a new straw hat shaped like a Prussian helmet and decorated with a crimson band; the baby is decorated in as much of the fashion of the day as its size will permit; the nurse, the neatest of the party, wears a spotless white cap and a short dark dress. An old dame, seated at her doorstep, taking a bountiful pinch of snuff, emits a harsh sound, more like "Jah!" or "Yah!" than the customary approving "Jolie!" which comes so trippingly on every French tongue. The Breton woman, in her old-fashioned gown, black stockings, and neat stout shoes, who owns the house she lives in, and perhaps half a dozen others, regards the fashionable visitors with anything but pleasure, and resists the advance of fashion into Lannion as an evil almost equal to an inroad of Prussians.

Every one makes a short stay at Lannion, in order to visit the thirteenth-century castle of Tonquédec, in a valley about eight miles south of the town. This castle is one of the best preserved specimens of military architecture in all France, and it is one of the beauty spots in Brittany.

Travelling in a south-westerly direction, by road to the busy city of Morlaix, and by rail to Landerneau (leaving to the north the wild district of St. Pol de Léon indicated in the sketch), we come to the department of Finisterre and have a different aspect of Brittany altogether. At Landerneau we are on the high-road to Brest. The railway from Landerneau to Brest is carried for the most part at a high level, and from the windows on the *left hand* we obtain beautiful views of the scenery of the bay. Below we can see the stores of timber for naval use, and are otherwise reminded of our approach to a sea-port by

TOWERS OF ST. POL DE LEON.

the company which collect at the small stations *en route*. In the crowded carriage are weather-beaten fishermen and countrywomen with market baskets, and, in one corner, two boys with fair fresh faces, set in wide straw hats, bearing upon them the inscriptions of *Vulcan* and *Vengeance*.

Brest is a naval station of such importance that even travellers in search of the picturesque should not pass it by without a short visit; the arsenal, docks, and harbour are on a scale of completeness second only to Cherbourg; moreover, Brest is the most convenient point from which to visit other parts of the coast of Finistère, especially the fishing village of Le Conquet, the abbey of St. Mathieu on the extreme western point of Brittany, and the island of Ouëssant. Brest is situated on an elevated position on the north side of one of the finest natural harbours in the world.

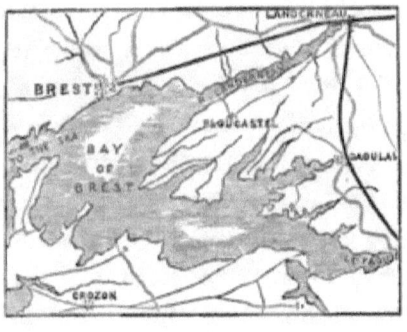

In order to realise the beauty of the inland bay of Brest, we must look down again from our imaginary *ballon captif*, and see its blue waters, green banks and woods coming down to the water's edge; the country dotted with white villas and little wooden châlets belonging to the wealthy traders of Brest, and here and there the sombre avenues of a château with grey, high-pitched roofs and pointed turrets peeping through the trees.

Across this inland sea, traversed by little steamers and dotted with white sails—raised high upon the heath-clad hills which form the western spur of the Monts d'Arrée— is the little town of Plougastel.

Plougastel.

It is too late to cross the bay on the occasion of our visit to Plougastel, and so we take the last train to Kerhuon station, where there is a ferry. A vessel has just been paid off at Brest, and in the railway carriage are several sailors on their way home. One of them gets out with us at Kerhuon, and we go down together to the river. By some mischance the ferry-boat is missing, and all is darkness at the little boathouse. The young sailor, ready at expedients, puts down his pack, collects some furze, and lights a fire as a signal. We sit and wait and shout at intervals, burning the fuel, until just about midnight, when we hear the plash of oars, and a dark object glides past; it is a fishing-boat with one mast, with three men in the stern, and two women rowing. After a little parleying they agree to take us across for thirty centimes each, and the women turn the boat round, running it heavily against the stones of the causeway. We get in quickly and stand in the bows, whilst we silently cross the Landerneau river. It is a strange, mysterious boat-load; not a word is uttered, there is no sound but the heavy plodding and working of the oars, and the night is so dark we cannot see the faces of the men or the nature of the packages that weigh down the stern. The moon, rising through the clouds, just illumines the darkness as we near the shore; it shines on the smooth, wet mast, on the waterproof hat of the marine standing up in the boat, and reveals close to us the strong, stout arms of a girl, bared to the shoulder, her head concealed in a dark, tight-fitting headdress, with lappets like an Egyptian sphinx; the head is raised for a moment, and eyes are turned upon us as we leave, but no word is uttered, scarcely a "Bon soir!" as the boat drifts away into the night.

GOING TO A PARDON.

Face p. 95.

The moon shines as we ascend the hill—winding up a path between great rocks and under the shadow of stunted trees, to Plougastel—revealing a poor-looking town of plain stone houses, silent and deserted at this midnight hour. At a corner of two streets our companion points out the inn and takes leave, having to go to his home at the further end of the town. We knock for admittance, but without avail; heads are put out of various windows, but the answer is that every house is crowded, for "to-morrow is the fête"; and, truth to tell, curses are heaped upon the strangers for disturbing the dogs, who begin to howl as they trot by on their midnight errands. There is nothing to be done until daybreak, and so the night is spent in the open air.

We have come to Plougastel to see the people, and also its famous calvary, which stands in the middle of a desolate churchyard strewn with newly cut stone. As the day begins to dawn, we make our way to the church, and to the spot where we can just discern the calvary, with its carved figures standing darkly against the sky. There is a flutter at our approach, for birds have been nestling behind the headless horsemen, and sheltering in the nooks and corners of the ancient pile. We leave them to silence a little longer, and stroll out to the highest ground to see the sun rise. Soon there is a streak of light from the east, which gives shape and outline to the church tower and the grey roofs of Plougastel, and, as we reach the high ground outside the town, the landscape southward is lighting in the morning sun; we see cultivated valleys and park-like views, with pleasant green slopes leading down to the sea. But beautiful as is the foreground, with its undulating green, interspersed with granite boulders, with dew upon gossamer webs and little clouds of vapour stealing between clumps of grass, the view across the bay, where the distant headlands (indicated on the map on page 93) take a pearly tinge, is the best sight of all. A little northward and westward are the masts, chimneys, and church spires, and the smoke and steam, of Brest, for the morning is breaking over a busy scene at the arsenal and dockyards; but here, as the sun shines out, the sounds in the long grass are of grasshoppers, birds, and bees.

It is the morning of the fête; the thrush clears his throat, and so do the peasants in their own way, as they come slowly up the hill. Let us leave the view and go into the streets of Plougastel, already full of people, some of whom might be the descendants of Eastern races wearing Egyptian or Phrygian head-dresses, caps from Albania, embroideries from Greece, and sashes from Arabia. Here, then, for the first time in our travels in Brittany, we find colour predominating in the costumes of the people. Some of the women wear close-fitting dark green caps embroidered with gold thread, their dark skirts also bordered with embroideries or stripes of colour; some wear white stockings and neat-fitting, red or black slippers or shoes. But the prevailing headdress of the women is the white cambric *coiffe* with large side lappets and wide collars which we see elsewhere in Finistère; the men have broad-brimmed hats with embroidered strings or ribbons. Some of the men who come from the south wear striped trousers with a red sash, and spare blue jacket with numerous silver buttons, as in the sketch opposite. Some are dressed entirely in blue cloth or serge, with sashes and red caps, but others have broad white trousers and belts, their jackets and blouses embroidered on the shoulders and sleeves. There is colour everywhere, subdued by the dark blue of blouses and the sober brown and green stuff gowns of the older women.

It is said that the people of Plougastel, preserving many

of their old costumes and traditions, still live much apart from their neighbours; a life half seafaring, half agricultural, whose origin is traced to some early immigration of Eastern races.

THE GAVOTTE.

The Breton *ronde* or round dance, of which the gavotte is a good example, is one of the most characteristic scenes to be witnessed in Brittany. At nearly every fête and gathering—in the streets, in the fields, or in the town-hall—we see the peasants dancing the gavotte, the musicians being generally two, one with the ancient Armorican bag-pipe (*biniou*), the other with a flageolet.

The dancers generally keep good time, going through a variety of figures, but always returning to the *ronde*, dancing together, hand in hand, with great precision and animation, and a certain kind of grace. The gravity of manner and the downward look of the women in certain figures, as they advance and retire with hands down, give a peculiar quaintness to the gavotte, which, apparently rollicking and unrestrained, is in fact, orderly and regular in every movement. The circular motion of the dancers, now revolving in several circles, now in one *grande ronde*, is traced by M. Emile Souvestre, and other writers, to Druidic origin and the movements of the stars.

But as the dancers come swinging down the centre of the hall, hand in hand, now meeting, now parting; as fresh couples join and others fall into the rear; as we hear the measured tread and the voices which never seem to tire, we should be content to describe the "gavotte" as a good old country dance of singular animation and picturesqueness; a scene of jollity and at the same time of good order, of which the sketches by Caldecott give an admirable idea.

We give a few bars of a favourite air, played at Châteauneuf du Faou, which seemed to give the performers intense enjoyment, for they returned to it again and again.

There was one figure dressed in the latest fashion of Quimper, who was looked upon with doubtful admiration by the other dancers, but who will serve to remind us that distinctive costume, even in these out-of-the-way places, is a flickering flame, and that in a few years such scenes as these will have lost their character.

At dusk oil lamps are lighted, a crowd fills the hall, and, late into the night when far away from the scene, we can see the steam rising between the rafters and hear the clatter of sabots.

THE GAVOTTE.

QUIMPER—DOUARNENEZ.

IN the valley of the Odet and the Steir, where two rivers join in their southern course to the sea, there rise the beautiful spires of Quimper, the present capital of Finistère; a town containing about 13,000 inhabitants, now the centre of the commerce and industry of southern Finistère. This ancient capital of Cornouaille, with its warlike and romantic history of the middle ages, the centre of historic associations in the times of the War of the Succession, preserves many landmarks and monuments that will interest the traveller and the antiquarian. The fine Gothic cathedral has a richly sculptured porch with foliated carving of the fourteenth century. Above and between the two towers is an equestrian statue of the somewhat mythical King Gradlon, who held a court at Kemper in the fifth century, whose prowess is recorded in

the early chronicles of Brittany, and in the romances of the Round Table.

In spite of railways, telegraphs, and newspapers, and the bustle of commerce that fills the streets and market of Quimper, some of the inhabitants of the neighbouring valleys find time, on St. Cecilia's Day, to perform a pilgrimage to this cathedral and to sing songs in honour of St. Corentin. Thus we see how conservative Brittany clings to its monuments and legends, and how its people still dwell in the past.

The cathedral of Quimper is the centre and rallying-point for all the country round, the home of Catholicism, the "one church" to the inhabitants of Finistère. No picture of the wide *Place* by the river, where the great gatherings take place on fête-days, and where so many curious costumes are to be seen together, is complete without the two modern spires of the cathedral rearing high above the town. The procession of people passing up the wide street on a Sunday morning leading to its doors—a dense mass of figures, fringed with white caps, like foam on a heaving sea, the figures framed by projecting gables nearly meeting overhead—forms another picture which has also for its background the two noble spires. The old houses in the market-place in the cathedral square, and the old inn, the Hôtel du Lion d'Or (this last well worthy of a sketch), are overshadowed by the pile. The people that come in by the old-fashioned diligences and the country carts and waggons go straight to the cathedral on arrival in the square.

One of the most complete and characteristic of Mr. Caldecott's sketches during our stay in Brittany was a scene in a *cabaret*, or wine-shop, where the farmers who have come in to market, whose carts we may see on the cathedral square, meet and discuss the topics of the day. It was the nearest approach to an open political discussion that we could witness on our travels, and a good opportunity to see the conservative Breton farmer, the "owner of the soil," one who troubles himself little about "politics," in the true sense of the word, and is scarcely a match in argument for the more advanced republican trader and manufacturer of Quimper; but who, from hereditary instinct, if from no other motive, is generally an upholder of legitimist doctrines and a royalist at heart.

Seated on the carved oak bench on the left is a young

Breton clodhopper or farm-help, whose ill-luck it has been to be drawn this year; who leaves his farm with regret—a home where he worked from sunrise to sunset for two francs a week, living on coarse food and lodging in the dark with the pigs. As he sits and listens with perplexed attention to the principal speaker, and others gather round in the common room to hear the oracle, we have a picture which tells its story with singular eloquence, and presents to us the common everyday life of the people of lower Brittany with a truthfulness and vivacity seldom, if ever, exceeded. The only bright colour in the picture is in the red sashes of the men and in one or two small ornaments worn by the women.

It is worth while for every one who stays in Quimper to see something of the coast, and to make a tour of at least two or three days to Pont l'Abbé, Penmarch, Pont Croix, the Pointe du Raz, and Douarnenez. In this short journey the traveller will see some of the finest coast scenery in Brittany, and people differing in character and costume from other parts of Finistère; a hardy fishing population, tempted to dangers and hardships by the riches to be found in the sea.

On the roads in this neighbourhood we obtain fine views of open landscape, with solitary figures here and there working in the fields, and occasional glimpses of the sea. It is a windy land; the colour is sombre, and the clouds which come up in heavy masses from the sea cast deep shadows over the ground.

If we try to recall the impression of the scene, it is principally of clouds, as in landscapes by Ruysdael or Géricault. The land for miles is without sign of habitation, the highest point of interest is a bank of furze, a stunted tree, or a heap of broken stones, chipped perhaps from a fallen menhir; a solitude that seems more

CAVALIERS AND ROUNDHEAD.

hopeless and remote from the tumultuous aspect of the heavens.

It is a dreary road from Audierne to the Pointe du Raz, passing the villages of Plogoff and Lescoff. At this point the rocks are higher above the sea than at Penmarch, and the scene is altogether more extensive and magnificent. We are on an elevation of eighty or ninety feet, and almost surrounded by the sea. To the south and east is the wide bay of Audierne, to the west the Île de Sein, the ancient home of Druidesses, and the horizon line of the Atlantic.

A cloud of sea-birds rises from the rocks below, and floats away like a puff of steam; there is an orange tint in the seaweed piled upon the shore, and a purple tinge upon the distant hills across the bay of Douarnenez; but the green upon the scanty grass in the foreground is cold in colour, and almost the only flowers are yellow sea-poppies and the little white bells of the convolvulus. On every side are piles of rocks stretching out seaward as barriers against the waves of the Atlantic; a dangerous, desolate shore, on which many a vessel has been wrecked. To the north is the Druids' "Baie des Trépassés," where, according to ancient legends, the spirits of the departed wait on the shore to be taken in boats to the Île de Sein. It is a Celtic legend, recounted in every history of Brittany.

The exposed position of the Pointe du Raz, the strange fantastic grandeur of the rocks, and the wildness of the waves that beat upon the shore in almost all weathers, are alone worth a visit. The numerous artists who stay at Quimper, Douarnenez, and Pont-Aven, in the summer months would do well to pitch their tents for a time near the Pointe du Raz, if only to watch from this elevation the changing aspects of sea and sky, to see the sea, calm and blue in the distance, but dashing spray in sunshine over walls of rock, and seaweed gatherers on a summer evening getting in their harvest, as deep in colour as the corn.

It is a fine drive over undulating hills to Douarnenez, with views of landscape more fertile than any we have seen since leaving Quimper; landscape with open moorland, interspersed with fields of corn, where harvesting is being actively carried on, as in the sketch. Here we get a glimpse

of one of the old farmhouses of Finistère, and (on a very small scale) of the farmer himself approaching in the distance to superintend operations.

A few miles farther, and the landscape is again bare and uncultivated; we see peasants in the fields at rare intervals; flocks of black and brown sheep feeding on the open land. There is a charm of wildness and a peculiar beauty about this scenery here that we who write for artists should insist upon with all the power of the pen.

DOUARNENEZ.

DOUARNENEZ, the headquarters of the sardine-fisheries, has a population of about 9000, almost entirely given up to this industry; the men in their boats, and the women and girls in the factories. It is a busy, dirty, and not very

SARDINE FISHING-BOATS, DOUARNENEZ.

attractive town, with one principal street leading down to the port; but walk out of it in any direction, so as to escape the odours of the sardine factories, and the views from the high ground are most rewarding.

There is no prettier sight, for instance, than to watch the arrival of a fleet of several hundred fishing-boats rounding the last promontory, racing in whilst they are eagerly watched from the shore. At one point the little fleet divides, to come to anchor at different inlets of the bay. Of the scene down at the port where the boats unload; of the massing of a forest of masts against the evening sky, with rocks and houses high above as a background, we can only hint in these pages.

At Douarnenez, in summer, the inhabitants are accustomed to an inroad of visitors who come for the bathing season, and there is a little colony of artists who live comfortably at the principal inns *en pension* for five or six francs a day, but it is not as quiet as Pont-Aven, near Quimperlé (the French artists' favourite haunt), for the streets are closely built and badly paved, and the busy inhabitants wear sabots which are rattled down to the shore at all hours of the day and night, according to the tide. Moreover the inhabitants of the town are scarcely typical Bretons; they are a little demoralised by success in trade, a little inclined to smuggling, and decidedly fond of drinking. The men, living hard lives, facing the most fearful storms of the Atlantic in their exposed little boats, out sometimes for days without a 'take,' are apt to be uproarious when on shore. The hardy, bright-featured women of Cornouaille have a rather sad and reckless look at Douarnenez; their homes are not too tidy as a rule; the little children play in narrow streets steaming with refuse from the sardine factories, where their elder sisters are working in gangs, with bare feet and skirts tucked up to their knees, sifting, sorting, and cooking sardines, and singing snatches of Breton songs the while. The lower streets, steep and narrow, are blocked with fish-carts, and the port is crowded with boats with nets drying in festoons. But the view of Douarnenez seen at a little distance out at sea, with its high rocks and overhanging trees almost reaching to the water's edge, and above, the spire of the old church of Ploaré standing sharp against the sky, will remain best in the memory. There is no end to the beauties of the bay of Douarnenez, if we explore the neighbourhood, starting off early for the day and not returning until sundown.

The children of Douarnenez have learned to beg, and along the broad road which leads to Quimper, beggars are stationed at intervals to waylay the charitable. Driving home one afternoon in a little covered carriage, a dark object appears before us on the way. Near it, at the side of the road, is a little shed roughly made with poles and brambles, and protruding from it, two sabots filled with straw, two sticks, and a pair of *bragous bras*. The rest of the structure consists of dried ferns, and a poor deaf human creature propped up to receive the alms of the charitable, a grim figure watching and waiting in the sun and wind.

In the evening there is a great Bohemian gathering at the Hôtel du Commerce; its artistic visitors overflow into the street, and make themselves heard as well as seen. There is a clatter of tongues and a cloud of smoke issuing from the little café presided over by the neat figure in the sketch. Those who have been to the Hôtel du Commerce at Douarnenez will recognise the portrait at once; those who have not must picture to themselves a girl with dark hair and brown complexion, a headdress and bodice in which scarlet and gold are intermingled; a dark skirt with a border of yellow or orange, and a spotless white apron and sleeves. In soft shoes she flits silently through the rooms and supplies our clamorous wants in turn; neither remonstrance nor flattery will move her, or cause her to raise her eyes.

The picturesque town of QUIMPERLÉ, on the rivers Ellé and Isole, from which so many English travellers have been scared, in years gone by, by Murray's laconic admonition, "No good inn," is a most pleasant and comfortable resting-place. It is approached on a high level when coming by railway from Quimper, the road from the station winding round the hills down to the *Place*, where there is the comfortable Hôtel des Voyageurs. On arriving at Quimperlé, the aspect of the people is more cosmopolitan, for we are approaching the borders of the province of Morbihan, and are on the highway between Nantes and Brest.

The people at the station are not numerous, and they are nearly all third-class travellers. The quiet, almost taciturn company consists of a tourist, a *sergent de ville*, a commercial man of Quimperlé, the same old woman that we meet everywhere on our travels, in the comfortable dark hood and cape of the country, and a peasant-woman taking home her sack of meal.

Quimperlé contains about 6500 inhabitants, principally occupied in agriculture. It is surrounded by hills covered with orchards and gardens shut in by high walls; an old and sleepy place, full of memories of the past, and with, apparently, little ambition for the future. There is an ancient abbey church, built in the eleventh century, on the plan of the Holy Sepulchre at Jerusalem; in the crypt is the tomb of St. Gurloës, one of the early abbots of Quimperlé. The large grey-roofed building on the *Place* adjoining this church, now used as the Mairie, was formerly a convent of Benedictine nuns; and other buildings, such as the old inn, the Lion d'Or, were originally used by the abbots of St. Croix.

But Quimperlé, in spite of its railway, is a town where grass grows between the paving-stones of its streets; a place which owes much of its attraction to its picturesque site and its ancient buildings, to its market-days, its weddings and fêtes. In the lower town there are some old narrow streets, with most picturesque wooden gables, and there is one dilapidated square, called "the Place of Revolution," where there would seem little left to destroy.

A painter might well make Quimperlé a centre of operations, for its precincts are little known; the gardens shine with laden fruit-trees, and the hills are rich in colour until late in autumn; and in the evening there is no

PONT-AVEN NEAR QUIMPERLÉ.

better place for rest than under the trees on the Place Nationale. Here the people pass to and fro, there are more women than men to be seen, for the latter are resting from their labours, in the cafés; and beyond, and high above this group, are the houses of the old town, surmounted by the two square Gothic towers, with spires covered with lichen, of the church of St. Michel. Under the trees near the river Ellé are women selling sardines and fruit.

The great attraction to Quimperlé is in the country round; in the beauty of the woods and the windings of the streams. In this neighbourhood the artist and the angler may settle down together and spend the summer months delightfully.

We said that Quimperlé, a town with a railway station, on the great highway between Nantes and Brest, owes most of its life and picturesque attraction to women, weddings, fêtes, and flowers. Let us picture a prominent personage at the old Hôtel du Lion d'Or. She has a beautiful name, *Augustine*, pronounced with enviable accuracy by all the household. She hovered about us like a fairy, attending to our wants in the most delicate way; to outward seeming a ministering angel with pure white wings, but, in truth, a drudge, a methodical housewife, massive, and hard to the touch. She did the work of

three Parisian *garçons*, and walked upstairs unaided with portmanteaus which would require two men to lift, anywhere out of Brittany. She slept in a box in the kitchen, and dressed "somehow" in five minutes. She ate what was left, contentedly, at the end of the day, and rose at sunrise to do the laborious work of the house; helping also at harvest-time in the fields. She had the sweetest of smiles (when she liked), an unconquerable habit of taking snuff, and a murderous way of killing fowls in the early morning which we shall not easily forget.

How it comes to pass that this girl of nineteen occupies such an important position in the household is one of those things which are peculiar to Brittany. The strong individuality, industry, and force of character of the women make themselves felt wherever we go. Whilst the men slumber and smoke, the women are building little fortunes or propping up old ones. All through the land, in the houses, in the factories, and in the fields, the strong, firm hand and arm of a woman *does the work*.

The pedestrian or sportsman, in his wanderings through Brittany, will, if he knows the country, seek, at the end of a long day, the country *auberge* where a "household fairy" presides. The land is full of legends and tales of gnomes and witches, but the reality is a white-capped figure, that welcomes the traveller at the inn-door, the modern representative of "mine host." Her brightness and attraction, and at the same time her whole armour and coat of mail, are her stiffly starched cap, epaulets and apron of spotless white. She presides at the fêtes and weddings which are celebrated at the inns, and joins in the frolics at the end of the day, dancing with the rest up and down the street, and submitting with modest but hearty goodwill to some rather demonstrative tokens of esteem. "How is it that these widespread collars are never crumpled?" some one asks. "Oh, we just turn them round and throw them over the shoulder for a minute!" is the quick answer.

Let us refer to our notebook to see how one of these weddings is managed in Quimperlé. It is just after harvest, and the time for rest and festivity in many a village round. Coats and gowns that have been laid by for months are brought out, and many an antique-shaped garment sees the light for the first time for a year. Two or three weddings are arranged for the same day, and at early morning all meet at Quimperlé. The girls come on foot, dressed in their local costumes, excepting a little innovation of finery here and there; the "boys" for they are little more in age, have modernised themselves, and wear a clumsy imitation of the conventional suit of black, being especially proud of Parisian hats. But excepting in the matter of costume, they do as their forefathers did; they spend the day in the streets of Quimperlé, parading arm-in-arm with their brides, stopping to take, and to give, refreshment at every inn-door and at the homes of all their friends. We meet them early in the morning crossing the principal square; they have registered their marriages, and have taken the sacrament in the church of St. Michel, in the upper town, and for the rest of the long summer day and half into the night they dance the "De Rober" up and down the streets, hand in hand together, to the music of the bagpipe and the flageolet.

THE PARDON OF STE. ANNE D'AURAY.

ON the 24th of July we take up our quarters at the comfortable 'Hôtel Pavillon d'en Haut,' at Auray. To-morrow is the great day of the Pardon of Ste. Anne, the occasion of the annual pilgrimage to the miraculous well,

whither from far and near, on foot and on horseback, in carts and many strange road conveyances, and by excursion trains, come pilgrims to the shrine of Ste. Anne. Like the great annual gatherings at Guingamp and at Ste. Anne la Palue, the Pardon of Ste. Anne d'Auray attracts a strange medley of people, and thus it is that the ordinarily quiet little town, four miles from the shrine, is crowded to overflowing.

The town of Auray, which contains about 5000 inhabitants, is finely situated above the river which bears its name. It was formerly a port of commercial importance, but its trade has drifted to Vannes and L'Orient, and it is best known to travellers as a starting-point for visiting the fields of Carnac and Locmariaker; also as a pleasant and healthy place of residence, where fishing and shooting can be obtained. There are no objects of great antiquity to be seen at Auray itself; its historic castle has disappeared, but there is much to interest the traveller in the old streets with timbered houses, leading down to the river.

On a wide *Place* a few yards off, called the Belvédère, is a column to ascend to see the view, looking northward and eastward, in the direction of Vannes, over a wide stretch of cultivated land, pastures, and woods, dotted with white houses and church spires, one of which is Ste. Anne d'Auray. Immediately beneath is a rocky, precipitous path down to the river, with small vessels loading and unloading, and the grey roofs of toy-like houses and warehouses on the quay. A sudden cloud of smoke, which curls through the gorse and bushes which conceal the greater part of the river from view, comes from a little steamer which has arrived from Belle-Ile with the evening tide, and has brought another crowd of pilgrims for Ste. Anne. All is quiet and beautiful from this vantage-ground; the air is soft, and slowly waves the tree-tops in the avenue which skirts the Belvédère on its southern side; there is nothing to indicate the tumult of to-morrow.

The morning of the 25th of July is bright, and the gilt statue of Ste. Anne glitters above the trees. If at this moment we could look down from the spire of its church, upon the country round, we should see on every road, and across the open land, little dark specks, which are pilgrims all tending one way—to the shrine. They have been coming all through the night, camping in the fields and sleeping at the roadside. The broad Roman road from Vannes is covered with carts and carriages, and more people are arriving by the river.

The crowd that has assembled in the open square near the church of Ste. Anne at six in the morning numbers several thousands, and increases every hour. They are pilgrims of every grade, from the marquis and his family, who were driven from Vannes the evening before, and stay comfortably at the large hotel, to the solitary herdsman in goatskin coat and wooden shoes stuffed with straw, who has walked for two days and nights from his home in the Montagnes Noires. But they have come on the same errand, and will stand side by side before an altar in one of the side chapels, and burn their candles together. They both believe, or are taught to believe, in a legend that some time in the seventeenth century a saint appeared to one Nicolazic, who rented a farm near this spot, and commanded him to dig in a field for her image, and to erect a chapel to her memory. They both have heard of the

miraculous cures at the well of Ste. Anne, and believe that no household can prosper, no ships are safe at sea, no cattle or crops can thrive, unless once a year, at least, they come to burn candles to Ste. Anne; and they both have wife, mother, or sister christened *Anne*, the name in fact of nearly every child we see to-day.

The miraculous well of Ste. Anne is in a large inclosure at the western end of which is the Scala Santa, a small raised chapel, open to the air and covered by a cupola; a modern wooden erection about twenty feet from the ground, approached on either side by a covered flight of steps. It is from this platform that the opening ceremony of the Pardon takes place in the afternoon of the 25th of July, when after a procession round the town with a brass band and banners, the Bishop of Vannes, or other dignitary, addresses the people in the open square. The procession is a long one, gay with the green-and-gold embroidered vestments of the priests, and bright with the white robes of the acolytes with their crimson sashes; a quickly moving procession of bareheaded men singing the litany of Ste. Anne, with banners (representing different departments and communes) waving above them, and silver crosses and relics carried high in the air. The crowd presses forward to see, and forms a narrow lane to let them pass to the Scala Santa, where the head of the procession comes to a standstill, and as many of the priests and attendants as can crowd on to the steps stand as a sort of bodyguard, whilst the bishop addresses the multitude assembled in the square beneath.

Then the outsiders of the crowd get up and watch the proceedings (including a cook in white cap and apron, who sits upon the hotel wall), some eagerly from curiosity apparently, some with devotion, and some, it must be confessed, with an easy, jaunty air more appropriate to a show in a country fair. There are several hundreds on the grass before us in the bright sun, sitting together in parties kneeling in prayer, or standing close together intent upon the scene.

What those upturned faces were, and what the good bishop saw beneath him in the crowd, as he rolled forth a discourse full of earnestness and eloquence, Mr. Caldecott's pencil has recorded. The sketches give, as no words could do, the mingled expression of feeling on the faces of the pilgrims. The words spoken were the old story: first, the history of "the miracle of Ste. Anne," then an exhortation as to the importance of confession and of works of charity and masses for the dead. The costume of the people that listen is nearly the same as in 1623, when Ste. Anne "appeared in a wheat-field to a peasant"; and yet—and in spite of all accounts of the earnest devotion of the people—if we look at the aspect of the crowd, we seem to understand the matter better than we ever did before.

They stand bareheaded in the sunshine, old and young, rich and poor; on the left, a pretty *bourgeois* daughter from Auray, in plain cloth dress with velvet body, dark, green shawl, and neatest of shoes; behind her, in the background, a contingent from more remote districts, farmers and small traders, the majority being comfortable people who have come by train. A spare old woman with eccentric expression and worn hands, holding purchases, or plunder, in her apron, is not a pauper, but a hanger-on at a large household, who has saved money. Next, nearer to us, is a peasant farmer, with long grey hair, in white jacket and breeches and leathern girdle, who has come on foot from his home in the interior. He has walked all through the night to be present at the Pardon, as he has done every year, going through the round of services and exercises, contributing several francs in money to the church, buying a few charms and trinkets, and then plodding home.

Let us add a few notes of the scene on Sunday, the second day of the Pardon, when the crowd is greatest, and when there must be collected at least 5000 people; when, besides the peasants and country people, visitors from Paris and other parts of France have filled to overflowing the large modern hotel, the courtyard of which is full of carriages and conveyances of all kinds. In the streets and round the open square there are booths for the sale of trinkets and toys, rosaries, tapers, statuettes, and medals of Ste. Anne, besides the more common objects for sale at a country fair. In the roadway women cook fish and cakes (*galettes*) at charcoal fires; there are itinerant vendors of gigantic wax candles, there are peep-shows and other amusements, skittles and games like quoits, played with leaden counters of the size of a five-franc piece. There is every kind of amusement in honour of Ste. Anne, and the family meetings and gatherings that take place round the cafés and in the open fields, suggest a picnic more than a pilgrimage.

But it is in the street leading to the church door, and in the adjoining cloisters of a convent, that the more serious aspects of the Pardon are to be witnessed, some of which it would be impossible to record in a sketch.

From four o'clock in the morning masses have been said, and in and out of the church there has been a continual stream of people, all in holiday attire, and nearly all wearing strings of beads, crosses, or silver ornaments bearing the image of Ste. Anne. They form in

groups on the grass in the centre of the cloistered square, close together, some kneeling, some standing erect, with eyes strained upwards at a cracked and weather-worn statue of the Christ; they tell their beads, and drop sous into a box at the foot of the cross, the poorest contributing something.

They pass round the cloisters in a continual stream, missing nothing set down for them, but stopping and kneeling at each "station" with expressions of devotion and awe at some grotesque paintings on the walls representing the Passion. They stop and pray, some on one knee only with beads in hand, some kneeling low on the pavement, sitting on the heels of their sabots for rest.

They have come a long and weary march, they are at the end of their pilgrimage, and so it happens that sitting and praying they fall asleep. A heavy thwack from a neighbour's umbrella falls upon the shoulders of the sleepers, and again they go the round.

By midday the crowd has increased so that movement in the road is difficult. Coming slowly up the narrow street—blocked by carriages, by vendors of "objets de dévotion," and by the crowd that passes up and down—is an apparently very poor, old man with long dark hair, a white sheepskin jacket and *bragous bras*, a leather girdle and sabots, holding in his hand a hollow candle three feet high; it has cost him six sous, and he will place it presently at the altar in the church with the rest. Following him is a farmer and his wife, well-to-do people, who have come by train, and combine a little marketing with their religious observances. Following them are two young married people with their child, all dressed in the latest costumes of Paris, the father manfully taking off his light-kid gloves, and carrying his candle with the rest.

The scene in the church, where services have been held at intervals all day, and the people crowd to burn candles at the side altars, is of people handing up babies, beads, and trinkets to be blessed; of the flaring of candles, of the movements of tired priests, and the perpetual murmur of prayers.

We have spoken often of the simple, practical, and graceful dress of the women; but here at Auray we must confess that many of the country people in full holiday attire are anything but graceful in appearance. At a side altar of the chapel there is a young face, very fair, with large devotional eyes, deepened in colour and intensity by her white cap; but below it is a stiff, shapeless bodice as hard as wood, and a bundle of lower garments piled one upon the other, till the figure is a rather ungainly sight; her large capable hands hold her book, her rosary, and a stout umbrella; she is encumbered with clothing, but she differs from her modernised sisters in one thing: her dress is not on her mind when she says her prayers. She is on her knees nearly all day at Auray; but, working or praying, half her young life has been spent in this position.

In spite of the grotesque element, which is everywhere at Pardons, the sight is often a sad one; sad, especially, to see so many young faces clouded by superstitious awe. The saying would seem to apply to Brittany, that "national piety springs from a fountain of tears."

We have purposely said little of the repulsive side of the spectacle; of the terrible-looking men and women who have come out of their hiding-places to kneel at the shrine and to beg from strangers, who wander about like savages and are propitiated with beads. Figures strange, weird, and grotesque, the like of which we shall see nowhere else in the world, pass round the cloisters of Ste. Anne d'Auray for two days in the year.

There is one half-witted man from the sea-coast, evidently soon "going home"; as he drags himself along, the shadows seem to deepen, and the light from human eyes to burn more fiercely in their tenement.

Fed with seaweed, thatched with straw, exposed to the wildest winds of the Atlantic, his home little better than a hole in the rocks, what wonder that he comes across the hills once a year to the Pardon of Ste. Anne for a blessing; that he prays for a land beyond the sea, visioned in his mind by innumerable candles, and paid for in advance through weary years in his Passage to the Cross!

Many of the pilgrims go through other religious observances before leaving Auray, including washing in the well, going step by step up the Scala Santa on their hands and knees; and all—the poorest and most pitiable—leave *something* in the coffers of Ste. Anne.

And so the long day passes, and at last the tide recedes. What if a strong north wind and the running river Auray could bear them away seaward, to be seen no more! What if all the wretchedness, dirt, and disease, collected, as if by a miracle, at Ste. Anne for two days, could, by another miracle, be swept away for ever!

VANNES.

A FEW miles from Auray and Carnac is the ancient city of Vannes, the chief town of the department of Morbihan and the capital of Basse-Bretagne. This city, from its position, is the natural point of departure for travellers entering Brittany from the east, as it is also the natural place of rest when coming from the west.

The part of Vannes of most interest to travellers is the old city, with its narrow streets and overhanging houses, and the remains of its walls and gates. In the narrowest part, near the Place Henri-Quatre, there rises between the eaves of the houses the square tower and spire of the cathedral of St. Peter, a structure dating from the eleventh century, altered and almost rebuilt in the fifteenth. The interior of the cathedral is gloomy, and the streets which surround it are dark and old. There are some cloisters and a finely sculptured porch of dark stone. The principal chapel in the interior is dedicated to the Spanish Dominican monk St. Vincent Ferrier, who evangelised the province in the time of Duke John V., and died at Vannes in 1419. The relics of this saint are once a year carried in procession round the town.

There is one side chapel with an altar, on which are three glass cases, in one of which are relics, and in another, some wax models of bones and imitation jewels; above these, between the folds of a curtain half drawn aside, is a painting of Ste. Marie de Bon Secours, to whom the chapel is dedicated. The light through a narrow stained-glass window falls upon the figure of an old woman, holding beads in her worn hands, who kneels upon the scagliola steps before the altar. There is nothing uncommon in the sight; but there is a romantic story that this old woman and the beautiful Madonna are one and the same; that she had sat in her youth as a model for the Holy Virgin, and that she kneels every day before the portrait of her old self.

Vannes is an ecclesiastical city of much importance, the see of an ancient bishopric, and a radiating point for the church in Morbihan; but, as a matter of fact, we see and hear very little of the church at Vannes; and it seems by contrast with the country—where every wayside has its cross or holy fountain, every district its little chapel or altar with saints and relics amongst the trees, every group of peasant-women a pastor—that the country people have more than their share of homilies and exhortations.

Coming from the interior, we miss the attitude of religious awe amongst the women, which seems to be put off at the city gates; and we miss, also, the individuality of costume, which vanishes fast in towns. If we were to picture the people as we see them on Sunday in Vannes, they would be very ordinary indeed, with just a sprinkling of white caps, and a few touches of embroidery on a shawl or a blouse, to remind us that we are in Morbihan; and in their general attitude they would seem as much at a loss for occupation as in other centres of civilisation where galleries and museums are closed on Sundays.

There is a museum of Celtic antiquities at Vannes, containing a collection of ornaments, flints, &c., found in the cromlechs at Carnac and the neighbourhood, which is well worth visiting; and there are various shows and amusements for the people on the *Place* and in the public gardens; but the fact remains that the majority of the working inhabitants sidle off on Sunday morning, gravitating one by one towards every house of call, outside of which hangs a bunch of dried mistletoe or broom.

The people that we see are for the most part pleasant and prosperous-looking, busy in commerce or in agriculture. There is, it is true, more than one regiment of the line quartered here, and the cafés, bright with plate-glass and gilding, are full of warriors of various sizes; in the morning

THREE HOT MEN.

and in the evening the air vibrates with regimental drums, but there is little else to remind us that the inhabitants are the direct descendants of a warlike nation, and that barons and knights once defended the battlements and towers of Vannes. The morning is spent at billiards in most of the cafés, and near some, especially frequented by the townspeople, there are such groups as the above.

Before leaving Vannes, we should go down at night to the old Place Henri-Quatre, where the roofs of the houses meet overhead; where, in moonlight, the gables cast wonderful shadows across the square, and above our heads rise the towers of the cathedral with a grandeur of effect not to be seen at any other time, or from any other point of view. It is then that the cathedral precincts look most mysterious in their darkness; narrow, irregular streets, with open gutters, lighted only by a glimmer from latticed windows, and where, from old doorways, figures are dimly seen to pass in and out. It is a poor quarter, where a Dutch painter would find work for a lifetime.

We said that there was no light in the streets, but, passing round the cathedral, there is a strong light from a lantern held close to the ground; it is the chiffonnier of Vannes (who, like his Parisian *confrère*, has learned the art of pecking and discrimination from the fowls) wandering through the night with his basket and iron wand.

One more note made in Vannes in stormy autumn-time. We go down to the port, sheltered from the wind by a high wall, through which narrow passages have been made to reach the sea. It is nearly dusk, and the rough-hewn edges of the stone wall stand out sharply against the sky. As we pass one of these, facing the west, the narrow opening to the shore is illumined by a blood-red sunset light, so bright by contrast that three figures coming towards us from the seashore, step as it were out of a furnace. They have men's voices, and as they approach and pass us hurriedly, we see that their heads are bare, and that their robes touch the ground. Upon their shoulders they carry a "dear brother" to his rest—the drift of last night's storm-tide. Next morning a rough stone cottage-door just outside the town is hung round with black—the drapery giving an appearance of height,

and almost grandeur of dimensions, to the little interior—
and resting upon the step is the projecting end of a
wooden coffin painted white. There are candles burning
on either side; a metal crucifix is placed on the doorstep,
and on a little table on the ground in the road is a vase of
flowers. The neighbours pass up and down crossing
themselves, and muttering Latin words of prayer for the
dead, and the little children stand and stare. Two days
after there is a bright procession, headed by a priest and
acolytes in white robes, with hymns and incense, followed
by a little crowd bareheaded, all struggling against the
wind, to a plot of ground on a promontory near the
seashore, where the poor Breton is taken to his rest.

There is a crowd of his forefathers here before him, with
black wooden crosses where their heads should be; they
are planted out in rows, and labelled with wooden sticks
to mark their species, and the garden is walled in with
stones and great rock boulders to keep out the wind. But
it is a dreary place; the wind finds it out from behind the
stones, blows down the wooden crosses, and strews the
ground with seaweed and dead leaves; nothing resists the
havoc of the wind over the graves but some bright yellow
immortelles and some metal images of the Christ.

We have said little of the ancient châteaux of Brittany,
many of which are in good preservation, and are inhabited
by direct descendants of the barons of the fifteenth
century; but we would suggest to the traveller, before
leaving Vannes, to visit the picturesque castle of Elven,
where Henry of Richmond, afterwards king of England,
was confined for fifteen years; and, if possible, to go by
road to Josselin, where there is one of the finest châteaux
of the Renaissance.

What clings to our recollections of Brittany? Some

things that are not beautiful, and which by no stretch of fancy can be described *en couleur de rose*.

But the best and most lasting impression of Brittany is of a country, interesting for its isolation from the rest of Europe; of a people who are, as has been well said, "dwelling in an heroic past that possibly never existed, consoling the failures of their destiny by beautiful fancies, and throwing a grace over their hard, unhopeful lives with romantic dreams and traditions"; of a people who invest every road and fountain with a holy name—for wherever two roads meet, there is a cross or a sign, and wherever three streams meet, they are called La Trinité;—of a land that stands alone in Western Europe, its rocks unmoved by the shocks of tempest from without, and its manners unpolished by advancing civilization from within; of a land where men look to the sea as well as to the earth for their harvest, where the plough comes down to the water's edge and the nets of the fishermen are dried upon fig-trees, where laden orchards drop their fruit over weather-worn walls on to the sands, and fish, leaping from the sea, alight sometimes in a field of corn; of a land brightened for a few weeks in summer with the flower of buckwheat, and the coral of its stems, where the wind sweeps over waves of grass and grain, and scatters the harvest over the sea.

THE PYRENEES.

Face p. 129.

LES "LANDES" NEAR PAU.

THE PYRENEES.

PAU.

THERE are some places in the Pyrenees that we shall best describe by comparing them for an instant to their prototypes in Switzerland.

Thus, in its situation, and in the circumstance of its being chosen as one of the starting-places for the mountains, Pau is the *Berne* of the Pyrenees. Like Berne, it has its history, its monuments, its peculiar customs, its interest as the capital of an industrious and thriving province, and, above all, the view of distant mountains from its terraces and park.

From the terrace on the "Place Royale" at Pau, one of the principal public walks near the centre of the town, a view of the whole western range is spread out before us, with the fertile Val d'Ossau in the middle distance, and the roaring "Gave," fed by glacier streams and swollen by torrents, immediately at our feet; and we could not, if we would, choose a more fitting or delightful spot to make our first acquaintance with the Pyrenees. We are here, as it were, on the threshold of the sanctuary, at the very feet of the mountains; we feel their presence, and long to approach them.

How shall we picture the scene on a fine summer afternoon in August? A luxuriant beauty of landscape—in the middle distance an undulating sea, soft in outline, varied in tint, half cloud, half mountain-top; rich pasture-land in the

valleys, dotted here and there with pretty white cottages, and châteaux peeping through deep masses of foliage—a bright golden hue over the land, a purple mist amongst the hills, and a sweet wind coming from the south.

The Pic du Midi d'Ossau, which is the most prominent of the distant peaks, is about twenty-six miles from us, and is 9790 feet above the sea, but the outlines are so blended with the clouds, and the forms are altogether so indistinct, that we can form very little idea of their distance or height.

The population of Pau is about 30,000, of whom a large

PAU.

number are foreigners, attracted both by the natural beauty of the situation and the reputation of the town as a mild and healthy winter place of residence. There are three or four important streets, of which the principal is the "Rue de la Préfecture," but the majority are narrow and irregularly built, and have no particularly attractive features. There are, however, abundant signs of prosperity and wealth in the large new houses that are rising in every direction, and in the extent and almost Parisian variety of the wares in the shops, although at this time of year the streets are half deserted, and the principal ones have almost as silent an aspect as a fashionable street in London out of the season.

It is only in the busy market-place, and in some of the nooks and corners of industry in the town, that we find much sign of commercial activity: and it is only on Sundays and fêtes, that many of the Béarnais are to be seen. Their costume is now so thoroughly modernised, that if it were not for the peculiar caps (*bérets*) worn by the men, and the striped handkerchiefs of the women, there would be little in the groups of peasantry to distinguish them from the inhabitants of any town in France.

The climate of Pau, and its value to invalids as a place of winter residence, has, like that of other towns in the south of France, been a little over-rated, but statistically it is one of the most healthy, and it has natural attractions almost unequalled. We have only to spend a few weeks here, to walk in the evening in the beautiful Park, to see the moonlight view from its terraces, to explore the environs, and enjoy the air even in this hot summer-time, to understand what brings so many of our countrymen hither. The remarkable stillness of the atmosphere (which in summer is seldom close, and in winter is delicious) is ascribed to the peculiar position of the town, which is sheltered on the north by the distant rising ground of the

K 2

Landes, on the south and east by the mountains, and on the west by the Park itself, which presents a perfect wall of foliage against the wind. It is almost impossible to credit the story, that in spite of the traditional stillness of the atmosphere at Pau, seventy-nine oak and beech trees were once destroyed here in a day, during a storm.

To the passing visitor, the stillness of the air, the silence and somewhat neglected appearance of the town and its public walks, give it a mournful look. We see at once that Pau is not a favourite resort in summer, and are not

CHÂTEAU AT PAU.

long in perceiving (what we shall have plenty of evidence of by-and-by) that the French people care little or nothing for scenery, and continually turn their backs upon the mountains.

If the public walks and buildings have a generally neglected air; if the pavement of the principal streets is so much out of repair that "au bout de cinq minutes vos pieds vous disent d'une manière très-intelligible, que vous êtes à deux cents lieues de Paris;" if the Park in autumn time is so strewn with dead leaves that its paths are obliterated—there is little sign of neglect or decay at the château. Here, if anywhere, we should have hailed any marks of dilapidation, but everything is new and bright; for—as a half-satirical Frenchman expressed it, as nearly as we can remember his poetic simile—" as the snow falls, obliterating landmarks and leaving all pure and white to view, so has an imperial providence, watching over Pau, covered these tottering ruins with fresh white stone, to the despair of the antiquary and the comfort of the custodian."

It is impossible to wander about Pau and the neighbourhood without being struck with the continual allusions to the memory of Henri IV., as if he had reigned only yesterday, and also at the same time without noticing the absence of anything like a noble monument to his memory. On the terrace of the Place Royale, the Béarnais have erected a white marble statue to their beloved monarch; there are three bas-reliefs

"A WALL OF FOLIAGE."

on the pedestal, representing, first, the infancy of the

prince, passed in the neighbouring mountains ; second, his humanity at the siege of Paris ; and third, his bravery at the battle of Ivry. As a work of art it is altogether poor and feeble, and in character and expression fails completely ; we cannot realize either the "Solomon of peace" or the "Cæsar of war," nor trace any signs of that intrepidity of character, energy, or *bonhomie* of which we hear so much. M. Taine asks why they have made him look so sad, and suggests, perhaps with some reason, that he was tired of hearing his praises sung by a faithful people!

The following, written in especial praise of "*noust Henri*," "our Henry," as they loved to call him, is worth quoting—

> "D'autres du grand Henri, on raconte la gloire,
> Un poète fameux,[1] au temple du mémoire,
> Entre les meilleurs rois, a placé son beau nom ;
> Sa vertu, sa valeur, ont partout grand renom.
> Moi, je vais le montrer sortant de la coquille
> Parmi ses Béarnais, au sein de sa famille.
> Je dirai dans mes vers, comment ce roi nouveau
> Fut soigné par nos mains en quittant son berceau.
> O France ! ce bon prince, objet de ton ivresse,
> Ce prince à qui le peuple a gardé sa tendresse,
> Tu le dois au *Béarn*.
> * * * * *
> Pretês-nous la couleur et une style fleurie,
> Allons, ne tarde pas ; c'est pour notre Henri."

The Béarnais poems and ballads are exotic, and do not bear transplanting ; we would suggest, however, to those who care for these things, that there is something very like true poetry—stored up or thrown aside—in the old song-books of the Béarnais, which visitors may discover for themselves, on high shelves, in the old book-shops at Pau, covered with the dust of time.

But we have come to see the mountains rather than the

---

[1] Voltaire.

towns, and, having taken our places for to-morrow for Eaux Bonnes, will go once more to the Place Royale, to see the view.

The air is perfectly still on the terrace, but a few miles from us we can see tree-tops bending in the breeze, and the light fleecy clouds that surround the summits of the more distant mountains keep changing form as we watch them, now descending into far-off valleys, nestling in their darkness for a while, like little snow-fields—then dispersing suddenly, and casting soft shadows in their flight across the plain.

As we linger until sunset, the outlines of the mountains have gradually blended with fresh companies of dark clouds coming from the south, leaving the valley half hidden in a veil of mist, and the Pic du Midi d'Ossau alone above them shining in the sun. The aspect of the clouds is rather ominous for the journey, but of this we take little heed. The air, so pure, so soft, so still, seems to us perfection; we can do nothing but marvel at the beauty of the scene and thank from our hearts the princes of Béarn, for planting their *palis* by the Gave de Pau.

EAUX CHAUDES.

IN a little corner, on the right bank of the Gave, where the mountain sides are almost perpendicular, and the river roars below; at a point where from a mixed bed of granite and limestone the hot sulphurous springs burst forth, we find the historic watering-place called Eaux Chaudes, consisting of a little street of poorly-built houses, two or three hotels, and a massive marble "Établissement des Bains." The latter is built on a platform almost overhanging the torrent, it has a large hall or pump-room, and promenade, fitted up with seats and stalls for the sale of all kinds of knicknacks; there are a number of private baths, and accommodation for patients suffering from rheumatism and other ailments, who are under the care of a resident physician. There are people sitting in a little garden trimly laid out, in front of the "Établissement," and others walking about with tumblers, going through a course of the waters; following the routine of the last three hundred years, since the time when the bishop of Oloron, Chancellor of Béarn, first established here a "maison d'habitation," by order of Henry of Navarre.

The situation of Eaux Chaudes is so confined that every square yard of space has had to be utilised, and at the side of one of the hotels a little terrace or promenade has been constructed almost over the Gave. On this the "administration" have planted trees and placed seats, and it is between this spot and the Établissement that the

ENVIRONS OF EAUX CHAUDES.

Face p. 136.

valetudinarian, who is not robust enough to clamber up the mountains, has a small piece of level ground where he can spend his days, varied only by a drive up the valley to Gabas, or down by the route we have just come.

If there is a gloomy and deserted appearance about Eaux Chaudes, even on a fine summer's afternoon, when the sun, which only shines upon the town for a few hours, is lighting up the trees above our heads with that peculiar golden green that tinges orange groves in the setting sun; when the cattle are returning from the high pastures and the tinkle of bells is heard in every direction, and the visitors (perhaps a hundred, in the summer) are moving about in their confined area; what must it be like when the clouds come down, as they do nearly every other day, and completely shut the inhabitants off from all view, either of the sky, or of the route up the valley, and when the roar of the wind is added to that of the torrent?

It has been frequently urged in guide-books that it is better for travellers to take up their quarters here, than at Eaux Bonnes, but after repeated visits we decidedly recommend the latter. Eaux Chaudes is cheaper, and is not overwhelmed with the "haut monde"; but it is situated in a gloomy, thorough draught.[1]

The environs are wild and beautiful in the extreme, and it is to explore these at leisure, to sketch the valley from different points, to examine the extraordinary stratifications of granite and limestone, to mark the traces of extinct glaciers, to collect fossils or wild flowers, to fish in the Gave, or to hunt the izzard (each one according to his taste), that this valley especially recommends itself for a lengthened visit.

The finest excursion is up the valley, southwards, past

---

[1] Eaux Chaudes and Eaux Bonnes are situated 27 miles and 24 miles south of Pau at the upper end of the Val d'Ossau.

Gabas, a little hamlet five miles from Eaux Chaudes, to the "Plateau de Bioux Artiques," three miles further, from which we obtain a fine view of the Pic du Midi d'Ossau, that famous mountain (9800 feet high) the proximity of which we are liable to forget when shut up in these valleys. There is a good carriage road to Gabas, and the valley, notwithstanding its height, and the sterile aspect of the gorge we have just left, is one of the most varied and beautiful in the Pyrenees. As the valley opens out again we see the sides of the mountains covered with green pastures and wild flowers.

Gabas itself is a lonely little hamlet, the last on the French side of the Pyrenees, a halting-place for travellers, and for the carriers who pass here on their way into Spain.

The stern, cold appearance of this part of the valley, with its grey rocks and forests of pines, is relieved by the beautiful purple iris that sheds a bloom over the lower slopes of grass, and by occasional patches of snow in the crevices of the rocks.

THE PYRENEES. 139

EAUX BONNES.

THE distance from Eaux Chaudes to Eaux Bonnes by the road, is not more than five miles, and there is constant communication by carriages and diligences during the summer months; but on the path over the Col de Gourzy, the mountain that separates us from Eaux Bonnes (6000 feet high), we obtain such splendid views, that it is the route to be recommended for riding or walking, although rather rough and steep.

As we approach Eaux Bonnes, the view of the valley is more beautiful and forms a fresh picture at almost every turn of the road, and our attention is so entirely fixed upon what is passing below, (where we can just distinguish the figures of the peasantry arriving at, and leaving Laruns,) that we have scarcely once looked upwards. What is it that we see immediately overhead? What are those little specks of red and white moving amongst the trees? They are the picquets, or outposts, of a " high civilisation " to which we must now introduce the reader.

A few more turns in the ascent, and we can distinguish people riding or walking, first by twos and threes, then a crowd. Where do they come from? We can see no sign of a town—nothing but a smooth path and a few yards of a carriage-road, neatly swept and railed off like the drive in a private park. We are no longer mountaineers; we are "en promenade." "Je comptais trouver ici la campagne," writes M. Taine; "je rencontre une rue de Paris, et les promenades du Bois de Boulogne!" We were of course somewhat prepared for this, but not altogether for the extraordinary sight that burst upon us on turning the road once more, and coming suddenly upon Eaux Bonnes.

Here in a cleft in the mountain-side, overhung and overshadowed by rocks and trees, is this famous, fashionable little hotel-village. On an area of not much more than two or three acres, the ingenious founders of this little town have managed to lay out a "Place" with trees and fountains, and two rows of hotels and pensions on either side, forming what is called the Grande Rue. At the upper end, built into the rock, is the Thermal Establishment, with its courtyards and promenades for bathers, and near it a little church. One or two streets lead out wherever a nook and cranny could be found for them. One is called the Rue des Cascades, and another, which resembles nothing so much as the shape of a slice cut out of a cake, is dignified with the name of Rue de Cauterets. In whichever direction we turn there are houses built into, and often forming part of, the mountain, resting on ledges of rock, like the eyries; but so cleverly contrived is the arrangement of the place, so admirably has space been economised, that there is a feeling of freedom about it, quite inconsistent with living in a bird's-nest.

Thus with the mountains several thousand feet above our heads, and the Val d'Ossau stretching away for many miles at our feet, with rocks overhanging and tree-tops waving below through which we can see the blue sky—with scarcely a foot of level ground anywhere (save the " Promenade Horizontale," of which we shall speak presently), with cascades and waterfalls almost at our windows, we find ourselves as comfortably and luxuriously housed as in any city of the plains.

As we approach the door of the Hôtel de France, we are blocked several times by a crowd on foot and on horseback; and in the gardens, or " Place," in front of the hotels, there are at least a hundred and fifty people making holiday after the manner of their respective nations.

Looking down upon this Place from our hotel window

on a bright sunny afternoon, it is the gayest scene imaginable, and we scarcely know which to admire most, the costumes of the fair riders who about this hour (five p.m.) come flocking in, some dressed in white riding-habits and scarlet hats, or their cavaliers in buff and green, like members of the "Ancient Order of Foresters," or their dandy guides, in embroidered Spanish costumes, silk sashes, and white stockings; or the gay trappings of their thin steeds; or the motley little crowd that stands about to see the arrivals. This last comprises every Parisian *fantaisie* and extravagance in attire, brought up here in those huge "Noah's-ark" boxes (the "bêtes noires" of all occupants of the diligence banquette), bright plumage for the inhabitants of our little nest—strange importation into the Vale of Bears!

The noise and bustle in the square,—instruments playing more discordant music than any Italian organs, the squeaks and rattles of juvenile civilization, the chattering of their *bonnes*, the incessant ringing of bells, the shouts and cracking of whips, the voices of different nations—all confined within a limited space, and echoed back from the surrounding rocks, can scarcely be conceived.

But everything is sunshine, politeness, and apparent gaiety, "la vie aux eaux;" a scene thoroughly unique, curious and grotesque—"grotesque qu'un peu d'eau chaude ait transporté dans ses fondrières la cuisine et la civilisation!"

The cuisine is well provided, as we shall find presently if we join the company who are now assembling in the handsome salon of the hotel for the table d'hôte. They consist principally of French people; there are a few Spaniards, and fewer English, Germans and Russians. The English are in a decided minority at Eaux Bonnes, as elsewhere in the Pyrenees, and are, to tell the truth, not too popular. The ruddy English face does not command universal sympathy and attention here, as in Switzerland, even amongst the class most open to impressions—waiters, servants, and guides. For once, and perhaps it is good for us, we do not have everything our own way.

The table is laid for about eighty people, and sixty or seventy sit down. The French—the habitués ("pensionnaires")—occupy one end, nearest the head of the table. They are elegantly dressed, courteous, and well bred, belonging principally to the well-to-do classes of French society. There are a few notabilities, in fact were we to mention the names of some assembled to-day, they would be familiar in the diplomatic and literary circles of several European capitals. That M. Fould is here, is a fact considered worthy of large type in the local papers, with the intelligence that "chaque matin il vient en calèche comme un simple mortel, prend son bain, déjeûne et s'en retournerait à la fin de la saison avec une nouvelle jeunesse!" Next to the French sit the Spaniards, who are also well dressed but far less talkative; then there is a hiatus, with the Russians, Americans, English, Germans, and "casuals" at the bottom.

As we are a holiday party, and have brought the latest Parisian fashions, the toilettes are not only handsome, but there is a distinguished air about the company which one rarely sees at an hotel in France, excepting at the capital.

We are merry and noisy, we might almost say uproarious, in spite of nationalities, and the gaps in our ranks. A wonderful clamour of plates and dishes, snatches of conversation, lively sallies across the table, disjointed accounts of "ascensions" more or less exciting according to the style of the narrator, a rather peculiar manner of eating, and an unparalleled consumption of vin ordinaire, is roughly what is passing at the further end of the table.

Our own part of the company, at the lower end of the table, is scarcely so brilliant in appearance, or so fluent in French, nevertheless we are sociable enough. There are grave "patres familiarum," who are here with their families, for the benefit of the waters, one or two members of the Alpine Club, who have "come down" to Eaux

Bonnes for a change, and entertain us with accounts of their guides, who seem to be a peculiarly lazy race, and soon "knock up," as the saying is; London physicians, taking a brief but vigorous holiday, forgetting appointments, breathing the free air of unpunctuality, and revelling in a suit of tweed; a few ordinary tourists, and the two English ladies that we meet almost everywhere in Europe travelling together.

It is now past seven o'clock and most of our party have dispersed, the majority betaking themselves to the "Promenade Horizontale." This walk, which we will call by the less prosaic title of the Lady's Mile, is a perfectly level and smooth promenade cut round the mountain side for nearly half a mile, and is the only level ground at Eaux Bonnes. It is lined for  some distance with little shops and stalls, where bright-coloured Spanish wools, trinkets, and toys are sold, where bagatelle and *tir au pistolet*, round-abouts and peep-shows —all the "fun of the fair" in fact, is set out for the amusement of idle Eaux Bonnes. From the seats placed at intervals on this wonderful platform the views down the valley, northwards, are most beautiful, with the little villages like specks in the distance, and the town of Laruns spread out in the shape of a cross at our feet.

As soon as it is dark the stalls and little wooden shops are lighted up, and promenading continues until about nine o'clock. The evenings are cold by contrast—colder than anything we have yet experienced, and many retire to the salons of the hotels, or to a little "café chantant" in a hole cut in the rock. There is a Cabinet de Lecture, but there are not many readers, and a Casino, which is also rather thinly attended.

The little square in front of the hotels is also full of people, who assemble in the evening with their families, to hear a band that we have already heard too often; there are a great many guides and couriers sauntering about, and considerable interest seems to be taken in an

L

expedition to hunt the izzard, which is to take place to-morrow.

But it is not until later in the night, when Eaux Bonnes has gone to sleep that we can appreciate the beauty of our mountain home, when the universal hubbub has subsided, and we can hear for the first time the sound of innumerable cascades, and the rustle of invisible tree-tops in the evening breeze; when the smoke from this great seething kitchen has ceased to curl up the rocks, revealing the stars shining down with a brightness that we never see in the plains.

The weather seemed so favourable for seeing the mountains, that we determined to make our first excursion the very next day, intending, if possible to ascend the Pic de Ger, the extraordinary conical mountain that we see in the illustration at page 144. With some difficulty, and at a high rate of pay, we had managed to obtain guides who would *walk*, and carry our provisions without extra porters to help them. Our chief guide prophesied a clear day for the excursion (which did not strike us as exhibiting much wisdom or foresight), adding that "il faut profiter du temps" in this treacherous Val d'Ossau, for that "there was no knowing what might happen."

What did happen may be judged from the next illustration, and to what an unwelcome sound we awoke next morning—the sound of pattering of feet and the pattering of rain. Water everywhere—clouds resting upon the housetops, shutting off all view beyond our little square, and the brave army of invalids taking the waters.

Let us follow them to the "Établissement," that we can just see through the rain, at the end of the street. It is a plain building of no architectural pretensions, which was once considered large, but is now quite inadequate to the requirements of Eaux Bonnes in the height of the season.

Visitors complain loudly of want of accommodation, especially in bad weather, when they have to stand upon the damp ground to wait their turn to drink the waters, and often find it difficult to get baths at the prescribed hours. There are three sulphurous springs that supply these baths: La Source Nouvelle, 86°, La Source Vieille, 88°, from which they drink, and La Source de la Douche, 91°.

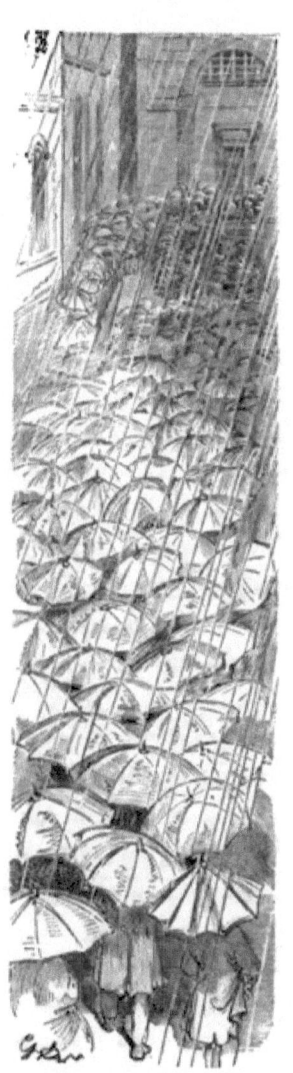

Whether it be good for any one, especially those affected with pulmonary complaints (these waters being prescribed in the early stages of consumption), to stand about here in the damp, on these cold wet mornings, we will not stay to inquire, regretting only with our French friends that "l'économie de l'administration suppose qu'il faisait toujours beau temps!" and does not provide for bad weather.

About ten o'clock we return to breakfast, and for an hour afterwards there is nothing to do on this wet morning but to listen to the German band, who, prisoners like ourselves, take up their position in the salon of the principal hotel, and discourse most eloquent music.

At eleven, it being a fête-day, and the weather slightly clearing, there is a general movement to the chapel, which is also much too small for the wants of the visitors, many of whom have come from the village of Aas.

"Cette église," says Taine, "est une boîte ronde, en pierres et en plâtre, faite pour cinquante personnes, où l'on en met deux cents. Chaque demi-heure entre et sort un flot de fidèles. Les prêtres malades abondent, et disent des messes autant qu'il en faut : tout souffre aux Eaux Bonnes du défaut d'espace, et on fait queue pour prier comme pour boire."

Soon after noon the cloud that had so completely encompassed us, disperses, and in half an hour has disappeared altogether. The streets and walks quickly dry up, and are again crowded with people. The day is too far advanced, and the weather too uncertain to make any long excursions, so that we may as well employ our time in looking about us a little, and observing a few of the peculiarities of "Les Eaux."

Everything, we notice, seems adapted for a long stay; people who come here are evidently expected to remain for the season, and visitors who wish to see the chief places of interest and hurry off again, meet with various opposing forces. If you wish to take a bath, you are expected to subscribe for a "course," available for the season; at the Casino and reading-rooms the system is the same, and hotel prices are exorbitant by the day, but moderate by the week. To get a good mount you must hire your steed by the week or month, and take him for better or for worse; and there are cascades to be viewed on the same principle.

We are all kept in good order here, everything is *en règle* and *au règle*, and if we stay a whole season, we need not be at a loss how to get through the days. It is all arranged. There is the particular promenade for the early morning facing the east, the exact spot where you are to

walk (and no further) between the time of taking each
glass of water, the morning cascade, the noon siesta, the
ride at three ; another cascade and more water, or a bath,
at four, promenade at five, dinner at six, " promenade
horizontale " until eight, then the Casino, dancing, " société,"
écarté, or more moonlight walks—and then, decidedly
early to bed.

How little the French people really know of the
Pyrenees, beyond the walks round their favourite watering-

place, can only be judged of by those who have met
them on their travels, and conversed much on such
subjects.

It has been said that the modern Parisian is "too much
at ease, too much protected, that his life is scattered about
in too many little delicate sensations," that he is unfitted
either physically or mentally for a mountain life, and that
the true zest for the enjoyment of nature is wanting in
him. Whether this be quite true or not, there is no doubt

that he suffers dreadfully from ennui. M. Taine admits the fact, and says:—

"Cet ennui prouve que la vie ressemble à l'Opéra ; pour y être heureux il faut l'argent d'entrée, mais aussi *le sentiment de la musique*. Si l'argent vous manque, vous restez dehors à la pluie parmi les décrotteurs ; si le sentiment vous manque, vous dormez maussadement dans votre superbe loge."

In spite of the theory (encouraged in French journals) that in society here, conversation is "extrêmement spirituelle," that one meets only "artistes, hommes supérieurs, et les gens du grand monde," that grace, elegance, and "la fleur de tous les plaisirs" flourish and abound, M. Taine finds the fact very different, and sums up the habits of visitors with the remark that they seem "to wear a great many hats, to eat a great many peaches, and to talk "immensely," but that in the matter of men and ideas they differ little from the rest of the world."

We have been to-day to see the Cascade du Valentin, and met plenty of people on the way thither. There is quite an assemblage at each of the favourite places of resort, and the roar of the waterfall cannot altogether drown the voices, or the orders for "cognac" and "sirops" at the little cafés which command the best view. The draught of air rushes down with a chilling sensation after walking in the sun, that renders it dangerous to sit long together in one spot ; yet in spite of the cold and spray, which falls like rain, we see several figures muffled up in cloaks, sketching the various points of interest.

These cascades, which Murray speaks of as "the pretty but trifling waterfalls of the Valentin," have seldom, we believe, been depicted with more power of the pencil than in these drawings by M. Doré. He has succeeded in giving the variety of form and undulating surface of this enormous mass of water, as it forces its way through rocks and trees, now a broad and overwhelming cataract, now a pool of smooth water reflecting the branches of the overhanging beech-trees, now escaping again in a hundred different ways, bounding from rock to rock, catching the sunshine in its course, and shedding prismatic colours on the rocks, now gathering its forces again, and roaring down into the valley far below, where we can trace it, a broad river, hurrying to the sea.

We have hitherto spoken of Eaux Bonnes in its summer

aspect, when it is crowded and gay, but perhaps the best time to see and to enjoy the scenery, is in the fine weather that we often have towards the middle of October, when all the little shops that lined the allées and promenades are not only shut up, but have departed bodily, and been trundled down to Pau; when the rows of seats that command the best views are untenanted; when, in short, "la vie" has departed, and there is only one hotel open for the solitary traveller—then, indeed, there is not a more pleasant or peaceful spot in which to spend the autumn days. The natural beauty of its situation, the forms of the surrounding mountains, the variety of interest in its walks, leave an abiding sense of beauty in the mind, long after the sounds of bells and whistles, and penny trumpets, the shouts and screams, and the perpetual *fanfare* making holiday, have died away.

CAUTERETS.

Face p. 153.

CAUTERETS.

"Cauterets est un bourg au fond d'une vallée, assez triste, pavé, muni d'un octroi. Hôteliers, guides, tout un peuple affamé nous investit ; nous sommes raccrochés par des servantes, des enfants, des loueurs d'ânes, des garçons qui par hasard viennent se promener autour de nous."

It is nearly dusk when (in about twelve hours after leaving Eaux Bonnes) we drive into the garden in front of the Hôtel de France at Cauterets. The rooms are brilliantly lighted up, and in the salon we see people dancing; in the gardens and under the trees we hear laughter and the voices of women, and, here and there, glow-worm lights betray the presence of the smoking sex.[1]

The extraordinary cures effected by the waters of Cauterets are the constant theme of conversation in the Pyrenees, and they are particularly esteemed by Spaniards, who come here in such numbers as to give Cauterets quite the appearance of a town on the other side of the frontier.

There are several sources of the waters, varying in temperature and slightly in composition. The Établissement called *La Raillère*, which is considered one of the most efficacious in pulmonary complaints, is built upon a raised terrace about a mile from the town, at the foot of Mont Regnère, on the road to the Lac de Gaube, to and

---

[1] This by courtesy and in ignorance of facts ; for we afterwards found that cigarettes were in request, both with Spanish and French ladies.

from which omnibuses are passing with patients all day. The thermal building comprises, according to Dr. Taylor, "twenty-three cabinets de bain, a fountain for the water-drinkers, an ascending and descending douche, a large peristyle in marble arches, and an extensive terrace in front to take exercise in dry or wet weather."

The best excursion in the neighbourhood—the one, in fact, which has brought us to Cauterets—is to see one of the few lakes of which the Pyrenees can boast, the Lac de Gaube (5866 feet above the sea), for there is nothing wanting so much, in the scenery of the Pyrenees, as lakes reflecting the blue sky. Even the waterfalls, numerous and picturesque as they are, appear somewhat insignificant compared with those of Switzerland, although there is a softness and luxuriant beauty in their surroundings that compensates in great measure for any lack of grandeur. At the hotel we announce our intention to walk to the Lac de Gaube, and to dispense with guides and ponies.

"Ces Anglais will ruin the Pyrenees!" is muttered sotto voce.

It takes about two hours and a half to reach the Lac de Gaube; the path is easily found, and is well trodden during the season. Leaving the valley of Latour (in which Cauterets is situated) on our left hand, the road ascends, first through a wood and by several cascades, then through pine-forests by a steep path for about six miles, when we reach the Pont d'Espagne. Here we make a halt before crossing into Spain, and wander about amongst the moss-grown rocks and débris through which the Gave rushes down, casting up a shower of spray which keeps the trees and shrubs in perpetual freshness.

From the Pont d'Espagne to the Lac de Gaube is about two miles—first by a steep ascent leading through a pine-wood, thence over a path strewn with rocks and loose stones—in a little less than an hour we reach the lonely mountain lake, so solitary, so still, and so different from all we have passed on our way, as to take us quite by surprise.

It is about two miles in circumference, and is said to be the largest in the Pyrenees. At one end is a little cabin, and hard by, on a rock, a white marble monument to the memory of an Englishman and his wife who were drowned here when on their wedding tour. The guides and the people who live in the little cabin tell the story, and, almost in the same breath, ask if we will not take a row across the lake.

The Lac de Gaube is a perfect mountain-basin, the water being prevented from escaping into the valley by a natural granite wall, which forms a sort of embankment at the northern end. From this point we obtain a grand view of the snow-covered Vignemale, reflected in the still water. The sides of the lake are steep and rugged, with masses of fir-trees reaching almost to the water's edge, making a dark sombre foreground.

At the upper end of the lake, we can just trace the waterfall which winds down from its glacier source; and if we were to sleep in the little cabin, and row across the lake in early morning, we might, with a good guide, reach the summit of one at least of the snowy peaks we see in the next illustration (between 10,000 and 11,000 feet), commanding a more extensive view than from the Maladetta, or other accessible mountain of the High Pyrenees.

The variety and beauty of the excursions in the neighbourhood of the Lac de Gaube, and the pleasant valley of Cauterets, by woods and waterfalls, to the snow-clad summits of the great chain, have detained many of our countrymen for weeks, and it is only to be regretted that we have still but imperfect information about some of the routes. The local guides prefer keeping to the beaten tracks, and require much persuasion and good pay, before undertaking any new expedition. There is one other excursion that should not be missed by those who are good climbers, and are favoured with clear weather, viz., to the Lac d'Estom by the Valley of Latour.

Every day during our stay is occupied in some picturesque excursion in the environs, which we never seem to have exhausted, and every evening we are launched on a sea of small dissipations, the like of which we could never have imagined possible on the steep side of a mountain 3000 feet above the level of the sea.

We had donkey-races, running in sacks, and climbing poles; in fact, it was more like a village merry-making in England than anything else. There were "courses de cruches," races with vessels full of water carried on the heads of young girls, most of whom were drenched in a most pitiless manner; whilst one, "Mademoiselle Sophie," the most active and spirited of the party, carried off a prize of 10 francs for having maintained the "cruche en équilibre."

Our remembrances of Cauterets are (independently of the fair) of an expensive residence, of a most fashionable promenade, of the noises of whips cracking, pianos jingling, of singing, of smoking ad libitum; of tall men riding diminutive ponies, and "les grandes dames" gaily capari-

LAC DE GAUBE.

soned mules; of the town looking as if it was perpetually going out to dinner in sedan-chairs, of salons, of "journals pour rire et pour instruire," with articles diluted to holiday calibre, of cascades and springs, of water—water, everywhere; of English scrambling up the rocks, of Frenchmen "en promenade," and of Spaniards sitting under the trees.

Our thoughts, if we analyse them, are not so much of the mountains and of the pine-forests that overhang its streets, as of smooth lawns and parterres; not of torrents,

but of the prettiest artificial cascades; not of rocks in their natural beauty, but of granite, smoothed and "faced," and turned into dwellings for the lords of the creation; of waters bottled off and stamped with the seal of the empire; and of the very stones at the road-side, numbered and registered like citizens of France.

In short, everything was civilised at Cauterets, they had civilised a bear; and nothing will leave a more mournful memory, not even the tragedy at the Lac de Gaube, than the picture of this dancing bear (performing almost in sight of his comrades looming down from the mountains), and of his fellow in misfortune, the monkey that took the money.

A satire upon society—a thing to be remembered, was the appearance of this last little figure, a type of the artificial atmosphere of the place—the "fun of the fair" for one sou; a strange, sad-looking being (wearing a red "béret" on his head and a bright embroidered sash), with very little of the animal about him—altogether a forlorn and most dissipated-looking little monkey, thus overdressed and out of his element—the image, in little, of many who crowd round him, the perfect type of "la vie."

Luz—Barèges—Bagnères.

The situation of Luz, in a large natural basin surrounded on all sides by mountains, is preferred by many visitors to St. Sauveur. It is more open, and the walks are more varied ; it is less fashionable and pretentious, and once was much cheaper than St. Sauveur as a place of residence. But partly from its central situation, partly from the fame of Madame Cazeaux's dinners at the Hôtel des Pyrénées, and chiefly from the report of its cheapness, it has now become dear ; and we doubt if M. Taine saw it in its crowded, noisy state to-day, with its modern white houses and hotels, he would be disposed to call it any longer a "petit village, tout rustique et agréable."

An old fortified church, built in the time of the Templars, where service is still performed behind its ramparts, and the remains of a chateau which crown the heights, are the chief objects of interest at Luz ; but the majority of travellers pay it only a flying visit. The French people prefer St. Sauveur or Cauterets for a residence, and the tourists make it merely a place for a mid-day halt. In the heat of the day in summer its principal street is crowded with vehicles stopping at the hotels, with horses and guides

RUIN, NEAR LUZ.

Face p. 360.

and hangers-on of all descriptions, with beggars ad libitum and any number of pigs.

We scarcely know how to give an adequate impression of the importance of the pigs in a place like Luz. They occupy the principal position in the streets and in the doorways of buildings, and the inhabitants seem with one consent to give way to them. In driving into the town we must turn out of the way for fear of disturbing a group that are fast asleep in the middle of the road ; and when we alight at our hotel we shall probably find a crowd of loungers superintending the operation of washing them in the stream that flows through the street, water being poured over them with a large iron ladle as they repose in the sun, submitting placidly to the operation of basting before their time. At Granada, in Spain, every one keeps a pig in the autumn, to fatten for Christmas, and it is considered unlucky not to possess one. The Spanish gentlemen who sit about the doorways here and watch these operations, must be gratified at the adoption of at least one of their customs by the people of Luz.

There is a good carriage-road from Luz to Barèges, the distance being about five miles of continual ascent, through a somewhat gloomy valley, which is often flooded in spring and winter; giving it that forsaken and ruinous appearance that we see in the valley of the Rhone near Sion.

As we approach Barèges the mountains close in upon us, and their sides become more and more barren, the wind blows in gusts, and the air is quite cold in the shade.

The waters of Barèges are so much esteemed for their curative properties that the baths are crowded with invalids, and the French administration has established a military hospital here for the treatment of gun-shot wounds and

other injuries. It is said that as many as ten or twelve thousand persons take the waters here during a summer season. It is most disagreeable to the taste and smell, and this, added to the discomforts of a crowded place and a decidedly *triste* situation, does not appear very inviting to a visitor.

But the weather is fine, and warm in the middle of the day, and we find ourselves tolerably comfortable in our mountain lodging, nearly 4000 feet above the sea; in the midst of a community of sick men, old women, and decrepit, all huddled together on a ledge of rock, like birds in a nest. The stormy winds that blow down the valley in sudden gusts, and moan in the crevices of the rocks, sound rather drearily, it is true, but what will it be, in a few months' time, when, increased to a hurricane and accompanied with snow, they will sweep away in their winter strength both " man and his dwelling-place "; and Barèges will have a second season, with another class of visitors who are less fastidious perhaps, less infirm, less careful to

drink the waters, but otherwise not unimportant, and as certainly to be expected in season as their summer friends.

The presiding deity of Barèges is the " Pic du Midi de Bigorre." The inhabitants love, honour, and obey its teaching; they look to it for the signs of the times and seasons, and the sense of its presence is ever near them. In the lonely track over the Tourmalet, and down the valley of the Adour towards Bigorre, it is continually in sight, and by the movements of the clouds round its summit, or by the sharpness of its outline against the sky, the wayfarer is encouraged or cautioned on his route.

Before we leave Barèges we take advantage of a clear

day to see the view from the Pic du Midi, where there is now an observatory with telegraphic communication with Bagnères de Bigorre which is considered to be unequalled in the Pyrenees for its extent. Its extraordinary position, standing considerably northward of the central chain, with no mountains of equal height (9439 feet) near it, and its accessibility to the summit, render it more worth ascending than any other of equal height. It takes three hours on foot, and nearly four on horseback. There is a clear path, and no guide is necessary.

We first follow the route leading over the Tourmalet, and then, turning to our left, ascend a shoulder of the mountain until we come to a little lake, and a cabin, where it is possible to get a night's lodging. From this point, where we make a short halt, the path leads in a zigzag direction, up the now steep and barren side of the Pic, from whence we occasionally obtain distant views of the valley.

The view from the summit, which is at least 1500 feet above the lake, and more than 5000 above Barèges, surpassed all expectation in its grandeur and extent. Our position here was so isolated, that even the vast chain of the Pyrenees, to the south, seemed to be separated from us, and so precipitous were the sides of the Pic du Midi that we scarcely felt as if we were on terra firma. Before us, the solitary Pic de Montaigu, and the plains of France extending into apparently illimitable space, and behind, all the most prominent peaks of the Pyrenees. It was like looking down upon a gigantic *carte relief*, showing the little towns, the bright green valleys, the dark rocks and the fields of snow. Immediately at our feet there was nothing but rock, but lower down there were slopes of grass, bright with gentian and other wild flowers; the base or frame of this giant mountain being "cast"—as Mr. Packe calls it—"in a brown micaceous schist, which, cropping out from the surface, sparkles with metallic brilliancy."

It is difficult to describe, without repetition, the views from these summits, as they must necessarily have so many points of similarity, but the reader may take the word of every one who has had a successful day for the expedition, that there is nothing comparable to it, at the same altitude in the Pyrenees.

As we said before, it is rare to get a clear day for these

"UNE ASCENSION."

ascents; let us now hear M. Taine's account of one on a cloudy day.

"Départ à quatre heures du matin dans la vapeur. Les pâturages à travers la vapeur ; on voit la vapeur. Le lac à travers la vapeur ; même vue !

"Commencement de l'escarpement ; montée au pas à la queue l'un de l'autre, chaque cheval ayant le nez contre la queue du précédent, et la queue contre le nez du suivant, comme au jour de sortie aux colléges d'équitation.

"*Première heure :* Vue du dos de mon guide et de la croupe de son cheval.

"*Deuxième heure :* La vue s'élargit ; j'aperçois l'œil gauche du cheval du guide. Cet œil est borgne, et il ne perd rien !

"*Troisième heure :* La vue s'élargit encore. Vue de deux croupes de chevaux et deux vestes de touristes, qui sont à quinze pieds au-dessus de nous. Ils jurent et je jure. Cela nous console un peu.

"*Quatrième heure :* Joie et transports ; le guide me promet, pour la cime, la vue d'une mer de nuages.

"*Arrivée :* Vue de la mer de nuages. Par malheur nous sommes dans un des nuages. Aspect d'un bain de vapeur quand on est dans le bain.

"*Bénéfices :* Rhume de cerveau, rhumatisme aux pieds, lumbago, congélation—bonheur d'un homme qui a fait une ascension ! "

Leaving Barèges and its invalids, it is with a certain sense of relief that we find ourselves once more winding slowly up the Bastan valley, on our way to Bigorre. The distance from Barèges to Bagnères de Bigorre is nearly twenty miles, but the steepness of the ascent, and the time occupied for resting, make it a journey of about eight hours.

Our path, which is nearly due eastward, passes between the Pic du Midi and the principal chain of the Pyrenees, the Tourmalet forming the connecting link between the mountains ; and it is not until we reach the col, which takes about two hours and a half, that we get any considerable view, or feel to some extent released from our prison-house.

When we have descended for about an hour, by some very steep and rough zigzags cut in the rock, we get a fine view of the Pic du Midi, and are once more amongst pleasant pastures watered by the river Adour, which here takes its rise and which we follow on its left bank almost to Bagnères.

Another hour's descent, and we meet gaily-dressed people, riding and walking about, who seem to belong, as it were, to another world (each valley is so shut in and distinct), and in the little town of Gripp, where we halt, there are carriages that have brought pleasure-parties from Bigorre, whose drivers are clamorous for a "back-fare." We drive down the valley in the cool of the evening, rattling through the streets of the town after dark, just sufficiently lighted to enable us to see the crowd that is walking up and down an "allée," shaded by two rows of fine trees, and bounded on either side by cafés and shops.

Bagnères de Bigorre is not only one of the most ancient, but it is one of the largest and most prosperous towns in the Pyrenees, having a resident population of upwards of 8000, besides accommodating in the season 4000 or 5000 visitors.[1] Its situation, neither in the mountains nor in the plains, the cheapness of provisions and other commodities, the moderate rent of houses, the mild saline springs, and the general character of the town for health, combine to recommend it to English people who reside permanently abroad.

It is a pleasant change to come down again towards the plains and spend a few days quietly in a town; and curious, to find the English language spoken continually, to hear the click of croquet ("le jeu d'arc," as the French call it), to see cricket bats, and to be asked in English at the shops if we will buy any "Pale Ale." On Sunday morning at the little English church, at the Club, and even in the streets, we might almost fancy ourselves in a country town in England, so familiar and so frequent are the signs of our nationality everywhere.

On market-days there is colour and some variety of

---

[1] Froissart speaks of it as "a goodly enclosed town called Bagnères, the inhabitants of which had a hard time of it in 1369, when war broke out between France and England."

costume. There are itinerant merchants in Spanish costume, with gay silk ribbons, woollen rugs, &c., for sale; and there are rows of shops for the display of woollen goods, which may be bought here much more reasonably than at Eaux Bonnes or Luchon. An old woman, with a large capulet over her head, in a fashion more picturesque than comfortable, one would imagine, offers us ten fine fresh figs for a sou (we have had to pay twice as much for the same at Seville), and young girls with pretty coloured handkerchiefs tied round their heads, sell flowers and fruit to passers-by.

If we were to go to market this morning, we could purchase ducks, fowls, and turkeys at prices that would make the British householder envious to hear of; and there is an air of plenty and contentment about the place that does one good to witness.

The people that come in from the neighbourhood in such numbers, that in the evening we can hardly force our way through the crowded allée, look healthy and prosperous; and we cannot help contrasting them in our minds, with the inhabitants of other beautiful valleys, such as Stachelberg in Switzerland, or Tintern on the Wye. Happy the people of such valleys as that through which the Adour flows, that they can live and thrive on agricultural labour, and put by for a rainy day, more in one month than a Dorset labourer is able to do in a year.

The walks in the neighbourhood are delightful; you cannot proceed in any direction for half an hour without coming upon some fresh view of the mountains. On one occasion we spent the day on the heights above Bagnères, sketching, and watching the changing aspects of the Pic du Midi, as it every now and then emerged from clouds (which never entirely left it, although it was clear elsewhere), and we were glad of any shade or wood in our path.

As we sat under the trees, there were sounds of voices, and, looking upwards, we discovered men and boys, and

even children, perched up sixty or seventy feet high in the air, either on the branches of the trees, or on three poles fixed triangularly in the ground.

Travellers see strange sights, in the Landes there were men literally "as trees walking"; here they seem to nestle in the branches, and cradle in the wind. They are spreading nets for the wood-pigeons that flock to this neighbourhood in great numbers in the autumn months, and are perched up aloft to throw their nets; the poles and branches bending with their weight, swaying backwards and forwards in the wind, in a manner that appears most dangerous to the uninitiated.

We had been wandering hither and thither, with that uncertainty which is the delight of a mountain ramble; we had come suddenly upon a flock of sheep, and had a sharp battle with the dogs in charge of them; we had nearly trodden upon a shepherd boy, who lay hidden in the long grass, and who, careless apparently of his flock, and heedless of us, was singing some quaint Béarnais air from memory.

We had passed up, far above pasture-land and trees, and gained a point where, if the eye could have penetrated the atmosphere that alone limited the horizon northward, it seemed as if we might have seen half over France; from the west towards the Bay of Biscay, and to the east almost to the Mediterranean shore, we could trace the line of mountains, and to the south a multitude of snowy peaks and promontories.

We sit down to rest for a while—to watch the effect of the sun leaving the highest peaks, whilst the town of Bagnères, several hundred feet below, is disappearing fast from view and sparkling with little glow-worm lights when —looking farther down the valley—we see a slowly-moving dark line, serpent-like in motion, winding noiselessly through the trees (some monster apparently, attracted by these earth-stars), now burrowing underground, and now, as it comes nearer, showing two flaming eyes, and a tail with glittering scales. This monster is a creation of the "Compagnie du Chemin de Fer du Midi," and in its sides there are lighted cells containing atoms of human life. What, we wonder, does the little shepherd boy, what do all the children of the mountains, think of steam?

"La gorge était illuminée dans ses profondeurs ; ses blocs entassés, ses arbres accrochés aux roches, ses ravines déchirées, son Gave écumant, apparaissaient dans une blancheur livide, et s'évanouissaient comme les visions fugitives d'un monde tourmenté et inconnu."—*Taine.*

STORM.

IT is not uncommon for travellers who have come to the Pyrenees in summer-time for health and recreation, and whose only chance of enjoyment is the continuance of fine weather, to regard with something of anxiety the slightest sign of clouds gathering round the distant peaks ; and it is also not uncommon to see, at the same time, a long procession headed by a priest, winding slowly up the valley.

The country, green and bright as it looks, is really suffering from drought, and, as a last resource, the curé, or priest, has been appealed to. A mass is celebrated, the hat is handed round, money is subscribed liberally, and—in due time, the rain comes.

In our wanderings in the Val d'Ossau and the Val de Luz, we had frequently noticed traces of the ravages of the storms, and in the windings of the Gave, the marks where in many places it had overflowed its banks; but the beauty of the weather, which continued day by day with almost a monotony of sunshine and blue sky, and the calm and peaceful aspect of security with which the inhabitants seemed to be gathering their harvest and tending their flocks, left us quite unprepared for the startling change that a few hours brought about.

The morning had been fine and cloudless, as usual, with a sun almost as powerful as in the tropics; it was too hot to do anything apparently, but work in the fields, as the women and young girls were doing, some bareheaded and barefooted, binding the sheaves of Indian corn, and struggling under loads of hay that an English labourer would hesitate to carry.

There was little to indicate a coming storm within half-an-hour of its breaking, but then the signs were unmistakable and not to be disregarded.

First of all, a few little clouds were seen to gather at the head of the valley in a wild, uncertain manner, and every now and then we heard trees rustling in the wind higher up the mountains, although not a leaf stirred near at hand; presently we seemed encompassed by four winds at once, and the dust and leaves, and sheaves of corn, were whirled in the air with the suddenness of an explosion. The sun was still shining brightly, and there were few clouds overhead, but, as if with a sudden instinct of self-preservation, every living thing in the valley and on the mountains hurried home. The women left the fields, the men their work in the forests, the birds were silent, the dogs disappeared, the cattle of their own accord drew away to shelter higher up the valley, and even the pigs (who sleep in companies by the roadside) roused themselves for once and shuffled home.

Down the narrow street of the little village, a herd of

A MOUNTAIN STORM.

Face p. 173.

goats are hustling and struggling, under the heels of a sullen grey pony, who, with his fore-feet planted firmly in the ground and his mane and tail spread out by the wind, stands immovable, without a purpose apparently but obstruction. A few of the most active of the inhabitants are tying their carts and implements to the trunks of trees and stowing away loose timber, but the majority are engaged in barring their doors, or peering furtively from dark windows and apertures, in a manner that suggests a Poussin or a Teniers.

Soon all interest is centred in the approaching storm, and it is a difficult task to describe the change, the almost dramatic suddenness with which a sunny smiling valley is turned into a howling wilderness. A shadow should be cast over these pages, something more expressive than words, more powerful even than Doré's pencil, should be enlisted in the service, and something should be done, were it possible, to give the moaning of the wind. The sound is piteous, and now almost constant, interrupted only by the thunder, and the distant roar of waterfalls.

The sun has not quite left the lower part of the valley, but the mountain-tops are in darkness, excepting when a sudden lightning flash reveals their outlines for a moment.

Another ten minutes and the clouds come down, closing over us, like a dark veil stretched completely across the valley. The wind that fanned us so gently but an hour since, sweeps past with the noise and fury of battle, bending the tall pine trees as it passes over them, dashing the waterfalls into spray, and scattering far and wide the sheaves of corn. Suddenly another element is added—a downpour as of a cataract, swelling the Gave to a roaring torrent, which now joins in the tumult.

Let us see what havoc is being made on its banks. Following its windings as far as we can discern through the clouds and rain, there are several companies of weather-beaten pines, against which the storm is raging in all its fury. As the clouds pass over they are continually concealed from view, as if in the smoke of battle, every here and there their ranks appearing—now resisting, now falling, bending, or snapping before the blast, but generally reappearing with a persistence that suggests to the spectator something human and heroic in the fight.

Nothing, however, that we have yet seen—not the

grandeur of the storm, its suddenness, or its power of destruction—is so extraordinary as the mass of water which has risen on every side. The lower parts of the valley have become one vast lake, dotted with island tree-tops, haystacks, timber, and wrecks of all kinds, carried down by the flood. The villages built on rising ground (with foreknowledge of these disasters), escape the deluge, but many outlying buildings and parts of the road have altogether disappeared. In scarcely less time than it takes to write it, we see acres of water where there were cultivated fields, and the rain that came with the thunder and the wind, now falls steadily and straight like a waterspout.

In half an hour all is again changed, the rain ceases as suddenly as it came, the mist clears, and the clouds drift away through the trees. The sides of the valley are streaked with torrents looking like veins of silver, every

little cascade has become for the time a torrent, and the swollen Gave, now dark, muddy, and turbulent, burdened with floating timber and débris of all kinds, has scarcely any limit, for there is water everywhere.

When the storm ceased, the water subsided in the upper

part of the valley almost as rapidly as it had risen; but the scene here was, if possible, more desolate, from the havoc that had been made amongst the trees in exposed situations.

One point was very striking, where we came to a piece of pasture-land separated on either side by a narrow gorge. This promontory was a complete mountain-wreck; it had been exposed to the full fury of two winds meeting in their downward course, and everything had "gone by the board"—trees were stripped of their branches, torn down, snapped and twisted into strange fantastic shapes, scarcely a whole stem out of a regiment of stately pines—nothing but waifs and strays, like a harvest-field when given up to the gleaners.

Nothing was to be heard at this spot but the rushing of waters, no human being was in sight, no cattle had returned to pasture, nothing living apparently, save two young eagles that flew low in the valley, and a solitary lizard (that had had much more water than was good for him) that came out of his hiding-place, and spread a spangled S upon the rock.

Then when the clouds had gathered up from the valley, there came a stream of light from the west, that, glancing from the rocks and torrents on either side, fell full upon this promontory, gilding the stems of the shattered pines, and marking in characters only too distinct the devastating work of storms.

A few hours only and the waters will subside, and it will again be "summer in the Pyrenees."

A word about Doré's illustrations of these storms, which seem to us some of the finest works of this character he has ever achieved. As we stood in our secure shelter, watching, what it did not require much stretch of the imagination to picture as a battle, we confess to have been completely

AFTER THE STORM.

carried away by the human aspect of the fight, and can hardly agree with those who think that in depicting such subjects, M. Doré has given too much scope to his fancy.

And the sunset after the storm, which is one of the grandest sights in the Pyrenees, calls to mind even more vividly the same groups of forest trees, not in war, but in peace—when their dark funereal plumes (tattered and weather-stained, like the colours and trophies of war) are tinged with a deep orange hue, and we see

> "The grace and glory of their feathery branches
> Spread like wings that love the light,"

and wish that any words of ours could induce more landscape painters to depict these scenes—scenes worthy of the full expression of a poet's heart either by his pencil or his pen.

LUCHON.

"Il est convenu que la vie aux eaux est fort poétique, et qu'on y trouve des aventures de toute sorte, surtout des aventures de cœur.

"Il est également convenu qu'aux eaux la conversation est extrêmement spirituelle, qu'on n'y rencontre que des artistes, des hommes supérieurs, des gens du grand monde ; qu'on y prodigue des idées, la grâce et l'élégance, et que la fleur de tous les plaisirs et de toutes les pensées y vient s'épanouir."—*Taine.*

IN the midst of a broad and fertile valley, with mountain slopes of pasture and wood on either side ; amidst groves of trees, from under banks covered with moss and lichen, burst forth the far-famed springs of Luchon ; the resort of invalids and "malades imaginaires,"—from the days when Roman emperors drank these waters and Fabia Festa paid her vow to the god Lixon, giving the name of Luchon to the little town built near the rocks, whence the healing waters flowed—to the present time, when several thousand people throng its streets.

Luchon is a favourite resort of nations both north and south of the Pyrenees. It is easily reached from Paris, and there are, also, several bridle-paths by which it may be approached from Spain. The latter are often taken—just as in the hot summer months the modern Florentine, who is stout of heart and strong in the chest, forsakes the dried-up banks of the Arno for the bracing air of Switzerland, making his way, as we have seen him, over the snows of the St. Theodule to Zermatt—so do certain brave-hearted Madrileños come over by the bridle-paths from Jaca, Pantecosa and the Port de Venasque, and make their sudden appearance on horseback at Luchon.

How shall we describe this shrine—the object of so many pious pilgrimages? Perhaps we cannot do better than compare it, for an instant, with Chamounix, in Savoy.

If we can imagine Chamounix, a town consisting of about two hundred hotels and lodging-houses, in the midst of a fertile valley, and surrounded with trees; if we can picture (a stretch of imagination, we admit) a little park outside the town, with trim lawns, beds of flowers, fountains, an artificial lake with gaily-painted boats upon it à la Bois de Boulogne, and a pretty boulevard (lighted by gas at night), with trees planted at regular intervals; and if we can further picture Chamounix without Mont Blanc, without its glaciers or any ice or snow, and without its bracing air that is born of them, a place where guides are *raræ aves* and ice-axes almost unknown; where guns are fired indeed often enough—not to signalise an ascent of Mont Blanc, but of a fire balloon; where kid gloves are more the *mode* than suits of tweed, and where Frenchmen take the place of Englishmen in native esteem—we get some idea of Luchon.

There is a certain similarity in the two places; they are both the head-quarters from which to make excursions; both are situated on rivers in the midst of a broad valley, with high mountains each side. There is a drive up to the

ENVIRONS OF LUCHON.

end of the Val de Lys, as to the Col de Balme; and there is a climb, to the Port de Venasque, nearly as steep and precipitous as to the Breven, (see page 196), with a view therefrom of the Mont Blanc of the Pyrenees with its snowfields and glaciers.

The comparative heights, &c., of the two places are thus—but the snow-level is more than 1000 feet higher, in the Pyrenees:

	Height above Sea-level.	Average height of surrounding Mountains.	Average Temperature.	Population about
LUCHON . . .	2064	8000	52° Fahr.	3000
CHAMOUNIX . .	3300	11,000	37° Fahr.	3000

The town of Luchon, as far as visitors are concerned, consists chiefly of one long street lined with old trees, and furnished with hotels, cafés, lodging-houses, and shops. At the upper end is the little park just mentioned, with the Thermal Establishment, a handsome building erected close under the mountain-side, and in front of which is the principal promenade. The opposite end of this street, called the "Allée d'Étigny," leads to the old town of Luchon, and to the road down the valley towards Toulouse.

The noise, dust, and bustle, in the Allée d'Étigny in the height of the season, when more than a thousand visitors are added to the native population, is extraordinary. There are several wide roads leading from it, and many chalets and houses dotted about the plain, but as it is the fashion to live in the Allée d'Étigny, the crowd is concentrated on this narrow little slip of land, whether riding or walking, reading or sleeping—day or night, there is hardly any peace upon it.

The scene is a very brilliant one on a sunny day, with

the perpetual movement of the gaily dressed crowds of French and Spanish holiday loungers. There is more local colour and variety here than at Eaux Bonnes; there are more Spaniards, more red berrets, gay sashes, and more striking feminine costumes. The shops are filled with Spanish wools and Parisian goods; signboards are festooned from the trees, and a thousand coloured objects arrest the eye. The middle of the roadway is crowded with carriages and horses; the trappings are gay, of course, and the drivers not the least dandified of the party. The horses or ponies they ride, or drive, are little, lean, attenuated animals, of a breed unknown elsewhere, averaging about twelve or fourteen hands high—narrow-chested and stiff-looking like wooden toys, certainly not worth more than 3*l*. or 4*l*. a piece. But how they scamper all day up and down this Allée, jingling their little bells; how their drivers shout and crack their whips, asking less and less for a "course" as the sun goes down; and how popular they are, in spite of the danger to life and limb as they career along, is something almost indescribable.

All this we see at a first glance as we drive at a hand-gallop up the avenue, and with shouts and cracking of whips turn into the courtyard of the Hôtel d'Angleterre. It is situated about the centre of the Allée d'Étigny, in a pleasant little garden, slightly sheltered from the road, and we are fortunate at this time of year in getting good rooms at the back. We are near the stables, and there are fowls, pigeons and peacocks in the courtyard, all favourable to early rising.

The hotel is full of visitors, chiefly "pensionnaires"— French and Spaniards, and two or three English—all methodical in their habits of early rising, taking baths and exercise, and punctual to a fault in assembling to breakfast at ten, and dinner at half-past six.

" Tout en haut, entre les troncs, brille un pan de ciel blue ; l'ombre et la lumière se coupent sur la mousse grise comme des dessins de soieries sur un fond de velours."

Face p. 183.

We have not been many hours in Luchon when we are besieged with enquiries as to what "*ascensions*" we have made, and it is quite clear that we shall have no peace until we have gone the "regular round." But before exploring the environs, or indeed going very far beyond the little "parc" we must see more of the people.

It is about eight o'clock on a summer's morning when we first walk out in Luchon. The mountains look fresh and green from the late rains, little flakes of cloud just touch their tops, and here and there some detached portions float down and nestle amongst the trees, or on projecting slopes of grass, where we can distinguish (through a telescope) sheep grazing, and children gathering wood into the chalets.

The streets are full of bathers hurrying to and from the "Établissement"; and as it is rather too early to see the habitués to perfection, we stroll up the "Allée des Soupirs," behind the baths for a couple of hours, by a steep, smooth path through a wood, towards Super-Bagnères. Every five minutes we get more lovely views of the valley, and of the peaks that rise on every side above Luchon. The town is almost *under* our feet, so precipitous are the sides of the mountain, and we see little of it besides slate-roofs and chimney-pots, with one straight row of tree-tops peeping through the smoke and steam, that rise from the town. If we were not bound to see the company to-day, we could well spend all our time in sketching here, or in wandering about Super-Bagnères.[1]

---

[1] It is a pity so little is said in English guide-books about Super-Bagnères; the distance to the cabin at the summit is only five miles, and it is an easy ascent. The beautiful walks through the forests, which M. Doré has sketched for us, and the panoramic view from the summit, taking in the plains of France on one side, and the Maladetta on the other, are well known to those who stay at Luchon.

It is now half-past ten o'clock. Luchon has taken its bath, has drunk the waters, has breakfasted well, and is prepared to promenade, or to make a *petite excursion;* let us descend to the "Allée d'Étigny" and see "the world." The street is more crowded than ever, and the costumes more brilliant and extravagant than any we have yet seen in the Pyrenees. The general effect of the colours of the figures, on foot and on horseback, is certainly very pretty; and if some of the ladies' dresses startle us a little by their originality—and if we are rather taken aback by seeing a French gentleman in a suit of scarlet, walking along swinging a child's rattle, or riding a diminutive pony, with his legs nearly reaching to the ground—the *tout-ensemble* we must admit to be charming.

Here is a group just starting for a ride; and what strikes us most of all is, perhaps, the size and length of spike of their spurs, the formidable weight of their whips, and the insignificant, meek-looking little animals they are going to mount. Four French gentlemen are about to ride a few miles up the valley, and the concourse to see them start, and the interest taken in the matter, is wondrous. There are perhaps a hundred spectators on foot, and fifty men and boys on horseback waiting for hire. These last keep up a constant shouting and cracking with their whips, which irritates the ear like irregular line-firing. The start takes about half an hour, but the crowd is an admiring one, and in no hurry.

With the departure of the cavalcade the crowd disperses, the majority tending towards the park, or "English garden"; where, under the shade of the trees, by the aid of syrups and ices, and to the sound of falling water, the next few hours may be dozed away.

It would be almost impossible to give to any one who had not seen the Bois de Boulogne near Paris within the

LAC D'OO.

Face p. 185.

last few years, a just idea of the ingenuity displayed in turning the bed of a mountain valley, covered but a few years since with débris (as seen in the illustration at p. 180), into a perfect promenade, and miniature park, with its artificial lake, dainty walks lined with tulip trees and beds of flowers, real waterfalls imprisoned and turned into "cascades"; fountains and grottoes, chalets and arbours— all designedly pretty and in order. The little boats that pass to and fro on the lake, trail their awnings in the water, purposely, to reflect their bright colours; and the Swiss chalets on its banks, and the houses in the town—white, with green shutters and red curtains at their windows—are all decorated with an eye to the picturesque.

As the afternoon draws on, there comes an almost continual sound of wheels, and horses' feet; the jingle of bells, and cracking of whips, drown the noise of the cascades again, and clouds of dust now roll down the valley, marking the track of carriages returning from the "Val de Lys" and the "Lac de Oo."

It is only four o'clock. Why do they return so soon?

"*C'est le temps de promenade.*"

Is it then *all* "promenade"? But let us follow in the direction of the people that we see assembling on a raised walk near the Établissement, where a brass band is the centre of attraction, and around which the numerous chairs are fast becoming occupied. The gaiety of this promenade is even more striking than that of the morning, and we are introduced to many fresh varieties of the "butterfly" species.

How we all wander up and down, and talk and pay little attention to the music, may be easily understood; but how we dress, how demonstrative and how brilliant we are in this clear bright sunny air, can hardly be conceived at a distance. Nor can we altogether picture to the reader the effect of the Señoras and Señoritas who have doffed the charming black mantilla and red camellia in the hair, and come abroad in all the glory of modern Parisian costume; nor the knowing little hats with peacock's feathers worn by pretty *Parisiennes;* nor the children—children only in size and love for bonbons; nor the Spanish dons in white paletôts and chimney-pot hats; nor the dogs, whose "paradise of whelping and wagging of tails" is clearly not here, for they also are on good behaviour, and can do neither one nor the other. They are muzzled, wrapped in flannel, and carried in baskets, and generally so clipped and washed, that in appearance they belie their origin.

Before five o'clock the numbers increase to a crowd, and at this fashionable hour the habitués—what in modern slang would be called the swell—make their appearance.

There were two figures who always walked arm-in-arm together, and came on the scene about this time, who were as familiar to us as the rocks and the trees; one a tall Spaniard, faultlessly dressed in a black velvet costume of the time of Charles II., with black silk stockings, shoe-buckles, collars, and ruff. His friend, a Frenchman, (we presume as a contrast), was the most perfect presentment of an English cattle-drover it has ever been our lot to encounter, the intention of the "get-up" being to signify a gentleman who was fond of "le sport," and as such he evidently found favour amongst the ladies. These two young gentlemen carried everything before them. They were in society, they knew everybody, and disported themselves in the park every afternoon, to the perfect contentment of Luchon.

The band plays well, but it does not matter: we come

to see, and not to hear. It adds, however, to the dramatic effect, and it is difficult to get rid of the idea that this raised platform is not the stage of some Italian opera, with all these gay moving figures the performers; the background the scenery to "Guillaume Tell," and the audience the group seated on the chairs.

But it is not all gaiety. If we look about us a little we shall see at this time of day numbers of strangers who occupy the chairs; for, just as the heat of the sun at noon draws forth myriads of insects and atoms of mysterious life, so does this afternoon promenade attract to it visitors seldom seen at any other time. Amongst them are the ennuyés—"ennuyés parce qu'ils ont trop de fortune et trop peu de chagrin"—men of middle age, and old, in as great numbers, and put to as great straits in the task of killing time, as may be seen in any city in Europe. Old and faded dandies, preserved with the greatest care, made "youthful for ever" by art, lounging away their days in that difficult time between *déjeuner* and *dîner*, alleviated only by this afternoon promenade, which may bring with it, perchance, a timely little flirtation, or something exciting to read in the feuilleton of the "Petit Journal," which is sold to the company for a sou. Curious anomaly of life!—strange indeed that men should wish to kill the hours and not the years; that those who find most difficulty in getting through the day, should, above all others, dread growing old!

Some of the Frenchwomen that we meet with at these watering-places, on the contrary, are very merry and industrious; they knit and knit as if for their very lives. The family group near us, consisting of *maman* and her four daughters, are shouting with laughter; they are delighted with bonbons and with the gambols of a pet poodle. Their happiness is harmless, and certainly unique;

but the majority of the people at Luchon are, truth to tell, suffering from the terrible "ennui."

Is this really so? Is it possible that in the midst of beautiful scenery, in a delightful climate, and surrounded with every luxury, we can be weary of existence; or, with so many resources, be at any loss for a topic of conversation?

Let us take the testimony of a Frenchman. "Avancez!—écoutez," says M. Taine, to two people who have just sat down:—

"Le monsieur est arrivé avec entrain; il a souri finement et avec un geste d'inventeur heureux; il a remarqué, qu'il faisait chaud. Les yeux de la dame ont jeté un éclair. Avec un sourire ravissant d'approbation, elle a répondu que c'était vrai.

"Jugez comme ils ont dû se contraindre. Le monsieur a trente ans—il y a douze qu'il sait sa phrase. La dame en a vingt-deux—il y a sept ans qu'elle sait sa phrase. Chacun a fait entendre trois ou quatre mille fois la demande et la réponse. Pourtant ils ont eu l'air d'être intéressés—surpris!"[1]

* * * * *

The time now draws near six o'clock, and there is a sound of relief; and up and down the Allée d'Étigny alarm-bells are rung as if there was a general conflagration. It is

---

[1] What a characteristic contrast to the bored young Englishman at Chamounix! His resources are not great—he is not *stoïque*, but he cannot help being energetic. "We were compelled," he writes home, "to spend some days unprofitably at that modern Capua, Chamounix —bargaining for artificial agates, eating heavy dinners, racing to the Montanvert against time, and feeding our imaginations on all sorts of ambitious schemes against the neighbouring passes and peaks."

needless to add that Luchon listens with willing ears to the voice of the charmer.

After dinner we go again to the Parc, and stroll about amongst the crowd, which is much more numerous and miscellaneous in its character.

The inhabitants of the old town, whom in our gaiety we had altogether forgotten, now join the throng. Groups of peasants—men and women, and hundreds whose occupations are to minister to the various wants of the visitors now take their evening holiday, and promenade and romp, or listen to the band.

As soon as it is dark the gardens are prettily lighted by gas, fire-balloons are sent up, rockets fly about, and dancing *al fresco* is commenced; and it is then, when the mountains are hidden from sight, and there is nothing to remind us of their presence, that we see how perfect is the likeness to the "Bois de Boulogne" or the "Champs Élysées." It is also perfect in its similarity to Paris in the various little out-door amusements—roundabouts, "tir au pistolet," little games of chance, and the various devices for getting rid of small change, for which the Champs Élysées are famous.

To complete the illusion, we pay twopence for a chair, and six sous for "La Presse" of yesterday (which has just arrived by the evening post), and listen, as well as we can in the hubbub, to a rather harsh interpretation of some well-known operatic airs, which comes from an elevated wooden kiosk hard by. The shrill discordant sounds of some of the notes we attribute to the dampness of the little wooden house in which, pending the erection of a ".grand casino," some of the stringed instruments are kept.

But we are not to be left long in meditation, we (visitors) are all, as we said before, essentially dramatic, and have our parts to fill ; if we are good for nothing else, we can buy flowers and sugar-plums as long as our purse holds out, and contribute something for the general good.

We had done our duty this evening—we had bought little books of native costume which were utterly untrue, we had bought red " bérets " which we could not wear, we had steadily refused, and afterwards purchased, knick-knacks and bouquets innumerable and inconvenient to carry ; and now, having successfully resisted a demand to pay twice for the same chair, and having lighted a last cigar, would be at peace.

But it is not to be. A neat little woman, with a white apron, a shining face, and a white handkerchief round her head, suddenly makes her way through the crowd, and bringing a chair, seats herself close beside us. She has brought with her a small round box, which placed on end makes a table ; it is gaily painted, fitted at the top with a little brass roulette, and lighted with a well-trimmed lamp. With a brief introduction, and the faintest apology for intruding upon " Monsieur," she commences conversation ; and in less time than it takes to write it, the whole history and gossip of Luchon, of its distinguished and undistinguished visitors, has been told, and told so well, and the family trials and hopes of " son mari " and " les petits enfants," are so skilfully interwoven into the story, that we find ourselves, unconsciously as it were, in the confidence of this little woman, and could not put her off with a word, or explain that we hate bonbons and never gamble.

And now will not Monsieur begin—see, all the wheels are spinning ? And so we follow suit and turn the wheel. The chances are dead against us, of course, but what matters it that the wrong numbers always turn up—what heed of the feigned astonishment on the patient face at our side? Before the light goes out we shall have an empty purse and a pocket full of bonbons, and perhaps have made a home happy.

These games of chance are considered the especial "fun of the fair," and every one joins in them. Look at the party of little girls seated in a circle near us; and kneeling on the ground before them a grey-haired mountebank, dressed in a half Spanish, half Basque costume, who is telling them love stories, and enlivening the dull parts with interludes of a little game of chance, which might in the half-light be thimble-rigging, but which is innocent enough; and when the band leaves off playing, and there is a general movement homewards, see with what a gentle, courtly grace this knight of other days takes leave of his friends with an " au revoir."

It is now past nine—in half-an-hour the Parc will be deserted, and at ten Luchon proper will be in bed.

The atmosphere is so close and hot sometimes at Luchon, that we can do little in the middle of the day besides sit about in the garden of the hotel looking on to the road, or stroll into the beautiful woods hard by. But there is plenty to amuse, if we remain at our own doors. At the windows of the white houses opposite we may see Spanish women seated, working, or leaning out upon red cushions, which gives the street quite an Eastern effect, and every now and then there is an "arrival." If perchance it should be by the mountains, if some intrepid Señor, having braved the mountain journey, rides up the Allée, preceded by his guide, suggesting in his imposing appearance and por-

tentous mien, Bon Gaultier's lines, in the ballad of the
"Broken Pitcher"—

> "When up there rode a valiant knight,
> From the town of Oviedo,
> Alonzo Guzman was he hight,
> The Count of Tol-lol-ledo'—

we are delighted at the "distraction," and throng round to watch the proceedings with an air of intense interest. We amuse ourselves with feeding the peacocks in the garden, we read the one local paper over and over again, and wish heartily, for the sake of an excitement, that a paragraph—stating that the Empress of the French is expected at Luchon would prove true to-day.

We go out again to the Parc, where "les élégants, couchés sur les chaises, lisent leur journal, et fument superbement leur cigare," and endeavour to solve the mystery, why the women of all classes are so much more cheery than the men, why we so seldom meet a sad French woman, why the young ladies never seem tired of discoursing of 'les paysanneries adorables de George Sand,' why their elders are never weary of embroidering, and why nearly every French visitor we meet bears a decoration, which might be that of the Legion of Honour!

We stroll up one of the paths through the trees behind the "Établissement," where the stifling sulphurous air ascends from the vast caverns which undermine the mountain-side, and come suddenly upon a French artist sketching, as we supposed, the valley of Luchon. No, his subject was neither rocks nor trees, neither the distant mountains, nor the sunset in the valley; it was "Still Life," an elaborate painting on ivory, of grapes and peaches, silver, and dead birds! A "pot-boiler," probably, a work of necessity, and more certain to find a purchaser than sketches of mountains or trees, but all of a piece with this artificial life and atmosphere, of which perhaps the reader has heard enough.

The weather is uncertain, but fine enough for short

excursions, so we will be off to-morrow to the Port de Venasque, bidding farewell to Luchon, where we have seen "le monde"—"le monde illustré," le monde parisien," and, to be truthful chroniclers—"le demi-monde."

Port de Venasque.

The journey to the Port de Venasque occupies usually ten or eleven hours. We leave Luchon soon after seven a.m., taking a light pony carriage a distance of six miles and a half to the open ground where the Hospice de Luchon is situated—a large, low building, affording shelter, and rough accommodation, for those who need it on their passage to and from Spain; a snug, dirty, smuggling-looking dwelling, the headquarters probably of all kinds of expeditions, hunting, shooting, pedestrian, and contraband.

Here we left the carriage to wait our return; and, crossing the river Pique (now quite a narrow stream) by a bridge a little below on the right, we got to work at once, and commenced the wild ascent of the Port de Venasque. From the Hospice we could see our route winding up, in irregular zigzags, several thousand feet above, just visible here and there, as it rounded a promontory, or when a string of laden mules, that were ascending before us, turned the sharp corners and appeared for an instant on the extreme overhanging edge of the mountain-side. The path, which led by a more gentle ascent through woods and over green pastures, immediately in front of us as we stood at the Hospice, was the route to the Port de Picade;

another and more circuitous route into Spain, by which we may return.

For the first half-hour after leaving the Hospice, we walk over grassy slopes, keeping well under the shadow of the rocks, but are soon obliged to emerge upon the more exposed part of the path, where the sun's rays are so powerful that if we had had a guide, we should have been glad to have given him our coats to carry.

As we get higher (still keeping in sight of the Hospice), the air becomes more rarefied, and we are surprised to find a wind. The path is one continual ascent, winding up and

up without a break, or scarcely an unexposed position on the side of the rock, and we can now easily understand the danger of this pass in stormy weather, and almost believe in the pathetic story of the fate of nine tinkers, who are said to have been carried down by an avalanche. After reaching a spot where we halt for a few minutes by the banks of five little blue lakes that we find nestling in the mountain-side, close to our path, the work begins in earnest, and it would be safer for every one to trust to his own feet. The way, so far, has been one that could easily

be taken on horseback in fine weather, but as we near the summit it is nothing but a steep shelving path, cut in the wall of rock, narrow and slippery, covered with loose shale, and here and there some snow. We have to keep quite close to the rocks to get any foothold and can at times scarcely hear each other's voices for a rushing sound, like falling water, but which is only the wind amongst the pines.

We have lost sight of the Hospice for half-an-hour, and can see neither where we came from nor whither we are tending. At every turn of the zigzag path the wind becomes more powerful, and it is necessary to make a steady stand against each gust as it sweeps down, bringing with it a shower of small stones, which strike against our faces as sharp and cold as hail; and thus on we plod, with the bright blue sky above, and clouds and the four little lakes apparently still close to our feet; when suddenly a

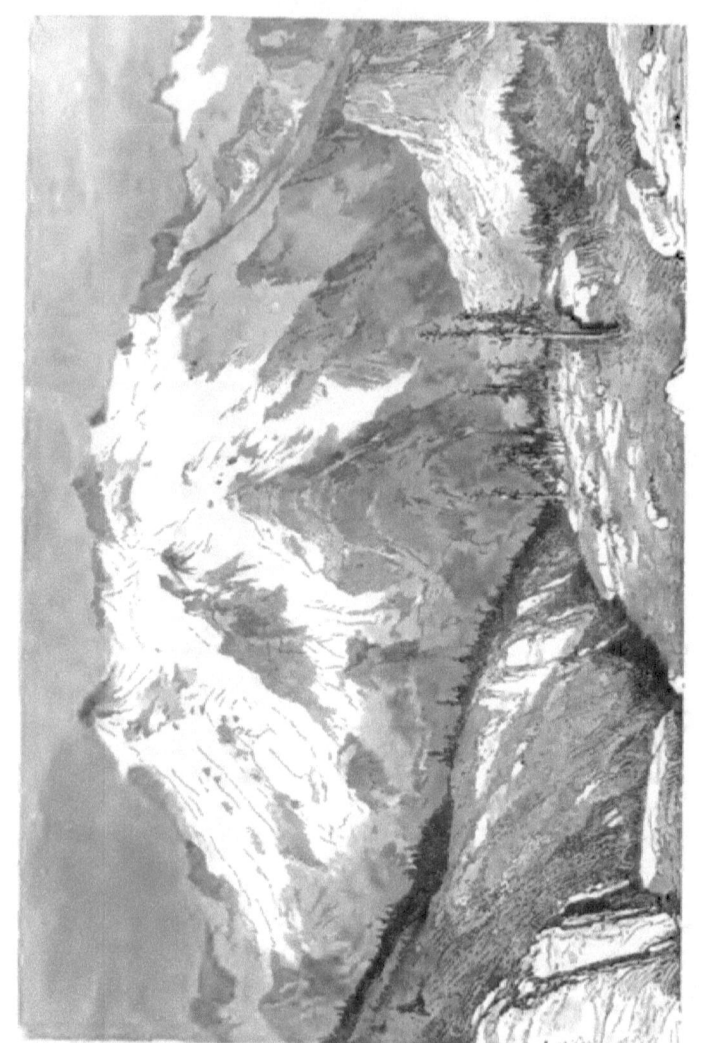

THE MALADETTA.

door opens in the great wall of rock, and we are ushered into Spain by the wind!

The view that has suddenly burst upon us is so magnificent from this elevation, that in spite of the hurricane (for it is here no less, although it is a calm, sultry day in the valley), we steady ourselves by joining hands, and stand in the *Brèche*. The Maladetta, taken from a spot not far below, is the prominent feature, surrounded by the grandest ranges of the Pyrenees. The intervening valley is desolate-looking, a sort of "no-man's land"—Spanish soil, indeed, but territory which no Spaniard is likely to take the trouble to dispute possession of.

M. Doré's drawing of the Maladetta is almost photographic in its truth and accuracy of outline, and in giving the sterile, desolate aspect of the intervening valley, a scene which has been described by many pens but by few pencils. Its isolated position, and the extent of glaciers and snowfields, that we can see to best advantage from a point a little above the "Port," where we attain an elevation of upwards of 8000 feet, give the Maladetta an appearance of height that is quite illusory, and the reader who is only familiar with Swiss mountains may be surprised to learn that the highest peak, the "Pic de Nethou" (the one on the left in the illustration) is only 11,168 feet above the sea.

There is one solitary hut, on the Spanish side, that we see below, with just sufficient accommodation to shelter a passer-by, but scarcely to give him a night's lodging with a chance of rest; for the rafters are loose, and the hay that formed a bed for some of our friends (who spent the night here when on an expedition to ascend the Maladetta) was nearly blown away when we last visited it. On the calmest, brightest day in summer there comes up the dark valley we have passed a cold and bitter wind—a wind that those who have once felt seldom forget—the same that haunts to this day the capital of Spain, and sweeps in chilling gusts through the corridors of the Palace at Madrid.

Leaving this scene of dreary magnificence, we descend to the cabin, and making a short halt to dispatch a bottle of most excellent Malaga wine, we continue our journey, in an easterly direction, keeping close to the spur, or ridge

dividing France and Spain, having the Maladetta on our right hand. Looking back, we can see with our glass far down into the valley leading to Venasque, and distinguish one or two bright moving specks, which prove to be a party of Spaniards on their way to Luchon, having sent their families and luggage, by a détour of several hundred miles, by Perpignan and Toulouse. They do not halt at the cabin, but moving slowly up to the door of rock, silently disappear.

Nothing can be more extraordinary than the contrast between the French and the Spanish side of the Port de Venasque; the latter (called the Peña Blanca, or white rock) shelving up the serrated ridge of a sheer precipice as shown in the sketch.

Continuing our route, over rocks and loose boulders and

patches of coarse grass, we pass a few huts for shelter for cattle, and meet a number of baggage-mules on their way to Spain, with their drivers in picturesque rags—each furnished with a red sash, and generally a pistol or a knife in his belt—and in about half-an-hour reach the Port de Picade, where we obtain an altogether different view, looking towards the Catalonian mountains, which is in many respects finer, and more varied, than that from the Port de Venasque. We now re-enter France, and, descending rapidly through a wood, rattling down with a hundred goats at our heels, keeping well to windward of them as a matter of comfort, we arrive again at the Hospice just as the sun's rays are leaving the valley, and the old man and the fowls are going to roost.

It takes some time to find our 'cocher' (who has been enjoying a long nap under the trees) and to get our horses put to, but once started we make up for lost time. The two hind wheels of our little basket carriage are closely locked, the whip is cracked until the lash has a large tuft at the end and will crack no more, and all the izzards, foxes, and bears in the neighbourhood are put on the *qui vive;* the reins are thrown loosely over the backs of our two little lean coursers, and away we go—winding down the side of the valley on the smooth steep road with the silent swiftness of sleighing, the gay trappings, and the fox-tails at the horses' heads, flying in the wind, and the bells jingling merrily. We nearly knock over one or two peasants with laden mules, and once are nearly overturned ourselves, but are so near the ground, and leaning back so comfortably in our little land-sleigh, that we would not slacken pace for the world; and thus glide into Luchon a little after dusk, having made a run of six knots in about half-an-hour.

And so we end our mountain journeys as we began them, riding and driving where, according to the muscular theory, we ought to have been on foot, enjoying these excursions much more for the little spurt at the beginning and the end!

There are many other walks, and rides, in the neighbourhood of Luchon, of which we should like to speak, but space will not permit; moreover, we are reminded by our French friends that we have done all that is expected of us, and may rest content—that, in short, we may enjoy the "bonheur d'un homme qui a fait une ascension," and repose in peace after the labours of the climb.

SPAIN.

Burgos.

The "*Parador de las Diligencias Generales*" is probably a good specimen of the old inns of Spain on the great high roads; constructed to accommodate a large number of people, providing them with tolerable fare at not very extortionate prices. It is, as the guide-books say, "an old-fashioned '*parador*,' decent and humble"; a rambling old building, with some of the bedrooms below the level of the road, and as we were late arrivals we were honoured with one of these.

It was nearly twelve o'clock at night and bitterly cold, and it certainly seemed an age before any one could be prevailed upon to show the weary travellers their rooms. We were led up and down an infinite number of stairs, through dark passages, and finally under an archway into an enormous bedroom. The furniture was modern, and took up so little space that it suggested the idea of a prison cell. The windows were barred with iron, the floor was cement or stone, coloured red, and the ceiling supported by massive pillars. Our next-door neighbours were mules and their drivers, whom we could hear distinctly all night, as well as the noise of rats chasing each other down the damp white-washed walls. The very stolid Señora who lighted us down assured us that the other rooms were all occupied, and that we had the best in the Fonda. There was nothing for it, therefore, but to thank her for her attention (which she evidently expected) and to wait for the morning.

"*Sunday, Oct. 9th*, 1864.—Our first morning in 'sunny Spain.' We find our cellar very dull and cold, and 'tis raining fast. Through the bars of our prison we can just see the leaden sky and part of a low barrack wall.[1]

"When we at last found our way out and into '*el comedor*' (a low, dingy, and most dirty *salle à manger* on the first floor, ornamented with an almanac several years old, and a few gaudy prints of saints upon the walls), we got some good chocolate and bread, and later in the day there was a table-d'hôte, to which about thirty people sat down. They were chiefly Spaniards, of all ages and degrees; and they

---

[1] The passages with inverted commas are extracts from an old diary, printed verbatim, in order to give the exact impressions of places visited. We went purposely to one of the old Spanish inns.

smoked between the courses, filling the room gradually until we lost sight of our opposite neighbours. It was interesting to watch the efforts of small boys of ten or twelve to make one cigarette last out between three or four of them, smoking it in turns, and placing the damp morsels on the edge of their plates whilst they had an interlude of dinner. Other habits less tolerable and less appetising kept us on the *qui vive* throughout the meal. The fare was good for Spain (as we afterwards discovered); there were a number of dishes dressed with oil, very coarse meats, poor fruit, and wine."

It is right to mention here, for the benefit of future visitors, that this " Fonda " is now by no means the best in Burgos; and is itself much modernised.

Burgos is well described as dull, damp, cold, and wind-blown, and from its elevation and scarcity of trees, very much exposed to the northerly winds. The cold lasts for seven or eight months in the year, and even in summer there is none of that softness in the air that we should expect in 42° 21' north latitude. After travelling in the south of France, and being burnt with the heat of the sun in the Pyrenees, this sudden change was as striking as it was unexpected.

" The whole aspect of the town was so very dull and cheerless on this cold Sunday morning, and the costume of nearly every one we met in the streets so modern and familiar-looking, that, after all we had read and expected of Burgos, we almost wished we had never come.

" Could this really be the city of the ballad of ' The Cid's Wedding ' ?—

' Within his hall of Burgos, the King prepares the feast ;
He makes his preparation for many a noble guest.
It is a joyful city, it is a gallant day,
'Tis the Campeador's wedding, and who will bide away ?

* * * * *

> 'They have scattered olive-branches and rushes on the street,
> And the ladies fling down garlands at the Campeador's feet.
> With tapestry and broidery their balconies between,
> To do his bridal honour, their walls the burghers screen.
>
> 'They lead the bulls before them all covered o'er with trappings;
> The little boys pursue them with hootings and with clappings;
> The fool, with cap and bladder, upon his ass goes prancing
> 'Midst troops of captive maidens, with bells and cymbals dancing.
>
> 'With antics and with fooleries, with shouting and with laughter,
> They fill the streets of Burgos—and the Devil, he comes after;
> For the King has hired the horned fiend for twenty maravedis,
> And there he goes, with hoofs for toes, to terrify the ladies.'

"Was it then *all* romance? Could the life and beauty of a place have so completely vanished, if it ever was anything more than a myth? 'Cold, damp and windblown' is almost all that modern writers have to say for a city which in centuries past was one of the glories of Spain! Had the climate changed? Did the worthy citizens of Burgos go about in the month of October (as we see them now) muffled up to their eyes to keep out the keen and terrible wind? And is all this mud, damp, and dreariness a modern innovation, the result of railways and improvements which the Burgalese hates with all his heart?"

But if all local colour and apparent life and gaiety have vanished, and the monotonous lines of modern buildings disappoint one at first sight, there is much that is curious and picturesque to be found.

The town is built on the side of a hill, in the form of a semicircle, sloping gently down to the river Arlanzon, which is crossed by three fine bridges. Remains exist of the citadel and of the old ramparts, and there are one or two Moorish archways in a good state of preservation.

The "*Calle Espolon*" is one of the principal streets facing the river, not far from our *Fonda*, but most of the buildings are modern; and it is not until we go up to the central square or market-place, with its massive arcades and old curiosity shops, that we meet with anything particularly characteristic or Castilian. Here we read that in former times public festivals and bull-fights were held, and "lords and ladies crowded the balconies in gay attire," and that the "arcades were thronged with the people." It is now a rather tumble-down-looking market-place, surrounded by curiosity-shops, and others filled for the most part with trinkets and odd wares, sham Toledo blades (made in Birmingham), counterfeit coins and relics, odds and ends from all countries, but, curiously, *nothing of Spain.* We count twenty shops where they seem to sell nothing, but which are open, and their proprietors stand smoking in the doorways. Peep inside, and you will most likely see four or five figures seated round a *brazero*, roasting chestnuts. But it is all so dark that you cannot make out what wares they have.

One of these little shops, by the sign over the door, is a bookseller's, and we venture in. We have evidently disturbed a family party, and feel conscious of having intruded.

"What did the Señores want?"

"A Guide to Burgos—a book of any kind about Spain—or a map. Perhaps 'Don Quixotte,' or a rare edition of the 'Cid'?—Might we look at his collection?"

A light was held by a woman whilst we hastily ran over the titles of the books that were ranged on the shelves. There were a few educational works for the use of the colleges at Burgos; one or two descriptions of the cathedral; "The History of Cristo de Burgos"; an account of some recent religious ceremonial at the cathedral, with poor illustrations on wood; a Spanish drama in six acts, with marginal directions to the players as to attitude and expression, on each page; "Cæsar's Commentaries"; and a few works of fiction, which appeared at a hasty glance to be new, and published at Burgos. There were piles of worthless-looking prints and song-books—the latter untranslatable into English—and one or two copies of an attempt at an illustrated magazine, full of advertisements of certain "*funcions*" to be held at various churches in the province of Burgos, and to all appearance very uninteresting, and a poor speculation for the proprietors. Poor, indeed, seemed the prospect for the proud "caballero," who scarcely acknowledged our presence (and who, by the way, looked entirely out of place, and superior to his position), and for the group round the *brazero*, if they had to subsist on the profits of the sale of books in that little shop! Here and elsewhere on the Plaza the people were very quiet and civil, and, if we gave no trouble and lifted anything down ourselves that we wanted to see, we were free to look about us as long as we pleased; for your Castilian, true aristocrat that he is, will lay his hand to nothing menial.

There are numerous stores and old-clothes shops where nearly everything sold is in the modern European style. It is true that a few mantas and red sashes hang in the doorways, and we see one rusty Castilian sword and a pair of Moorish spurs; but the peasantry evidently prefer trumpery French trinkets and "sham" jewellery, which is sold in abundance. We search in vain for much sign of industry or serious commerce, and cannot get rid of the impression that even the people themselves seem masquerading.

Spaniards seem to suffer in appearance more than any other European nation by adopting the modern costume. A swarthy, stout *Señor*, in a scanty paletôt, badly-made trousers, and "chimney-pot" hat, loses what he most prizes and depends upon,—his dignity of bearing; and there is no question that "*las Señoras*," who look grand in

BURGOS CATHEDRAL.

Face p. 207.

their dark dresses and black lace mantillas (which are still *de rigueur* in the churches), do not appear to advantage in Parisian bonnets and bright colours.

The Cathedral of Burgos is renowned as one of the finest in Europe. As in many other cities, this noble pile is so built up against and crowded by dwellings that it is almost impossible to get any good view. But in whatever direction we approach, nothing can conceal the lofty spires, towering above the town, models of lightness, symmetry, and beauty. An old Spanish ballad speaks of the stars shining through their perforated stone, as the pride of Burgos. The effect reminds one of the tower of Strasburg, although the latter appears higher from standing alone.

Commenced in the thirteenth century, this cathedral has been modified and added to down to the sixteenth, in the style of the Renaissance.

Our illustration is taken from a considerable elevation, and shows the west front; the only point where a good exterior view can be obtained. The architectural details are from photographs, and are as accurately drawn as was possible on a small scale.

An examination of the cathedral and its chapels, as indicated by Mr. Ford or Mr. Street, would have been a week's work, which we did not attempt; the ordinary visitor will be content probably, as we were, to be shown its chief beauties in one day. The sculpture in the chapels and on some of the monuments, the exquisite carving of figures and flowers in walnut-wood in the choir, and the general proportion and lines of the building, seemed to us most worthy of observation. The pictures are not very remarkable, as far as we were permitted to see them, but the interior was undergoing repair, and some of the chapels were covered up. The stained glass windows have nearly all been destroyed, and the flooring is at present greatly out of repair. Those who ascend to the summit of one of the spires will be repaid by an examination of the beautiful exterior carvings, and also of the statues which decorate its pinnacles.

We spent nearly all day in the cathedral and its cloisters and chapels. We went into the sacristy, and were hurried through several rooms without being allowed time to examine their contents, but saw the worm-eaten coffin of the Cid, which is chained up against a wall.

There were several services during the day; the women, in black and wearing the mantilla, knelt in groups on mats on the floor at the base of the pillars; the men chiefly stood and crowded round the altars and chapels. Every group was picturesque; the kneeling figures dimly seen along the dark aisles, the men in their cloaks or mantas standing in indistinct masses, had the effect which the unknown architect probably had in his mind when he designed this nave, 200 feet long, with a vaulted roof supported by twenty pillars, nearly 200 feet high.

The absence of all chairs and seats, and consequently the easy, natural attitudes of the worshippers, give solemnity and grandeur to the scene which the modern costumes, partitions, and heaps of chairs, in most European cathedrals, prevent us from obtaining.

"Some of the peasantry looked as if they had stepped out of a picture by Murillo or Velasquez. One man especially we made a note of. He sat upon a marble tomb like an emperor, and looked as regal. He wore a coloured handkerchief bound turban-wise round his head, a Veronese-green vest, a red sash, and long quaint-shaped shoes, fastened to his feet and legs with dark sandals; his cloak was brown, lined with a plaid, which he wore in such a manner as if, unconsciously, to show the lining,

VESPERS.—BY E. LUNDGREN.

Face p. 208.

throwing it over one shoulder in graceful folds. Every time he moved he fell into a grander attitude, looking like the figure on the tomb of Lorenzo de' Medici—a poor, proud Castilian he, of the old type, little heeding that an irreverent nineteenth-century artist was taking notes of him.

"Another man, whom Murillo would have delighted to honour—ragged, dirty, proud of course—the colour of an old canvas, knelt down by our side in one of the chapels, and 'abstractedly' disappeared with the wide-awake hat belonging to one of our party."

There are several fine churches in Burgos to be visited, and we are told not to omit to see the tomb of the Cid, whose bones are kept in a "common walnut urn" in a room fitted up as a chapel in the Town Hall. But perhaps our time will be better occupied in a drive of a few miles towards the hills to see the tomb of Juan II. and Isabella of Portugal. It is here, in a Gothic church of the *Cartuja* of *Miraflores*, that we can appreciate the magnificence of carved alabaster. Two recumbent figures, raised about six feet from the ground, on a pedestal of the same material (the ground-plan of which is in the shape of a star), form one mass of carving in bold relief and most delicate ornamentation. Figures of saints surround it, whilst lions and other animals crouching in different attitudes, in the recesses and niches beneath them, group boldly and effectively. The modelling of the animals is excellent, and is only surpassed in workmanship by the wonderful imitation of lace and embroidery on the figures.

Close to these monuments is the tomb of Don Alonzo, their son, around which the clustering branches of a vine are festooned upon a Gothic arch; and here again the workmanship is most elaborate. There were other monuments and specimens of carving in the chapel, and several

P

stained glass windows; but all the riches and magnificence crowded together here, could not dissipate the desolate air of everything about this almost deserted convent.

It was sad to walk in the lonely cloisters and hear from the poor monks (the two or three remaining ones who conduct strangers over the convent) what the "*Miraflores*" must once have been, and suggestive as a contrast, after the alabaster tombs of kings, to visit the "*champ de repos*," of 419 Carthusian monks "who lie here in death, as they lived, humble and forgotten, without a name or a date, amongst the weeds, shaded by tall and sombre cypresses, which raise their arrowy spires to heaven."

Quitting Burgos at half-past ten at night, we went direct to Madrid. The following is a note on the journey.

"A very lovely sunrise, the next morning, over the Guadarama mountains, presenting one of those strange bright contrasts between the deep-red glow of the waving lines of hills, and the cold, clear, blue sky, that is seldom seen in any other country. Warmth of colour, and cold photographic hardness of form and outline, with a background of the most tender, delicate blue."

At this part of our journey we might have been in the East, for all the signs of life or vegetation that could be seen; nothing but ridges of brown, barren mountains, rising one behind the other in dreary monotony; no towns, no villages of any importance, and hardly any inhabitants.

There are fifty-seven tunnels between Irun and Madrid, and the railway winds in and out between the mountain ranges, keeping an average level of 1500 feet above the sea. As we approach Madrid there are more signs of cultivation, and we pass first something that looks like a farm, and then a manufactory with a chimney that reminds one of Manchester—the style is unmistakable.

About 9 A.M. we pass the "*Escorial*," the tomb of the

Spanish kings, and soon after 10 A.M. arrive at Madrid. We are late, of course. The "curves" and "gradients" that we have passed over during the night are not favourable to a high rate of speed, and we are fortunate if we average more than eighteen miles an hour. The time wasted at stations where there were no passengers, or any sign of a town; the listless way of doing everything connected with the traffic, and the national hatred of punctuality, all tend to the same end. Matters do not seem to improve, judging from a letter from a passenger by the "express" train, who writes of this part of the journey,—"On we plodded, up hill and down hill, as if drawn by short-winded and broken-kneed engines, the very dogs coming out, running along and barking at us in front and in rear, doubling us round and round as if we were some old *patache*, with which they could keep up races at will."

The fact is, that we are really travelling by a luggage-train, and that, owing to the poverty of the system of *one line of rails* for all traffic, the train is composed chiefly of cattle and goods trucks, which we have to "shunt" and take up at the various small stations, and which sometimes reach to an enormous length, with two or three passenger carriages in the middle. In winter, on steep gradients and with frequent snow on the Guadarama mountains, it is almost impossible to keep correct time, as one unpunctual train disarranges the whole system for the day or longer. In spring and autumn the traffic is greater than the railway company can properly undertake, and much crowding, discomfort, and delay, is the consequence : and all this on a line which at other times has not sufficient funds to pay working expenses.

MADRID.

EVERY traveller goes to the "Puerta del Sol," the great central "*place*," the life and heart of Madrid.

From our window in the "*Fonda de los Principes*" we look down upon a bright and brilliant scene, unlike anything in any other capital in Europe. The houses and public buildings are, it is true, of no particular style of architecture, and the shops and their contents are more Parisian than Spanish; but in spite of the prevailing modern European style of dress, there is colour and variety of costume in the crowd. The mantilla is still occasionally worn, and Spaniards of all degrees take care to display the gay-coloured silk linings to their cloaks; there are the tassels and bright worsted trappings to the mules, and the quaint dresses of the water-carriers continually passing with their loads; detachments of troops are moving about in every direction, and the crowd is as great at this spot as on the Paris Boulevards.

All the principal streets lead into or towards this spot, where there is constant traffic night and day. The "Puerta del Sol" is about 400 feet in length north and south, and 150 feet wide, being rather narrower at either end. The building which occupies the western side is the "*Palacio del Gobernacion*," the Home Office, and also the central depôt for troops. Opposite are shops, with one or two of the principal hotels above. The south end is formed by the "*Hôtel de Paris*," and the *Calle de Alcalá*.

Six other streets converge upon the "Puerta del Sol" (the Gate of the Sun), which seems to draw, irresistibly, towards itself the traffic of the city; and as the Madrileños are more alive by night than by day, the noises and movement seem incessant to any one unaccustomed to the place.

There is a fine fountain in the centre of the "Puerta" well supplied with water, which is now playing, as we write, at least sixty feet high, flashing in the moonlight, and giving that bright aspect to the place which strikes every visitor. The pavements are broad under our windows, and at twelve o'clock to-night there are at least five hundred people standing about or walking. We remarked that few people left the pavement or stood in the centre of the square, but were unaware at the time that there was a regulation prohibiting groups of persons standing together in the centre of the square.

On the "*Prado*" and the "*Fuente Castellana*," the chief afternoon promenades, an Englishman will be struck with the style of the carriages, and with the number of "thoroughbreds" that pass up and down over the half-mile of straight drive, the handling being of course after the manner of the "*Bois de Boulogne.*" It is not fashionable to walk anywhere; it is even thought better to sit in a closed cab which jolts you terribly, at the rate of four reals (less than one shilling) an hour, over the rough stones on their roadways.

Every day whilst we have been here some of the royal family drive past our hotel on the "Puerta del Sol" in closed carriages drawn by six mules with gay trappings. Their approach, long before the carriages are in sight, is heralded by a faint squeak from something between a penny trumpet and a French horn, issuing from the gate of the "*Palazzo del Gobernacion.*" The number of squeaks is regulated according to rank, thus :—three squeaks for the Queen, two for the Infanta, and so on. There is a perpetual interchange of visits between royal personages, who live at opposite sides of the city, and call on each other every day. A cradle and perambulator often follow on these visits in an open carriage, drawn by four mules with outriders and attendants. It is one of the sights for a stranger to see.

We should not omit to make mention here of the "*Guardias Civiles*" (Civil Guards) who are constantly on duty about the Palace and the Government Offices. They are a fine body of picked men (like the Irish constabulary), representatives of public order, the prop and stay of the Government, whatever party may be in power. We shall see them constantly in Andalusia, riding about the country, with their long cloaks covering both horse and man. The sketch of one of them, lounging about near the "Puerta del Sol" in his picturesque uniform, is by the late John Phillip.

A glance at the map of Spain will show how central is the capital of Spain, both by natural position and the formation of roads and railways. Everything is brought to the capital, and every one must go to the capital to supply his most ordinary wants. There is hardly any road in Spain that does not lead to Madrid. The adventures of a gentleman who journeyed from Oporto to Salamanca, an account of which appeared in the newspapers a few years ago, may be remembered. It gave a good idea of what travelling on cross-roads is like since the introduction of railways.

If the traveller when he enters Spain may be likened to a fly which has just stepped into a spider's web and must take the consequences, in Madrid he has arrived at the centre, and his enemy is upon him. There is no escape, he must pay—and pay. Twenty-five shillings a day, and even more in the height of the season, it costs each person at a good Fonda. The system of monster hotels—where there is no host to welcome you, or to care for your wants, where no one troubles himself whether you go or stay, and

A SKETCH.—BY THE LATE JOHN PHILLIP, R.A.

Face p. 214.

where you feel from the moment you enter that you are part of a huge machine, is not the ideal hostelry. But in Spain "everything does go by contraries," and a "*Grand Hôtel*" in Madrid is like a drop of water in a thirsty land.

In the common out-door life of Madrid, Paris is copied, and, if it were not for the unmistakable Spanish faces, the people might be Parisian. Their horses are splendid, their carriages are English-built, and both "fours-in-hand" and "tandems" are seen on the Prado.

But there is one special characteristic in the crowd near the "Puerta del Sol," a crowd that never disperses day or night. It is in the number of idlers, of dark men standing about from morning till night wrapped in cloaks. The majority are, to tell the truth, an ill-looking set (of the traditional stage villain type); they have scowling faces, a slouching aspect, and an ill-mannered address if spoken to. They loiter in all the frequented places in Madrid, and are very much in the way. They hardly speak to one another, and scarcely seem to have energy enough to light a cigarette, scratching their fusees sometimes (as we have seen them) on the coat of a passer-by, in a contemplative, patronising fashion, that takes a stranger rather aback.

Many a young Madrileño is content to lounge his life away in this fashion; and if he has an income sufficient to keep him in "*cigaritos*," to pay for his weekly seat at the "*Plaza del Toros*," and to provide him the bare means of subsistence, he will do no work. He is ready in case of an *émeute*, or for a place under Government—neither would come amiss to him. It is all he seems fitted for, and apparently the height of his ambition. In the morning a lounge on the "Puerta del Sol," in the afternoon a walk or ride on the "Prado," in the evening to a café or theatre, varied occasionally by a bull-fight or cock-fight—seem the average employment of half the young men in Madrid.

There is not much betting or "sporting" in our sense of the word, even at the bull-fights, and they seemed to us on most occasions to do what Englishmen alone have been accused of, " to take their pleasure sadly."

The women seem more cheerful and industrious, although we see comparatively few in the streets. In the early mornings they go in great numbers to the various churches, dressed in black and wearing the mantilla, but in the afternoon, bright, if not tawdry, colours are the "*mode*," and Spanish features and complexions are put through the forcing process of wearing Parisian bonnets.

Nothing is wonderful in Spain. The great café under the "Grand Hôtel de Paris" is crowded day and night with people, some of whom look so poor and spend so little that it is a marvel to the uninitiated how they all live.

Our lasting impression of the people of Madrid will be, that one-third spent their lives in carriages, one-third in cafés, and one-third begged their bread.

The beggars are a great feature in all the streets, and pursue you with loud clamours for "cuartos" in the name of "our Lady of Atocha." They lounge about in groups in the most public places, and thrust themselves before you with an insolent, and sometimes threatening aspect, that does not by any means incite to charity. But they are licensed and numbered, and beg "officially" in the name of "our holy mother the Church."

In the interests of art, with which we have here most concern, we may hope that those picturesque groups of men, women, and children of all ages, that obstruct the entrance to every church, and stain the very doors with their filthy garments, may "never cease out of the land"; but for the sake of order, and public decency, we might ask the authorities at Madrid to protect strangers from annoyance and often insult.

Notwithstanding the evident poverty and distress which existed in Madrid when we were there, the dearness of provisions, and the poor quality of nearly everything exposed for sale in the markets, it is cheering to have another proof of the truth of the saying that there are "two sides to every picture," and to learn from the newspapers that the Madrileños are not in the depths of despair :—

"In spite of all this distress," writes a correspondent, "we have had a very merry Christmas here in the capital; flocks of fat turkeys gobbling about the streets for weeks; the Plaza Mayor, and its adjacent districts, one vast show of meat and vegetables, with great piles of grapes, pomegranates, and oranges, endless stalls of turrons, marzapanes, and other sweetmeats of the season, booths of children's toys, with all the paraphernalia of the Holy Manger, angels, shepherds, wise men, and 'star in the East'; and all over town long strings of boys, as well as of grown-up men, with penny drums and farthing trumpets, keeping up a jolly noise for a day and a night, to the total murder of wholesome sleep."

If our "Lady Bountiful" smiles, all goes well; wherever be the secret springs—from whatever point the sun of prosperity shines—whether the good genius be a "patron-saint" of the Church, or a patron-sinner, who holds for the time the keys of the public treasury, certain it is that at Christmas-time at Madrid, and during the Holy Week at Seville, the tide of wealth flows—as it flows sometimes in the great oil cities of the West. If this be a puzzle to "*estranjeros*," it is a perfect mystery to the more thoughtful of the inhabitants of Madrid, who feel certain, and do not hesitate to express their opinion, that "a crash must come some day, when the pay of the Guardias Civiles will get too far into arrear; when the cry for bread will drown the noise of penny drums and farthing trumpets, and we shall no longer read of three hundred Members of the Upper House, each driving to save his country in a coach and pair"!

Two Bull-Fights.

WE were sitting one evening in a crowded café near the Puerta del Sol, wondering, for want of something better to do, by what mysterious means such an extensive establishment could manage to exist, when nearly every visitor contented himself with a glass of sugar and water, for which he paid a penny, and perhaps sat there the whole evening, smoking the *cigaritos* that he brought with him.

Flowers were offered for sale by most diminutive Señoritas; toys, books, songs, and newspapers, were handed about by itinerant vendors; and lottery tickets with such excellent numbers that we could have made a rapid fortune in a week if we had desired it and—*if* we were fortunate.[1] We were listening to a monotonous song from a rather demonstrative young lady in a short Andalusian costume, who accompanied herself on a guitar, and were becoming gradually confused with the noise of hundreds of voices and the fumes of cigarettes, when a group of men entered, on whom all eyes were instantly turned.

We heard the names of "*Cuchares*" and "*Dominguez*" whispered about, and soon learnt that these were the "Espadas" and the performers who were to appear at the bull-fight the next day. They were fine, athletic, well-made men, with bright eyes and manly bearing; quiet in demeanour, looking very clean and neat in their tight-fitting suits of black, with embroidered hussar jackets, Spanish "sombreros," and hair cut closely, with the exception of one little plaited pigtail hanging down the back.

---

[1] Lotteries are "Cosas de España," and are popular amongst all classes; there is a *Manual del Lotero* published at Madrid to guide the uninitiated.

LOTERIA NACIONALE.—BY JOHN PHILLIP, R.A.

Face p. 218

With them came in a crowd of young Madrileños, the sporting fraternity of Madrid, who discussed the chances of the morrow with much animation. The performers were by far the least excited of the group, and sat and sipped their coffee or "*agua*" with the greatest composure.

Before we left the café we noticed the sporting group in deep consultation with one Count ——, who it appeared had obtained permission to act as amateur "Espada." The man was no novice, having a private bull-ring.

On the following day we go early to obtain tickets, as it is supposed that some of the royal family will be present at the "funcion," and tickets will be difficult to procure in the afternoon, excepting at exorbitant prices.

The crowd, however, is here before us, in such numbers and apparently so eager that expectation is raised to the highest pitch, and the excitement is catching. It is no orderly *queue* of people waiting two and two for their turn, as is customary on the Continent, but a crushing, struggling, and surging mob, that sends up volumes of smoke, and ejaculations that are certainly not blessings. The majority fight their way to the "despacho" (a little wooden erection in the Calle de l'Alcala) and fight their way back; then, buying a fan for one real, and a little blue play-bill for a cuarto, they disappear until the afternoon. The chief cause of all this disturbance is not the genuine eagerness of the crowd, but the system of speculators buying up tickets to sell again at exorbitant rates.

Whilst we are watching and making up our minds for a struggle, a tall, bright-eyed *gamin* comes up and offers his services.

"Shall he get a 'carta' for us?"

"Yes, for the cheapest place on the *shady side.*"

In an instant he is plunging and crushing amongst the crowd, crawling, over their heads; and, holding out our money with a long arm, he succeeds in getting one of the few remaining seats for two reales.

"But this 'carta' is not marked '*al sombra*,' and we cannot sit in the sun."

"The Señor can have a fan for two reales, and it is the best side of the Plaza."

The seats on the sunny side are about half the price of those marked "*al sombra*," and the young gentleman, who kept a store of the former, had tried to foist one of them upon us, pocketing the difference. Paper fans are sold for those who take these seats, but it is almost impossible to see when facing the sun.

The performance commenced at three, and before two the whole population seemed to be moving towards the "Plaza de Toros."

> "For once all men seemed one way drawn,
> Saw nothing else—heard nothing."

Across the "Puerta del Sol," down the Calle de Alcala, past the deserted "Museo," the almost as solitary "Prado," and through the Puerta de Alcala, flowed the great river of men and women, gathering tributary streams at every street-corner, all eagerness and haste to see what they had seen a hundred times before.

There was one figure—and one only—in this crowd that told its purpose, and the sight was a sad one. A sorry steed, a veritable Rosinante, with gay tassels and trappings, was doing its best to prance and career up and down to attract the people, tottering under the weight of a lusty "picador," padded and covered with an arrangement of cork and leather to protect him from the bull's thrusts; followed by a boy on foot, whose office it would be to drive the poor beast when in the arena, and compel him to face the bull. The "picador" rides gaily along, bowing to the people on each side, until they reach the entrance to the arena.

In every book that we ever read on Spain, it is stated that the best bull-fights are to be seen at Seville; but having seen them both at Madrid and Seville, we venture to think that this is no longer correct. "Corridas de toros," like everything else in Spain, have been affected by over-centralisation and railways; and the influx of strangers to Madrid has attracted the most distinguished "Espadas" (with the fiercest bulls) to the capital, and caused more money to be spent upon performances here than in any part of Andalusia.

The "Plaza de Toros" at Madrid is a low, ugly-looking building outside, with the general poor appearance of a second-rate circus, but with the addition of a peculiar and terrible smell as of shambles. The entrance to our seats was through a narrow passage behind some stables, where there were ten or twelve horses, (some eating their last meal), and where harness and various "properties" were piled up ready for use.

"On entering the ring," says Mr. Ford, "the stranger finds his watch put back at once eighteen hundred years; he is transported to Rome under the Cæsars; and, in truth, the sight is glorious of the assembled thousands in their Spanish costume; the novelty of the spectacle, associated with our earliest classical studies, is enhanced by the blue expanse of the heavens spread above as a canopy."

The interior of the building is in the form of a Roman amphitheatre, with a ring of about 1100 feet in circumference. Its general appearance is shabby and ruinous. Round the lower part, where we had taken places purposely, in order to get a good general view, there are ten rows of open seats rising one behind the other, with the number of inches allotted to each person painted upon them; behind are two tiers of shabby boxes, separated from the rest by a wooden railing, as a still further protection from the bulls. There is a royal box on the principal tier, and a few spacious ones on each side, decorated with tawdry hangings and devices, are reserved for the Court. We are separated from the ring by two wooden barriers about five and six feet high respectively, with an alley or passage between, all round the ring, serving as a place of refuge for the performers when hotly pursued, and for adventurous "Madrileños" who wish to be near the scene of action. Opposite the royal box are the doors where the bulls enter, and at the sides two others for the performers. The seats about us and the benches above are worn and weather-beaten, and there seems to have been little attempt made to repair or redecorate the building.

There is, as has been truly said, a "business-like and murderous look about the whole building" which is unmistakable. When we entered, the arena was as crowded with people as the course at Epsom on the Derby Day before the great race; but at the sound of a trumpet the ring was gradually cleared, and we soon became tightly wedged up on all sides, beyond all possibility of retreat if we had desired it. In front, leaning on the ropes, were young men and boys armed with sticks and fireworks, ready to take part in the performance if they could get a chance, which they occasionally managed to do.

The crowd was not demonstrative or very noisy; it was, on the whole, a good-humoured holiday mob, which seemed to care more for a "*cigarito*" than anything else in the world; but there were a few connoisseurs near us and round the bull-contractor's box who were discussing the chances of the day, and might have been betting, but that there is so little real speculation or "sporting" amongst Spaniards. The excitement of real danger to the performers, and curiosity as to how each bull would behave, seemed to be the paramount attractions.

We said that the crowd was not noisy, but, when the seats were nearly full, the sound that went up from more than eight thousand people was almost deafening; and the smoking was a wonderful sight, resembling an enormous circle of burning peat, or the smouldering of camp fires. Almost the only distinguishable sounds were the scratching of fusees or matches, and the cry everywhere for water—*Agua! agua! agua!* The water-carriers were in constant requisition all through the performance, for the heat was very great. Many of the people were dressed in Spanish costume, and were evidently from the country and suburbs of Madrid; but all true Madrileños of course wore black coats and Paris hats, and the ladies in the boxes, of whom there were a number, wore hats as well as the mantilla.

Just before the commencement of the performance the sun shone out brilliantly, and in an instant a thousand paper fans of all colours fluttered in the breeze, looking in the distance, as if a swarm of butterflies had suddenly started into life.

At a signal from the trumpeter the band played, and from a general movement in the crowd we knew that the royal box had its occupant, and that the signal to commence had been given.

A side-door is opened, and the combatants enter in procession, led by two mounted officers of police in ancient Spanish costume, with black hats and cloaks. The procession itself, and the whole effect when the spectators rise to see the entry, is so imposing and unique, that we should recommend every one to see this, if not to stay for the fight. After the "*alguaciles*" or officers come the "*picadores*," mounted on their poor steeds and armed to the teeth, holding heavy lances in their hands; after them the "*banderillos*" and "*chulos*," or combatants on foot, fine, active men, in the costume we are accustomed to see in the opera of "Figaro" or "The Barber of Seville." Next follow the "*matadores*" (or "*espadas*," as they are generally called), the "maestros," whose office it is to kill the bull single-handed. Lastly, come a number of attendants, and a team of mules three abreast gaily caparisoned, which are afterwards employed to drag away the dead.

The performers bow before the royal box, and a key of the door by which the bulls are to enter is thrown to them by the president. All then retire from the ring excepting two "picadores" on horseback; the trumpet sounds again, and the door is thrown open.

This is the supreme moment; every eye and ear is on the stretch, and there is a general hush throughout the crowd. A low roaring is heard in the dark passage leading from the stables, and in a few seconds, with a plunging, awkward motion, the bull rushes into the centre of the ring and stands still; dazzled apparently with the brightness and sudden change from his dark prison, and startled with the shout that greets his entry. The first bull on this day was a handsome black beast, rather small, of Andalusian breed, with enormous horns, and apparently of great strength and activity. His coat was glossy and bright, and was decorated with ribbons of the colour of his owner (*azul turqui*), pinned on to his shoulder.

His first impulse seemed to be to find his way out of all this uproar, and get back to his den; but all such thoughts evidently vanished when he caught sight of the "picadores" drawn up near the barrier one on each side of the ring. He faced about at once, and with a motion, well described "as though body and legs were borne helplessly along by the enormous throat, which, working in every muscle, seemed to sway itself over the earth by its own mere weight," he rushed headlong at man and horse and threw them both to the ground with a crash. Instantly the "chulos" and "banderillos" entered the ring, and with their bright red flags drew away the bull from the fallen picador. Then commenced a chase and a series of passages and rushes, in which the chulos displayed marvellous dexterity in evading the bull, sometimes waiting for his approach, and, just as the animal stooped to toss, *stepping on its forehead*, walking along its back, and jumping easily off again. Sometimes they were so hotly pursued that they had to drop their flags and leap the barriers.

In the meantime the fallen "picador" had been dragged with difficulty from under his wounded horse and remounted, and the ring was again cleared of every one on foot. The same scene occurred with slight variations; the more skilful "picadores" managed sometimes to receive the charge of the bull with their lances and to drive him back; but, in the end, the horses were fearfully wounded by the bull's horns, often falling dead under their riders. The "picadores" appeared much shaken by the falls, and it looked dangerous work, but we heard that they were seldom seriously injured. After several horses had been killed, the "picadores" retired, and the more skilful and graceful part of the performance commenced.

The trumpet sounded again, and the "banderillos," advancing with two little barbed darts about a foot long, entered the ring, and, standing upright with their arms raised above their heads, received the charge of the bull, jumping aside and endeavouring at that instant to fix the darts on his shoulder—an operation which, as our neighbour informed us, "should be done neatly—one on each side,"

Q

This of course enrages the bull, and renders the sport most exciting to those who love it.

He roared and tore up the earth with rage, and rushed headlong after his tormentors, who had hairbreadth escapes, jumping the barriers when the bull was almost upon them. They immediately returned to the charge, and darted about the arena, waving their cloaks in the bull's face, and tormenting him until his rage was terrible to behold.

The excitement at this time was at its highest pitch, and to enter the ring at all seemed, to novices, most dangerous. Two "banderillos" advanced cautiously, holding their darts high in the air. They stood too close to each other, and when the bull rushed at them one tripped against the other and fell down. In an instant the ring was filled with "chulos" to the rescue, who, in their turn, were scattered right and left; several ran for the barrier within a few yards of us, and the bull followed them closely.

We saw him coming plunging towards us, and although several women shrieked and people jumped from their seats, we did not at the moment apprehend danger. Surely, we thought (if there was time to think), it is so arranged that the bull cannot leap *both* barriers and reach the seats. But this was one of the "*cosas de España*" that we had yet to learn; we did not know that this was a favourite part of the performance, and the "fun" that all those young gentlemen with red handkerchiefs and sticks like Smithfield cattle-drovers, had come out to see.

The bull tried to leap the barrier, and failed; he turned away with a sullen roar, and ploughed up the earth about him. The "banderillos" and "chulos" returned again to the ring, but he was either craven or obstinate, or (as we thought) out of breath, and nearly beaten; nothing would stir him.

Then the monotonous cry, that we had heard incessantly throughout the fight, of "*Agua! agua!*" was changed to another cry—for "fire." "*Fuega! fuega! fuega!*" was echoed round the ring, and in answer to the call a "banderillo" advanced with two darts, shaped like the others, but covered with white paper. He stealthily approached the bull, who stood motionless near the middle of the ring, and, skilfully planting the points of the darts in the bull's shoulder, beat a rapid retreat. The darts were loaded with hand-rockets, and immediately exploded on his back. He turned round and leaped into the air in terror and pain, while the people rose and screamed with excitement. Suddenly seeing his tormentor leaning over the barrier, he made after him, and getting his fore-feet and head on to the wood-work, he fairly toppled over and fell into the passage between the two partitions. Here he was immediately set upon by the young gentlemen, who with their sticks tried to drive him back. He turned upon them, however, and cleared the *second* barrier, how we know not, and, sooner than we can write it, was amongst us, and walking up the seats within a few feet of where we sat. The proverb that "he who hesitates is lost" was never better illustrated. To hesitate, to run away, or to make room for the bull, would have been fatal; the plan adopted instantly by all was to fasten upon him in a body, man, woman, or child, whoever was nearest, and so by sheer dead weight of numbers *walk him back* into the ring!

And now the third act commenced, the ring was cleared and one of the "espadas" entered alone. He was dressed as daintily as if he were going to a ball, with an embroidered suit of gay colours, and light silk stockings, exactly as we see him in the next illustration. He threw his cap to the ground, and, with his sword in his right hand,

and a "*muleta*" or red flag in his left, advanced to meet the bull, amidst the cheers of the people.

It was an exciting moment for any one to see for the first time (not realising that the animal was now thoroughly fatigued) this man standing alone before the bull, his life depending upon his quickness of eye and his trusty sword, his fine figure (clad with almost effeminate delicacy and grace) separated not three feet from his enraged antagonist. The bull hesitated, but soon made a rush at the "espada," who skilfully turned it off by waving the red flag in the bull's face and jumping aside. This was repeated a dozen or twenty times, during which the bull was slightly wounded; at last choosing his opportunity when the bull had lowered his head to the right position, the "espada" pointed his sword steadily at a spot behind the horns, and the bull ran upon it and *killed himself*,—falling dead at one blow. This was applauded vehemently; hats and caps were thrown by the spectators into the ring, which the performer had the trouble of throwing back again to the owners—a peculiar form of compliment which every one seemed to appreciate.

Immediately the gates were thrown open, and the mules were brought in to take away the dead: they were splendid animals, and galloped off rapidly with the bull and afterwards with the dead horses. In about ten minutes the ring was cleared and another victim rushed in. The second bull was a poor-looking animal—tame and frightened—that ran away from the "picadores," and tried to escape out of the ring. However, after a time, he turned upon his tormentors, and the same performances were gone through as before, but with less spirit. The only event of importance was the entry of the amateur "espada," whom we had seen in the café the previous evening. He was greatly cheered by the people, and

DOMINGUEZ THE "ESPADA."

Face p. 228.

showed plenty of courage and self-possession; but it was a wretched blundering business, wounding the bull cruelly with false thrusts, and failing to kill him in the required time. The poor beast had to be put out of his misery by a professional executioner.

This was enough; we had done our duty, and had seen a bull-fight as it is conducted in the capital of Spain.

A Burlesque Bull-Fight.

LET us now, very shortly, describe a burlesque bull-fight which took place at Seville on one of the red-letter days of the Church's calendar, "for the benefit of certain masses, and other acts of piety and charity."

The great attraction was the first appearance of an "intrepid *señorita*"—tauromaniac we should be disposed to call her—who was to face a bull singlehanded. This, of course, drew crowds of spectators; and when the ring was cleared, and the young lady entered, in a kind of "bloomer" costume, with a cap, red spangled tunic and trousers, the audience rose to welcome her. She bowed to the president, and was conducted at once into the centre of the arena, when lo! a great tub, with one end open, was brought and placed upright and the "intrepid" lifted into it! It reached to her armpits, and there she stood waving her banderillas or darts, when at a given signal a bull was let loose in the arena. It was a young bull, with horns cut short and padded at the ends; and as the animal could only toss or do any mischief by *lowering* its head to the ground, the risk did not seem great or the performance very promising.

For some time the bull would not have anything to do with the tub, evidently not considering it fair game, but after walking two or three times round the arena he turned suddenly, and without the slightest warning rushed headlong at the strange object. Away went the tub, rolling half across the arena, with our fair *señorita*, who had evidently rehearsed her part, coiled up inside!

This was all very well, and the lady might enjoy a sport usually confined to the hedgehog and other lower animals; but when the bull, who soon began to get angry, at last caught up the barrel on his horns, and rushed bellowing round the ring, it looked serious for the tenant. There was a general rush of "banderillos" and "chulos" to the rescue, but some minutes elapsed before they could surround the bull and release the performer from her perilous position. When extricated she was smuggled ignominiously out of the arena, and we saw the brave *señorita* no more: the bull was not killed, but "bundled" out of the ring.

The next act was "Skittles." Nine negroes ("Bedouins of the desert"), dressed grotesquely, stood up like ninepins, within a few feet of each other, and a frisky "*novillado*," or young bull, was let in to knock them over. They understood their duty, and went down flat at the first charge. The bull struck out right and left, and soon overturned them all. They then sat in rows in chairs, and were again bowled over, to the delight of the assembly. This was great fun and was repeated several times—the bull liked it, the "ninepins" *seemed* to like it, and the audience shouted with delight.

The third act was a burlesque of the "picadores." The trumpets sound again, the doors are thrown open and on they come in close phalanx, cheered by at least 5000 people; the five donkeys with their ears well forward, and their tails set closely between their legs; the ragged "picadores," without saddle or bridle, riding with a jaunty air, and a grim smile on their dirty faces, that was comical in the extreme. Would that Gustave Doré could have seen the group!

They ride once round the ring when the doors are opened again, and the bull goes to work. He charges them at once, but they are so closely packed that they resist the shock and the bull retires. He has broken one of the poor animal's legs, but they tie it up with a handkerchief, and continue marching slowly round, keeping well together as their only chance. A few more charges and down they all go. The men run for their lives and leap the barriers, and the donkeys are tossed up in the air!

The finale was a wonderful sight. Two or three young bulls (with their horns padded) were let into the ring, and then *all the people*. We left them there, rolling and tumbling over one another in the darkness, shouting and screaming, fighting and cursing—sending up sounds that might indeed make angels weep.

Such is a general outline of the performance, which had many variations and interludes, and lasted more than three hours.

But this scene of riot made, as so often happens in Spain, one of those pictures that delight an artist. The "Plaza de Toros" at Seville is half in ruins, one side of the wall being destroyed, and through this gap we could see the city. The foreground was an irregular mass of people, scarce distinguishable in the twilight, but twinkling with the light of thousands of "cigaritos," and covered with a complete canopy of smoke floating in the still air. Beyond, the city towers just tinged with the sun's departing rays, and "La Giralda," high above them all, glowing as if it were yet broad day.

Madrid to Cordova.

> "Swallow, swallow, flying, flying south,
> Fly to her, and fall upon her gilded eaves,
> And tell her—what I tell to thee."

To swallows flying from England's wintry winds, who, when summer is over, disperse like autumn leaves—to those who, dreading the sea passage to the south of Spain, think the overland route would be preferable, this chapter is dedicated. The general reader may pass over it as a mere chapter of accidents, incident to a journey before the completion of railways; but similar events are occurring on the cross-roads of Spain in 1892.

At one point on the road, where the railway ended temporarily between Madrid and Cordova, there were several diligences (great lumbering conveyances covered with mud, of which it would be difficult to say whether they were dirtier inside or out) drawn up in a line near the railway, in the middle of a pond, with their gaily caparisoned team of mules standing up to their knees in water. Seats were at last found for the ladies of our party in the "*intérieur*" and in the "*banquette*" on the top; the rest rode where they could, one with the driver on one diligence, and the others on the roof with the luggage.

A Spanish "*diligencia*" holds between twenty and thirty people, besides luggage and merchandise. On the chief high roads it is drawn by a team of ten or twelve mules, the country being hilly, and the roads heavy. They are harnessed two abreast, a boy riding on one of the leaders, and it is on his care, and the sagacity of the animals, that the guidance and safety of the vehicle depend. The driver holds loosely the reins of the two last, but he has little or no power to guide or control the movements of the vehicle with such a team, and it is only fair to say that he seldom attempts it.

Each diligence is accompanied by a "*mayoral*," or conductor, a very important personage, who has charge of the whole equipage, and who, with his embroidered jacket and gaiters with silver buttons, his red sash, and bright handkerchief round his head, is here, there, and everywhere during the journey; and if, as is generally the case, he is a

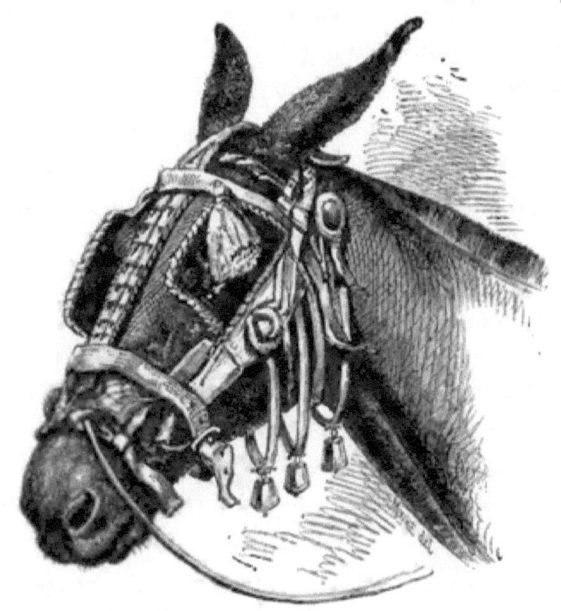

jolly fellow, he is the life of the party. He has the important office of assigning the passengers their seats, and deciding when the diligence is to stop.

There is a coupé, called a "*berlina*," holding three people; an "*intérieur*," a "*rotonde*," and a "*banquette*" above, called a "*coupé*," with seats for three or four. The roof is a sort of warehouse, where passengers' luggage and merchandise are stowed away, including provisions of all kinds, both alive and dead. When all other seats are taken, passengers are packed away on the roof, and often have an exciting time of it in warding off the charges of portmanteaus and boxes as the diligence sways from side to side, and when it becomes dark, as may be imagined, the combat thickens.

The pace is generally good, averaging eight miles an hour, including hills and short stoppages. But the roads are falling into neglect and disuse, and in many places between Madrid and Cordova the railway has destroyed the old road without leaving any substitute.

Accidents happen continually, but they are seldom serious, and are taken as a matter of course. As far as our experience goes, the chances are about equal as to whether you arrive at your journey's end without some sort of *contretemps*. A common one is this: the diligence is approaching a town after a long day, coming down hill at a swinging trot, at the rate of about ten miles an hour, sometimes even faster, for the Spaniard is like the traditional English postboy, who always reserved a gallop for the last mile; the postilion, who has perhaps been in the saddle for twenty or thirty hours without rest, takes this opportunity to doze, or more frequently to drop the reins, and concentrate his whole attention upon making a new thong to his whip. Suddenly his horse stumbles and falls; away rolls the postboy into a ditch or down an embankment; down go the mules, tumbling over and over one another, and pile up in an instant into a dusty, struggling heap, upon the top of which the heavy diligence rolls, and there stops, or falls, as sometimes happens, over on one side.

The scene of uproar and confusion that ensues can hardly be described. The struggles of the mules to extricate themselves, and of the passengers to get clear of their heels; the shouting and yelling of the driver and postboys; the groans of the wounded animals, who are often crushed under the diligence; and the apparently inextricable confusion of everything, must indeed be witnessed to be understood. Sometimes the diligence has to be unloaded, and some of the mules taken out of the team, causing a delay of several hours; but the journey is generally accomplished without any more serious mishap than a stunned postboy, or two or three mules left dead on the roadside.

It is very amusing, before it becomes monotonous, to sit in the *coupé*, or *berlina*, and listen to the compliments, threats, and expostulations in turn of the driver (called the "*moto*"), who has charge of the team, and who is perpetually jumping down and running by the side to keep them in a trot. Every animal has a name, and answers to it; and if the "mayoral" happens to mention to the driver in a low tone that "Brunella," or "Zitella," or some other delinquent, is not pulling properly, she immediately begins tugging and struggling as if she were doing half the work of the team; "Brunella" probably remembering well the penalty for non-fulfilment of duty, her tender driver thinking nothing of getting down and picking a handful of the sharpest stones that he can find, and throwing them at the animal's head.

At the stages where they change they often get into the greatest confusion, and much time is lost. Just as you are dozing, or in the middle of the night, you become gradually conscious of a sound of scuffling, shouting, and swearing, and the free use, apparently, of the names of all the saints in the calendar, and you wake up to find the nose of a mule rubbing against your window, and that he has his fore-feet on the body of another lying on the ground; and gradually, by the light of a lantern, you discover the whole team tied into an apparently inextricable knot, whilst the excited drivers are struggling to get them into line again.

Towards the end of our journey we were getting up into our seats again, when a tremendous noise of shouting was heard in the darkness near us. It turned out that the team of mules had started off down the mountain, dragging with them the boy who had been placed in charge. Then of course there was a grand chase, and they were finally brought back in a desperate state of entanglement and confusion. This caused another delay of nearly an hour, by which time many of us had again gone to sleep, when the signal was given to start. With a lurch and a crash (occasioned by our being pulled off the "jack," or lever, on which the diligence rested whilst the wheel was being fitted, tearing it to pieces by dragging the vehicle over it, because no one had taken the trouble to move it away), we started at once into a gallop, several of the animals having their legs over the traces, and for two or three hours without a halt kept rushing through the darkness; sometimes jolting against the bank, "shipping" earth and stones, and swinging from side to side in a manner which would have sent us all out of our seats if we had not been closely packed. The rain fell heavily, and we were soon ploughing through mud and crossing torrents, which made the latter part of our progress very slow and tedious. As we got farther south and began to descend, the air became much softer, the vegetation altered with the change of climate, and aloes and the prickly cactus grew on the road-side—and so on to Cordova.

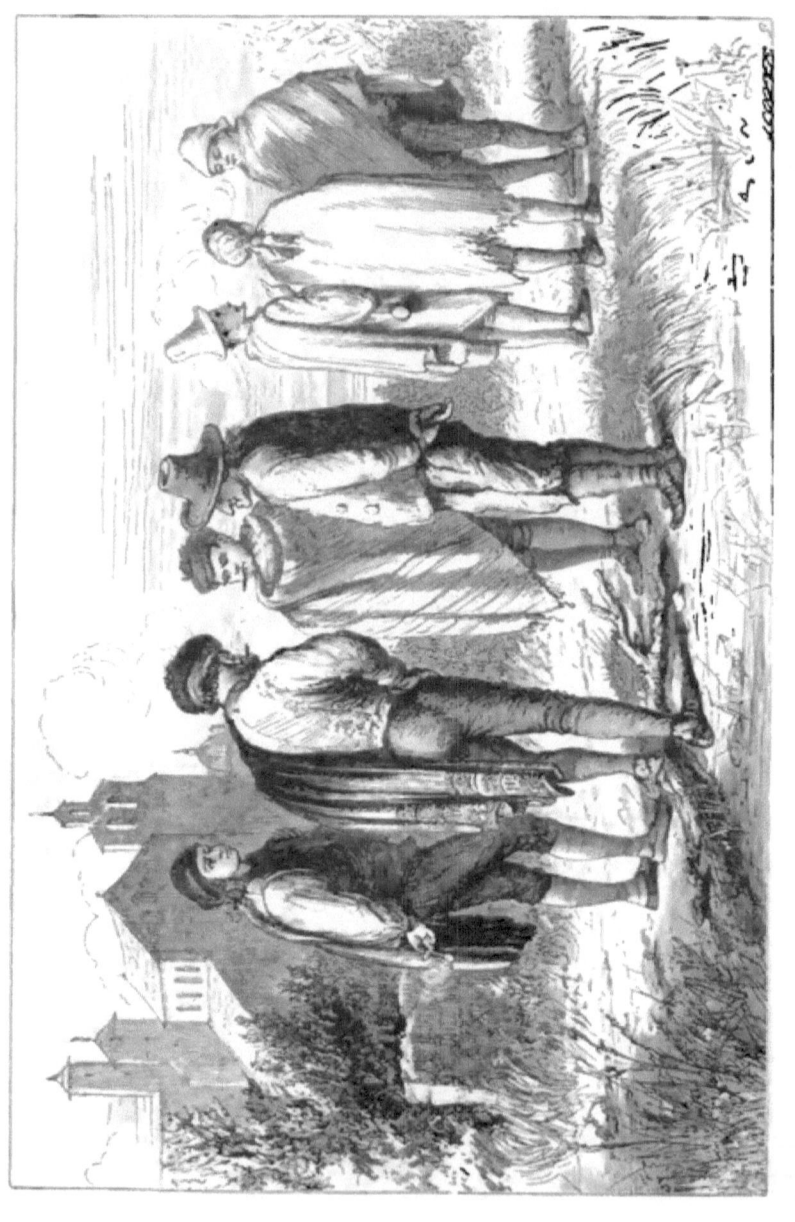

"CABALLEROS" AT JAEN, NEAR CORDOVA.

CORDOVA.

THE welcome sight of the towers of Cordova, as we turned the last hill a few miles east of the city, on our weary journey from Madrid, gave an impression of size and grandeur which was altogether unreal. As we approached its gates, the great mosque with its Moorish battlements towering above all other buildings, showed at a glance where the chief object of interest in Cordova was centred; but the most imposing entrance into this city is from the south, by the road from Malaga, crossing the Guadalquivir, near the ruins of an aqueduct and close to the walls of the mosque, which, from this point of view, appears like a town in itself.

When we look out of our window at the "*Fonda Rizzi*" the next morning, we find a half-ruined, half-deserted city. The houses are white and flat-roofed, the air is soft and balmy; we can see orange-gardens and "patios" filled with exotic plants, and the aspect is almost Oriental. There are several palm trees in the city, and in the distance olive-groves and fertile plains, through which we can trace the windings of the river Guadalquivir.

The aspect of the city when we walk through it is in keeping with its outward appearance. There is very little sign of bustle and activity, and here the only life it exhibits seems to be owing to the constant passage of travellers between Madrid and Seville. The manufacture of the famous Cordova leather is almost a thing of the past, although they are still at work in a few factories. The public buildings and the churches give evidence of poverty and neglect, and are not architecturally interesting; and it is only when we come to the mosque and the remains of Moorish buildings that we feel rewarded for the journey.

Directly on leaving the "*Fonda*" we find ourselves shut in, in a series of narrow courts or alleys, so narrow that we can touch both sides at once. The walls of the houses are whitewashed, with little narrow windows looking on to the street. In purely Oriental towns the charm of these little windows is, that they are often the framework for a magnificent pair of eyes that dart their glances upon the passers-by; many of these windows were once so illuminated, but times have changed.

But we have no time for reverie—a string of donkeys laden with paniers containing merchandise and fruits of all kinds; live fowls hanging down, a dozen together tied by the leg on one side and two or three little lambs on the other, thrown across a donkey's back like a sack, the cavalcade driven by muleteers in gay sashes, embroidered gaiters, and velvet hats; followed by water-carriers, men and women,—make us beat a retreat into the nearest doorway to let them pass. Following them to the "Plaza," or market-place, a large neglected-looking square, with arcades chiefly appropriated to tinkers and Jews' clothes-shops, we see what little there is left of native costume in Cordova. Its appearance, to tell the truth, is dilapidated and "seedy"—there is no better word. Italians are much more picturesque than the groups we see here, and are more consistent in their dress. The *Señoras* wear a red rose or sprig of jessamine in their hair, and throw a mantilla over their heads; but their dresses come from Lyons or Marseilles; and the poorer classes imitate their betters and buy all the modern finery they can.

A few of the old nobility still reside in Cordova and its environs, and it is fair to presume that that old lady that we see nearly every day, bumped and jolted over the stones through the very few wide and paved streets of which Cordova can boast, is a representative of some ancient house: she has imported a new open carriage from Madrid, and it is evident that the cobble-stones and the rather unscientific "whip," who is belabouring the mules that complete the equipage, will make short work with the springs. She is going to take her daily ride on the "alameda," and *promenade* by the banks of the Guadalquivir.

There was really little to see besides the mosque, which we went to every day. It occupies an immense area, surrounded by a high wall of Moorish work. We enter

THE COURT OF ORANGES.

first (under a horseshoe arch) the "Court of Oranges," an oblong court or garden, upwards of 400 feet long, with trees and fountains in the centre. Nothing can exceed the beauty of this court, with its orange trees, palms, and cypresses. To come suddenly out of the glare of the burning streets into the cool shade, where fountains are playing, birds singing, and breezes bearing upon them the most delicious odours, is what we read of in the "Arabian Nights," but seldom realise.

The first sight of the interior of this extraordinary place of worship is utterly unlike that of any other building in Western Europe. It has a very low roof, with the familiar horseshoe arch, supported by a forest of marble pillars. The area of the interior is 642 feet by 462 feet, and the roof cannot in some places be more than 30 feet high. Near the centre there is a lofty *capilla*, erected by the Christians when the mosque was first used as a cathedral. In this—especially in the "coro"—there is some fine carving, and also in a number of side chapels, dedicated to various saints.

There are some "treasures" in the sacristy, but not of great value, and scarcely worth the trouble of searching out. The real treasures are in the variety and beauty of the Moorish ornamentation to be met with at every turn, some of which is in excellent preservation.

Everything about Cordova had a dreamy, forsaken look, and a forsaken sound. Even at Toledo we sometimes heard the tones of the guitar, but at Cordova scarcely ever. From the few people that we saw altogether during our visit, it hardly seemed possible that the city should contain upwards of 40,000 inhabitants; and quite in the region of romance and fable that this same Cordova was once the "*largest city in the western world*, that it measured twenty-four miles by six, the whole space covered with houses, palaces, mosques, and gardens, down to the banks of the Guadalquivir."

SEVILLE.

> "O northern lotos, say a prayer for one
> Enthrall'd amidst these daughters of the sun!"

OUR first impressions of Seville were those of disappointment. As we drove through it we had glimpses of the noble tower "*La Giralda*," of which we have endeavoured to give the reader some idea in the next illustration; and we knew that in its cathedral, its "*Alcazar*," its collection of pictures, and in its associations, there were few cities to compare with it for interest—still, it fell far short of anticipations.

The houses are low, the streets are very narrow and badly paved, and there is no rising ground from which to get any good general view.

From the balcony of the "*Fonda de Paris*," in the "Plaza de Magdalena," we can see something of the city and its inhabitants. There is a little stall underneath our window where more cold water has been sold and consumed than we ever saw distributed gratis within the same space of time at any public fountain. The little bell tinkles incessantly, and the cry of "*Agua, agua*," is kept up all day—water, with a dash of sugar in it for the more luxurious—seems to be the "staff of life."

And what are the inhabitants like? Curiously like the rest of the civilized world, and with little variation in dress from our own people. The man who sells the water is a little gayer in his attire, and his hair is trimmed with a delicate pigtail like the Madrid dandies. His customers are, from Murillo's dirty street-boys upwards to grave *señores* in cloaks and bright-red umbrellas, embroidered with black. *Las señoras* wear the mantilla almost always, and very few bonnets are to be seen.

The buildings are substantial and bright-looking, with plain whitewashed walls, and courtyards opening to the street. There is much bustle and apparent business in the principal streets, and the shops are filled with French and foreign goods.

Our first visit was to the Cathedral, in the morning when the sun was high, as this is the only time when the pictures can be well seen.

The Cathedral, the Court of Oranges, with the chapter and offices, form a square pile of great extent, raised upon a platform or terrace. In the illustration we have given the best view of the "*Giralda*," and part of the Gothic Cathedral, which are seen towering above all other buildings. Those who have heard in Mahommedan countries the muezzin's cry from the towers of a mosque, calling upon the faithful to "come to prayers, come to prayers, it is better to pray than to sleep," cannot help thinking of that time, when Seville was "the beloved city of the Moslem— the gold and lace tent of the sensual Eastern—who planted it on the banks of the Guadalquivir to dream life away amid the enchantments of refined taste, which he lavished his gold and genius to adorn, and his blood to defend and fortify."

Nothing that we have yet seen in Spain brings more vividly before us the colossal scale on which the Moors worked than "*La Giralda*," which is a square Moorish tower, about 350 feet in height, ascended by a series of inclined planes, like the tower of St. Mark's at Venice. Remains of Moorish ornamentation may be traced upon it, but the upper part, the belfry, and the bronze figure of "Faith" on the top, are comparatively modern additions.

From this tower we obtain our only good view of Seville. We can distinguish a few of the principal streets and plazas; and the terraced houses, with their pretty balconies

LA GIRALDA, SEVILLE.

Face p. 243.

and green patios, but the buildings are so close to each other that they almost seem to touch. Immediately beneath is the Gothic cathedral, with its pinnacles and enormous roof with flying buttresses; near it is the *Alcazar*, the old Moorish palace, with its beautiful courts and gardens, extending as they once did to the river-side, to a spot where we see the "*Torre del Oro*," the famous tower of gold (a Moorish outwork or fortification); and the Guadalquivir winding for miles through olive-groves, and away towards Cadiz among the cork trees.

From "*La Giralda*" we can also take a distant view of the "Plaza de Toros," and see the performance and the multitude without being present at its horrors. Across the river is the rather disreputable suburb called Triana, inhabited by a race of gipsies, who live in a half-Arab fashion, conforming as little as possible to Spanish habits. It is the very place for picturesque old buildings, and for painters who wish to study the costumes and habits of the gipsies of Andalusia.

Two other features on the map beneath are the wide Campo Santo—the playground of Seville; and one enormous building, in itself almost a town, the tobacco manufactory, covering a quadrangle of 600 feet, where about 4000 persons are constantly employed.

Seville is situated in a flat country, with nothing remarkably pretty or attractive about it, on the banks of a narrow river with anything but a "crystal bosom," on which there are some barges, and a small steamer sending out volumes of smoke. Its streets are badly paved, and the roads in the environs are almost impassable after rain.

From the tower of St. Mark's at Venice the view is somewhat similar, but there is nothing here to compare with the "*Canale Grande*" and the broad lagunes; and we cannot, in whatever direction we look, discern much that is imposing, either in the situation or the buildings of Seville.

If in the twelfth century it was one of the most considerable cities in Spain, it is still the most favoured spot; the fertility of the soil and the beauty of the climate, rendering it at all times a desirable residence.

The Cathedral is in itself worthy of a pilgrimage.

The interior is sombre and blocked with the "coro," and it takes some minutes before one can appreciate its real extent. The ground-plan is enormous, 400 feet by 260 feet. It is divided into seven naves, the centre being 134 feet in height; **thirty-six pillars** support the roof, each 15 feet in diameter, and "around them are grouped shafts, slender, thin and light, like so many reeds around an oak-trunk, terminating in slender palm-branches, blending gently with each other."

"Bound with leaf garlands tender, rise stately and slender
The grand massive pillars." . . . .

On our first visit we were conducted in a dreamy manner through upwards of thirty chapels. We were shown the splendours of the "retablo" of the high altar; the "coro," with its statues of "prophets, priests, and kings"; and the "capilla real," with its tombs and arabesques.

Coming out through the beautiful "Puerta del Puerdon," (a remnant of the ancient mosque), into the "Court of Oranges," we see the "Giralda," with its fretted arabesque ornament glowing in the last rays of the sun, and are again, in imagination, in the land of the Moors.

Seville is the birthplace of Murillo, and the *Caridad* (a hospital and church in one) contains some of his finest works. Here is the great picture of the "Miracle of the Loaves and Fishes," and opposite to it "Moses in the Wilderness." They are well hung, but rather too high for close examination.

At the Museo, which is open free on Sundays and fête-days, there is a separate room set apart for the Murillos.

The Alcazar is part of a Moorish palace, rebuilt by "Pedro the Cruel" in 1353, with the aid of architects from the Alhambra. From the Cathedral tower we noticed traces of the original extent of this building, reaching to the "Torre del Oro" on the river side, and in several other directions. It has been added to at several periods and in different styles of architecture.

The other Moorish building that we visited was the *Casa de Pilato*, which is said to be like Pontius Pilate's house at Jerusalem. In parts of the interior it resembles the Alcazar, although of course much smaller. There is a beautiful patio paved with marble, with a fountain ornamented with dolphins, and statues of goddesses at the four angles. There are several handsome apartments and a magnificent staircase leading to a gallery. From the terrace-roof there is a good view over the city and into the now neglected gardens, giving a good idea of the "housetops" of the East, and the general character of the buildings at Jerusalem.

But are we sure that we have seen Seville—the Seville that we are to "see and die," the capital of Andalusia, the seat of refinement and learning, the chosen home of the ἄριστοι of the south of Spain? If in Madrid politics are uppermost in men's minds—if in Cadiz or Barcelona commerce is of the most importance—in Seville they should give place to poetry, music, and the "*belles lettres*." Seville is not itself without "*life*"—life in music, in dance, in song—animation everywhere.

Passing down almost any street in Seville, the senses are gratified with the most delightful perfumes issuing from the inner patios, and with sounds of music and dancing. Enter, by a door of open metal-work, through a hall paved with marble, into the inner court, filled with plants and flowers; a fountain is playing in the centre, and an awning overhangs, which keeps the air cool all the day long. There, with such surroundings as rare tropical plants, sculpture, antique hanging lamps, and prettily-tiled walls, the Sevillians spend their lives in their summer drawing-rooms, and in their cosy little "boudoirs" leading on to balconies, of which we just get a peep here and there.

All the principal rooms lead on to the central court, where visitors are received, concerts are held, and the main business of life is transacted; varying, of course, very much according to the position, or taste, or wealth of the owner. Everything has such an air of home comfort and luxury about it, that we, in our insular ignorance, are quite taken by surprise. Here at least is one continental nation that understands the meaning of the word "comfort," and can appreciate "home."

Would that we had had time to do Seville justice and to stay during the summer months, for the style of living of which we have spoken is peculiar to Seville and to Seville alone; but it is only in summer that it is seen to advantage, for "patio life ends in September and does not recommence until May."

GRANADA.

"The gardens of thy Vega, its fields and blooming bowers—
Woe, woe! I see their beauty gone, and scatter'd all their flowers."

THERE are some places in Europe, such as the Rhine, and the city of Rome, about which so much has been said, or sung, in praise, that they rarely fail to disappoint the traveller who sees them for the first time. There are some again, that realise more than almost any ideal. The Lake of Lucerne, Switzerland, in spring-time; St. Mark's Square, Venice, from the Grand Canal, by moonlight; "The Golden Horn," Constantinople, at sunset; and—at all times and seasons—Granada.

Whether it be from association, or the romantic beauty of the situation, everything seems to combine to satisfy the spectator. Poet, philosopher, antiquary, artist (or mere holiday lounger, who may be all, or none, of these), will each find something to his mind, and each, according to his taste and temper, will be more or less gratified.

The illustration is taken from the garden of the "Generaliffe," which is situated on the heights above the Alhambra, from which it is separated by a deep ravine; we can see a portion of the town and the plains beyond, and can form some idea of the general plan of the palace itself. We can trace the old walls and towers for a considerable distance, the latter—formerly the residences of the sultanas and their families—still bearing traces of rich decoration; we can see the conical roofs of the "Court of Lions," and beyond these the great square building erected by Charles V., for which a portion of the Moorish palace was removed.

It is evident from this drawing what a splendid situation the Moors selected to build upon, and what noble views they must have had from their windows over the Vega, thirty miles in extent. We see the town below, the rows of stately elms, the luxuriant gardens, and cornfields beyond; but even here, the pride and great glory of Granada we cannot see—the snow-capped mountains of the Sierra Nevada, which rise in the opposite direction, and form of themselves a perfect picture of Alpine beauty.

Here at least, at Granada, we can live quietly and enjoy ourselves. There is a little inn built into a part of the old walls of the Alhambra, called the "*Fonda de los Siete Suelos*"; it is nearly half a mile from the town, up a steep ascent, and, although a "perfect place" in summer for an artist to work, we could hardly recommend it as convenient for a short visit. It has, of course, the advantage of the moonlight walks on the terraces, but in winter (to be matter-of-fact) it is damp and extremely inconvenient to return to after dark from the town.

THE ALHAMBRA, GRANADA.

Face p. 248.

After a good night's rest, and considerable study of "Murray," perhaps the best way to see the sights of Granada is to engage the services of a guide by the day, as you are not allowed, without special permission, to visit the Alhambra alone. E. Bensaken (*père*), the same guide who assisted Ford and Owen Jones in their labours, was formerly to be heard of at this hotel, and seemed qualified to speak of the Alhambra. His information was not always accurate, but he knew more about the place than any other local guide. He had an especial attraction for us, because he had Moorish sympathies, and told his story of the ruin and degradation of the place with an earnestness that was partly genuine. It was like a voice from the dead—"the last wail of the banished Moor."

Bensaken was a "character." Born at Gibraltar, of Moorish parents, he was brought up as a money-changer; and afterwards served under the Count Montijo (uncle of the Empress Eugénie), whilst Captain-General of Granada, until he was put into the Inquisition. Twenty years ago Bensaken acted as chief guide and interpreter at Granada, and had the privilege of showing many royal personages over these buildings, our Prince of Wales amongst the number. He printed a short account of Granada, which he sold to travellers; but it was always better to draw him out and hear him talk.

Early on the first morning after our arrival, we set off to visit the apartments of the Alhambra. Fighting our way through the crowd of beggars, who lay in wait for our coming, we pass up some steep and irregularly paved streets, and under a massive archway built in the time of Charles V., and are immediately within the precincts of the Alhambra. We walk up long avenues, planted on either side with tall elms, between which we catch glimpses of the red towers far above us, and soon arrive at the

'Gate of Justice," with its horseshoe arch, and marble pillars, and the superscription—

"There is no power or strength but in Allah."

Thence by a path between high walls to a large open terrace, called "The Place of the Cisterns," commanding a fine view of the surrounding country; past the palace of Charles V. (the prominent building in the last illustration) to a little mean-looking door in one corner of the square, and are, without being aware of it, within six yards of the chief object of our pilgrimage. We are at once conducted through the "Patio de la Alberca," or the "Court of the Fishponds," oblong in shape, with a sheet of water in which are reflected the slender columns of a portico, rich with moresque decorations.

A few paces further, at the end of a corridor, is the "Court of Lions." Its appearance was quite familiar—having been so often described, pictured, modelled, and copied, in part and in whole ; there seemed as if there were nothing new to examine or discover ; and we could not help comparing notes, in our mind, with Owen Jones's restorations, and mentally admiring the fidelity of his copy of this court.

But here we have the marks of time, the mellow tints of age upon the marble shafts and conical roofs, and the deep-blue sky overhead ; and its proportions have an effect of elegance and lightness for which we were unprepared from Owen Jones's model. The open court is grass-grown, and the fountain is dry ; one side is under repair, and busy hands are at work *reproducing* (not restoring) what time and vandals have destroyed, or allowed to go to ruin. Some of the lace-like ornamentation is in wonderful preservation, and here and there we can trace the remains of the original colours with which this court was decorated.

No doubt sentiment and association have much to do with this; but even to the unlearned in styles of architecture, the principles on which the Moors built, seem to appeal more directly to the imagination. Simplicity, refinement, and truth are their chief characteristics. Looking at the severe exteriors of their towers and walls, giving no indication of the art, and luxury, and grace, that they concealed, we cannot admire too much the completeness of the general plan. Their palaces were formed, as Owen Jones remarks, "like those of the ancient Egyptians, to impress the beholder with respect for the power and majesty of the king, whilst within, the fragrant flowers and running streams, the porcelain mosaics and gilded halls, were constantly made to remind the owner how all that ministered to his happiness was the gift of God."

In decoration, both in form and colour, they worked on fixed principles. Owen Jones's analysis of their method of colouring has become well known in England since the Exhibition of 1851, and we can here judge for ourselves how valuable and true his teaching is. What he says about "form" cannot be too often repeated :—

"A still further charm is found in the works of the Arabs and Moors from their conventional treatment of ornament, which, forbidden as they were by their creed to represent living forms, they carried to the highest perfection. They ever worked as Nature worked but always avoided a direct transcript; they took her principles, but did not, as we do, attempt to copy her works. In this again they do not stand alone; in every period of faith in art, all ornamentation was ennobled by the ideal; never was the sense of propriety violated by a too faithful representation of nature."

Nothing in the architectural history of any nation is more remarkable than the orthodox spirit in which the Moors worked, scarcely showing any sign of contact with other nations, or even a trace of the influence of Christian art, in any of their buildings; preserving to the last their distinctive character, their refinement and exquisite taste.

The doorway of the "*Patio de la Mesquita*" is a good example of Moorish ornamentation; of suggested strength and fitness, combined with delicacy, and appropriateness of design. The upper portion is a specimen of relief work *without* colouring: the lower part, on each side, is white tiling, the patterns upon it being in blue, yellow, and black. At the capitals of the marble pillars may be observed portions of texts from the Koran, and it is interesting to notice how beautifully the cuneiform inscriptions blend with the other parts of the decoration.

We spoke of the general principles on which the Moors worked, and of their being forbidden by their creed to copy or to represent any living thing; but they have, in this instance, approached very closely to an imitation of nature, in the introduction of the form of a shell into the ornamentation.[1]

Many of the passages inscribed on the walls of the Alhambra are very appropiate and suggestive. In the "Hall of the two Sisters" there is a sentence that runs thus:

"Look attentively at my elegance, and thou wilt reap the advantage of a commentary on decoration."

And we may be sure that this would never have been written if the architects had not felt that, in so doing, they were not sounding their own praises, but inculcating a principle.

The Court of Lions measures 100 feet by 50, and is surrounded by a portico supported by 144 marble columns, arranged irregularly. The variety and beauty of the ornamentation are seen almost to better advantage in the

---

[1] The lions supporting the central fountain in the "Court of Lions" were made *purposely* unnatural, on the same principle.

PATIO DE LA MESQUITA, GRANADA.

brownish tint in which they now are, and it seemed to us that the whole aspect of this court could scarcely be improved by the addition of colour.

Leading from the Court of Lions is the "Hall of the Two Sisters," with its beautiful stalactite roof, a "profusion of vaults and miniature domes." The walls are richly decorated and inscribed with sentences from the Koran:

"There is no conqueror but God," &c., &c.

And on shields, several times repeated:

"God alone the conqueror."

In this hall it would seem as though the skill of Moorish artizans had been exerted to the utmost; the most precious woods and marbles, the rarest mosaics, and the most delicate carvings and sculpture having been employed to embellish it.

On the opposite side of the Court of Lions, and also leading out of it, is the "Court of the Abencerrages," and at the end, the Hall of Justice.

But what, perhaps, strikes the visitor most is the "Hall of Ambassadors." Its noble proportions (37 feet square by 75 feet high), its position, the views from its arched windows over the distant country, and also into the "Court of the Fishpond," with its flowers, seen through another corridor; the recesses in the windows, the proportion of every door and window, and the delicacy of the decorative work, interlaced, as usual, with inscriptions and praises to God.

We were shown the Baths—a suite of luxurious apartments, with a central patio or "chamber of rest," which has been richly "restored" in colour; also other chambers and the *Mosque*.

But time, and Charles V.'s furniture and whitewash,

(when he turned the Mosque into a chapel,) have obliterated nearly all the Moorish work, although the ceiling is very fine. In this chamber we were shown a beautiful recess where the Koran was kept.

When we look at the arrangement of the halls and chambers of the Alhambra, with separate apartments for each of the Sultanas, and think of the sumptuous accommodation provided for them, and indeed for every member of the enormous retinue of the Palace, our thoughts may turn for a moment to what we read of the interior arrangements of our own palaces in the sixteenth century.

Is it not chronicled somewhere that in the reign of "good Queen Bess" the maids of honour had to petition to "have their chambers ceiled, and the partition that was of boards, to be made higher, for that the servants looked over"; and that the chamber for the squires of the body was so "ruinous and cold," that they begged to have it "ceiled overhead and boarded under foot" to make it habitable?

Whatever be thought of Moorish architects, judged by the standard of other nations, may we not attribute, as least a part, of their great success to the fact that they were *artists* as well as architects; that their education comprised a knowledge of engineering, of chemistry, of painting, and indeed of everything that was directly or indirectly applicable to their art?

In the first visit to the Alhambra it is difficult to see and remember much more than we have indicated (for you are not permitted to stay long in one apartment), but after two or three visits the eye becomes accustomed to the style of architecture and decoration, and comprehends the intention and plan of many parts, of the building and ornamentation, which at first sight seemed confused.

So much injury has been done to the Alhambra by

visitors, that the custodian is *not permitted to let any one remain within the walls unattended*, and, of course, prefers showing the rooms to a large party at a time—a tiresome and irksome regulation that takes away from the pleasure of contemplating quietly the beauties of the place. It was only after repeated application, and by representing that we were artists anxious to make studies of portions of the building, that we obtained permission to remain a few hours alone in any of the courts.

To ascend the Alhambra towers, and walk on its terraces, was the chief delight of our stay at Granada, and we have endeavoured to give, in the illustration on p. 247, some idea of their effect by moonlight.

After some time has been spent in the study and examination of these ruins—a time ever to be remembered—we are naturally led to inquire what is the great charm about the works of the Moors, and about the Alhambra especially, which makes us love to linger within its walls?

In Castile—at Burgos, Segovia, and Toledo—we have seen some of the noblest examples of early Christian architecture; but if we are not mistaken, we have seen nothing, as striking in beauty and power, and assuredly nothing that will leave such an impression on the mind in after years, as the "Alhambra."

ALGERIA.

ALGIERS.

"Ah oui, c'est qu'elle est belle avec ces châteaux forts,
  Couchés dans les prés verts, comme les géants morts!
  C'est qu'elle est noble, ALGER la fille du corsaire!
  Un réseau de murs blancs la protége et l'enserre."

THE first view of the town of Algiers, in North Africa, with its pretty clusters of white houses set in bright green hills, or as the French express it, "like a diamond set in emeralds," the range of the lesser Atlas forming a background of purple waves rising one above the other until they are lost in cloud—was perhaps the most beautiful sight we had witnessed, and it is as well to record it at once, lest the experience of the next few hours might banish it from memory.

It was a good beginning to have a stately bare-footed

Arab to shoulder our baggage from the port, and wonderful to see the load he carried unassisted.[1] As he winds his way through the narrow and steep slippery streets (whilst we have enough to do to keep pace with him, and indeed to keep our footing), it is good to see how nobly the Arab bears his load, how beautifully balanced is his lithe figure, and with what grace and ease he stalks along. As he slightly bows, when taking our three francs (his "tariff" as he calls it), there is a dignity in his manner, and a composure about him that is almost embarrassing. How he came, in the course of circumstances, to be carrying our luggage instead of wandering with his tribe, is a question which may answer itself in the course of the narrative.

The first hurried glance, as we follow our cicerone up the landing steps—at the dazzlingly white flat-roofed houses without windows, at the mosques with their gaily painted towers, at the palm trees and orange trees, and at the crowd of miscellaneous costumes in which colour preponderated everywhere—gives the impression of a thoroughly Mahommedan city, and now as we walk down to the *Place* and look about us at leisure, we find to our astonishment and delight that the Oriental element is still most prominent.

The most striking and bewildering thing is undoubtedly the medley that meets the eye everywhere: the conflict of races, the contrast of colours, the extraordinary brightness of everything, the glare, the strange sounds and scenes that cannot be easily taken in at a first visit; the variety

---

[1] It is generally admitted, we believe, that "a vegetable diet will not produce heroes," and there is certainly a prejudice in England about the value of beef for navvies and others who put muscular power into their work. It is an interesting fact to note, and one which we think speaks volumes for the climate of Algeria, that this gentleman lives almost entirely on fruit, rice, and Indian corn.

of languages heard at the same time, and above all the striking beauty of some faces, and the luxurious richness of costume.

First in splendour come the Moors (traders looking like princes), promenading or lounging about under the trees, looking as important and as richly attired as was ever Caliph Haroun Alraschid. They are generally fair and slight of figure, with false effeminate faces, closely-shaven heads covered with fez and turban, loose baggy trousers, jacket and vest of blue or crimson cloth, embroidered with gold; round their waists are rich silken sashes, and their fingers are covered with a profusion of rings. Their legs are bare and their feet are enclosed in the usual Turkish slipper.

This is the prominent town type of Moor or Jew, the latter to be distinguished by wearing dark trousers, clean white stockings, French shoes, and a round cloth cap of European pattern. There are various grades, both of the Moor and Jew, some of course shabby and dirty enough; but the most dignified and picturesque figures are the tall dark Arabs and the Kabyles, with their flowing white bournouses and turbans of camel's hair, and their independent noble bearing. Here we see them walking side by side, and their conquerors in full military uniform and their conquerors' wives in the uniform of *Le Follet*, whilst white-robed female figures flit about closely veiled, and Marabouts (the Mahommedan priests) also promenade in their flowing robes. Arab women and children lounge about selling fruit or begging furtively, and others hurry to and fro carrying burdens; and everywhere and ever present in this motley throng, the black frock-coat and chimney-pot hat assert themselves, to remind us of what we might otherwise soon be forgetting—that we are but four days' journey from England.

There is noise enough altogether on the *Place* to bewilder any stranger; for besides the talking and singing, and the cries of vendors of fruit and wares, there is considerable traffic. Close to us as we sit under the trees (so close as almost to upset the little tables in front of the cafés), without any warning, a huge diligence will come lunging on to the *Place* groaning under a pile of merchandise, with a bevy of Arabs on the roof, and a party of Moorish women in the "rotonde"; presently there passes a company of Zouaves at quick step, looking hot and dusty enough, marching to their terrible tattoo; and next, by way of contrast again, come two Arab women with their children, mounted on camels, the beasts looking overworked and sulky; they edge their way through the crowd with the greatest nonchalance, and with an impatient croaking sound go shambling past.

The "Place Royale" faces the north, and is enclosed on three sides with modern French houses with arcades and shops, and when we have time to examine their contents, we shall find them also principally French. Next door to a bonnet-shop there is certainly the name of Mustapha over the door, and in the window are pipes, coral, and filigree work exposed for sale; but most of the goods come from France. Next door again is a French café, where Arabs, who can afford it, delight in being waited upon by their conquerors with white aprons and neck-ties.

The background of all this is superb: a calm sunlit sea, white sails glittering and flashing, and far to the eastward a noble bay, with the Kabyle Mountains stretching out their arms towards the north.

At four o'clock the band plays on the *Place*, and as we sit and watch the groups of Arabs and Moors listening attentively to the overture to "William Tell," or admiringly examining the gay uniforms and medals of the Chasseurs

THE GREAT MOSQUE, ALGIERS.

Face p. 261.

d'Afrique—as we see the children of both nations at high romps together—as the sweet sea-breeze that fans us so gently, bears into the newly constructed harbour together a corvette of the Imperial Marine and a suspicious-looking raking craft with latteen sails—as Marochetti's equestrian statue of the Duke of Orleans, and a mosque, stand side by side before us—we have Algiers presented in the easiest way imaginable, and obtain some idea of the general aspect of the place and the people, and of the relative position of conquerors and conquered.

As our business is principally with the Moorish, or picturesque side of things, let us first look at the great Mosque which we glanced at as we entered the harbour, part of which is sketched opposite.

Built close to the water's edge, so close that (before the new quay was built) the Mediterranean waves sapped its foundations—with plain white shining walls, nearly destitute of exterior ornament, it is perhaps the most perfect example of strength and beauty, and of fitness and grace of line, that we shall see in any building of this type.[1] It is thoroughly Moorish in style, although built by a Christian, if we may believe the story, of which there are several versions; how the Moors in old days took captive a Christian architect, and promised him his liberty on condition of his building them a mosque; how he, true to his own creed, dexterously introduced into the ground plan the form of a cross; and how the Moors, true also to their promise, gave him his liberty indeed, but at the cannon's mouth through a window, seaward.

The general outline of these mosques is familiar to most readers, the square white walls pierced at intervals with

---

[1] This beautiful architectural feature of the town has not escaped the civilising hand of the Frank; the oval window in the tower is gone, and in its place is an illuminated French clock!

quaint-shaped little windows, the flat cupola or dome, and the square tower often standing apart from the rest of the structure (as in the vignette on page 257), like an Italian campanile. Some of these towers are richly decorated with arabesque ornamentation, and glitter in the sun with colour and gilding, but the majority of the mosques are as plain and simple in design as shown in the large sketch.

Here, if we take off our shoes, we may enter and hear the Koran read, and we may kneel down to pray with Arabs and Moors; religious tolerance is equally exercised by both creeds. Altogether the Mahommedan places of worship seem by far the most prominent, and although there are Roman Catholic churches, and buildings held by other denominations of Christians, there is none of that predominant proselytising aspect which we might have expected after fifty years' occupation by the French. At Tetuan, for instance, where the proportion of Christians to Mahommedans is certainly smaller, the "Catholic church" rears its head much more conspicuously.

In Algiers the priestly element is undoubtedly active, and *Sœurs de Charité* are to be seen everywhere, but the buildings that first strike the eye are not churches but mosques; the sounds that become more familiar to the ear than peals of bells, are the Muezzin's morning and evening salutation from the tower of a mosque, calling upon all true believers to—

"Come to prayers, come to prayers,
It is better to pray than to sleep."

The principal streets in Algiers lead east and west from the *Place* to the principal gates, the Bab-Azoun and the Bab-el-Oued. They are for the most part French, with arcades like the Rue de Rivoli in Paris; many of the houses are lofty and built in the style perhaps best known as the "Haussman." But much of the upper town is still

Moorish, and is approached by narrow streets or lanes—steep, slippery, and tortuous, which we shall examine by-and-by. The names of some of the streets are curious, and suggestive of change. Thus we see the "Rue Royale," the "Rue Impérial"; there is, or was until lately, a "Place Nationale," and one street is still boldly proclaimed to be the "Rue de la Révolution"!

In passing through the French quarter, through the new wide streets, squares and inevitable boulevards, the number of shops for fancy goods and Parisian wares, especially those of hairdressers and modistes, seems rather extraordinary; remembering that the entire European population of Algeria, agricultural as well as urban, is not much more than that of Brighton in England.

Before we proceed further, let us glance at the general mode of living in Algiers, speaking first of the traveller who goes to the hotels.

The ordinary visitor of a month or two will drop down pleasantly enough into the system of hotel life in Algiers; and even if staying for the winter he will probably find it more convenient and amusing to take his meals in French fashion at the hotels, ringing the changes between three or four of the best, and one or two well-known cafés. There is generally a table-d'hôte, but strangers can walk in and have breakfast or dine very comfortably at little tables "*à part*," at a fixed hour and at a moderate price. The rooms are pleasant, cool, and airy, with large windows open to the sea. Everything is neatly and quietly served, the menu is varied enough, with good French dishes and game in abundance; the hosts being especially liberal in providing those delicious little birds that might be larks or quails—which in Algiers we see so often on the table and so seldom on the wing.

Half the people that are dining at the "Hôtel d'Orient," to-day are residents or habitués; they come in and take their accustomed places as cosily, and are almost as particular and fastidious, as if they were at their club.

There is the colonel of a cavalry regiment dining alone, and within joking distance, five young officers, whose various grades of rank are almost as evident from their manner as from the number of stripes on their bright red *kepis* ranged on the wall of the salon. A French doctor and his wife dine vis-à-vis, at one table, a lady *solitaire* at another; some gentlemen, whose minds are turned to commerce, chatter in a corner by themselves; whilst a group of newly-arrived English people in the middle of the room, are busily engaged in putting down the various questions with which they intend to bore the vice-consul on the morrow, as if he were some good-natured house-agent, valet-de-place, and interpreter in one—placed here by Providence for their especial behoof.

It is all very orderly, sociable, and comfortable, and by no means an unpleasant method of living for a time. There is the *cercle*, the club, at which we may dine sometimes; there are those pretty little villas amongst the orange trees at Mustapha Supérieure, where we may spend the most delightful evenings of all; and there are also the Governor's weekly balls, soirées at the consulate, and other pleasant devices for turning night into day, in Algiers as everywhere else—which we shall be wise if we join in but sparingly. And there are public amusements, concerts, balls, and the theatre—the latter with a company of operatic singers with weak lungs, but voices as sweet as any heard in Italy; and there are the moonlight walks by the sea, to many the greatest delight.

The ordinary daily occupations are decidedly social and domestic; and it may be truly said that for a stranger, until he becomes accustomed to the place, there is very little going on.

You must not bathe, for instance, on this beautiful shelving shore. "Nobody bathes, it gives fever," was the invariable answer to enquiries on this subject, and though it is not absolutely forbidden by the faculty, there are so many restrictions imposed upon bathers that few attempt it; moreover an Englishman is not likely to have brought an acrobatic suit with him, nor will he easily suit himself with a "costume de bain" in Algiers.

There is very little to do besides wander about the town, or make excursions in the environs or into the interior (in which latter case it is as well to take a fowling-piece, as there is plenty of game to be met with); and altogether, we may answer a question often asked about Algiers as to its attractions for visitors, that it has not many for the mere holiday lounger.

But for those who have resources of their own, for those who have work to do which they wish to do quietly, and who breathe more freely under a bright blue sky, Algiers seems to us to be *the* place to come to. The "bird of passage," who has unfortunately missed an earthquake, often reports that Algiers is a little dull; but even he should not find it so, for beyond the "distractions" we have hinted at, there is plenty to amuse him if he care little for what is picturesque. There are (or were when we were there), a troop of performing Arabs of the tribe of

"Beni Zouzoug," who performed nightly the most hideous atrocities in the name of religious rites: wounding their wretched limbs with knives, eating glass, holding burning coals in their mouths, standing on hot iron until the feet frizzled and gave forth sickening odours, and doing other things in an ecstasy of religious frenzy which we could not print, and which would scarcely be believed in if we did.

There are various Moorish ceremonies to be witnessed. There are the sacrifices at the time of the Ramadhan, when the negro priestesses go down to the water-side and offer up beasts and birds; the victims, after prolonged agonies which crowds assemble to witness, being finally handed over to a French *chef de cuisine*.

There are the mosques to be entered barefoot, and the native courts of law to be seen. Then, if possible, a Moor should be visited at home, and a glimpse obtained of his domestic economy, including dinner without knives or forks.

An entertainment consisting entirely of Moorish dances and music is easily got up, and is one of the characteristic sights of Algiers. The young trained dancing-girls, urged on to frenzy by the beating of the tom-tom, and falling exhausted at last into the arms of their masters (dancing with that monotonous motion peculiar to the East, the body swaying to and fro without much movement of the feet); the uncouth wild airs they sing, their shrieks dying away into a sigh or moan, will not soon be forgotten, and many other scenes of a like nature, on which we need not dwell—for are they not written in twenty books on Algeria already?

But there are two sights which are seldom mentioned by other writers, which should be alluded to in passing.

The Arab races, which take place in the autumn on the French racecourse near the town, are very curious, and well worth seeing. Their peculiarity consists in about thirty Arabs starting off pell-mell, knocking each other over in their first great rush, their bournouses mingling together and flying in the wind, but arriving at the goal generally singly, and at a slow trot, in anything but racing fashion.

Another event is the annual gathering of the tribes, when representatives from the various provinces camp on the hills of the Sahel, and the European can wander from one tent to another and spend his day enjoying Arab hospitality, in sipping coffee and smoking everywhere the pipe of peace.

These things we only hint at as resources for visitors, if they are fortunate enough to be in Algiers at the right time; but there are one or two other things that they are not likely to miss, whether they wish to do so or not.

They will probably meet one day, in the "Street of the Eastern Gate," the Sirocco wind, and they will have to take shelter from a sudden fearful darkness and heat, a blinding choking dust drying up as it were the very breath of life; penetrating every cavity, and into rooms closed as far as possible from the outer air. Man and beast lie down before it, and there is a sudden silence in the streets, as if they had been overwhelmed by the sea. For two or three hours this mysterious blight pours over the city, and its inhabitants hide their heads.

Another rather startling sensation for the first time is the "morning gun." In the old consulate, which was in a Moorish house in the upper town, the newly-arrived visitor may have been shown imbedded in the wall a large round shot, which he is informed was a messenger from one of Lord Exmouth's three-deckers in the days before the French occupation; and not many yards from it, in another street, he may have had pointed out to him certain fissures or chasms in the walls of the houses, as the havoc made by earthquakes; he may also have experienced in his travels the sudden and severe effect of a tropical thunderstorm.

Let him retire to rest with a dreamy recollection of such events in his mind, and let him have his windows open towards the port just before sunrise—when the earthquake, and the thunder, and the bombardment, will present themselves suddenly and fearfully to his sleepy senses.

But it may have roused him to see one of the sights of Algiers. Let him go out at once to the almost deserted *Place*, where a few tall figures wrapped in military cloaks are to be seen quietly sidling out of a door in the corner of a square under the arcades—coming from the club where the gas is not quite extinguished, and where the little green baize tables are not yet put away for the night;[1] and then let him hurry out by the *Bab-el-Oued* and mount the fortifications, and he will see a number of poor Arabs shivering in their white bournouses, perched on the highest points of the rocks like eagles, watching with eager eyes and strained aspect for the rising of the sun, for the coming of the second Mahomet. Let him look in the same direction, eastward, over the town and over the bay to the mountains far beyond. The sparks from the chariot-wheels of fire just fringe the outline of the Kabyle Hills, and in another minute, before all the Arabs have clambered up and reached their vantage ground, the whole bay is in a flood of light. The Arabs prostrate themselves before the sun, and "*Allah il*

---

[1] How often have we seen in the Tuileries gardens, the bronzed heroes of Algerian wars, and perhaps have pitied them for their worn appearance; but we shall begin to think that something more than the African sun and long marches have given them a prematurely aged appearance, and that absinthe and late hours in a temperature of 90° Fahrenheit may have something to do with it.

Allah" (God is great) is the burden of their psalm of praise.

But Mahomet's coming is not yet, and so they return down the hill, and crowd together to a very different scene.

The officers whom we saw just now leaving the *Place*, have arrived at the Champ de Mars, the drill-ground immediately below us, and here, in the cool morning air, they are exercising and manœuvring troops. There are several companies going through their drill, and the bugle and the drum drown the Muezzins' voices, who, from almost every mosque and turret in the city, repeat their cry to the faithful to "Come to prayers."

Our Moorish Home.

In the midst of the Moorish quarter, up a little narrow street (reached in five or six minutes from the centre of the town) passing under an archway and between white walls that nearly meet overhead, we come to a low dark door, with a heavy handle and latch which opens and shuts with a crashing sound ; and if we enter the courtyard and ascend a narrow staircase in one corner, we come suddenly upon the interior view of the first or principal floor of our Moorish home.

The house has two stories, and there is also an upper terrace from which we overlook the town. The arrangement of the rooms all opening inwards, is excellent ; they are cool in summer, and warm even on the coldest nights, and although we are in a noisy and thickly-populated part of the town, we are ignorant of what goes on outside, the massive walls keeping out nearly all sound. The floors and walls are tiled, so that they can be cleansed and cooled by water being thrown over them ; the carpets and cushions spread about invite one to the most luxurious repose, tables and chairs are unknown, there is nothing to offend the eye in shape or form, nothing to offend the ear—not even a door to slam. Above, there is an open terrace, where we sit in the mornings and evenings, and can realise the system of life on the house-tops of the East. Here we can cultivate the vine, grow roses and other flowers, build for ourselves extempore arbours, and live literally in the open air.

From this terrace we overlook the flat roofs of the houses of the Moorish part of the city, and if we peep over, down into the streets immediately below us, a curious hum of sounds comes up. Our neighbours are certainly industrious; they embroider, they make slippers, they hammer at metal work, they break earthenware and mend it, and appear to quarrel all day long, within a few feet of us; but as we sit in the room from which our sketch is taken, the sounds become mingled and subdued into a pleasant tinkle which is almost musical, and which we can, if we please, shut out entirely by dropping a curtain across the doorway. Our attendants are Moorish, and consist of one old woman, whom we see by accident (closely veiled) about once a month, and a bare-legged, bare-footed Arab boy who waits upon us. There are pigeons on the roof, a French poodle that frequents the lower regions, and a guardian of our doorstep who haunts it day and night, whose portrait is given at page 295.

Here we work with the greatest freedom and comfort, without interruption or any drawbacks that we can think of. The climate is so equal, warm, and pleasant—even in December and January—that by preference we generally sit on the upper terrace, where we have the perfection of light, and are at the same time sufficiently protected from sun and wind. At night we sleep almost in the open air, and need scarcely drop the curtains at the arched doorways of our rooms; there are no mosquitoes to trouble us, and there is certainly no fear of intrusion. There is also perfect stillness, for our neighbours are at rest soon after sundown.

Such is a general sketch of our dwelling in Algiers; let us for a moment, by way of contrast, return in imagination to London and picture to ourselves our friends as they are working at home. It is considered very desirable, if not essential, to an artist, that his immediate surroundings should be in some sort graceful and harmonious, and it is a lesson worth learning, to see what may be done, with ingenuity and taste, towards converting a single room, in a dingy street, into a fitting abode of the arts.

We know a certain painter well, one whose studio it is always a delight to enter, and whose devotion to Art (both music and painting) for its own sake has always stood in the way of his advancement and pecuniary success. He has converted a room in the neighbourhood of Gower Street into a charming nook where colour, form, and texture are all considered in the simplest details of decoration, where there is nothing inharmonious to eye or ear, but where perhaps the sound of the guitar may be heard a little too often. The walls of his studio are draped, the light falls softly from above, the doorway is arched, the seats are couches or carpets on a raised daïs, a Florentine lamp hangs from the ceiling, a medley of vases, costumes, old armour, etc., are grouped about in picturesque confusion, and our friend, in an easy undress of the last century, works away in the midst. Not to particularise further, let the reader consider for a moment what one step beyond his own door brings about, on an average winter's day. A straight, ungraceful, colourless costume of the latter half of the nineteenth century which he *must* assume, a hat of the period, an umbrella raised to keep off sleet and rain; and for landscape a damp, dreary, muddy, blackened street, with a vista of areas and lamp-posts, and, if perchance he be going to the Academy, a walk through the parish of St. Giles!

Perhaps the most depressing prospect in the world is that from a Gower Street doorstep on a November morning about nine o'clock; but of this enough. We think of our friend as we sit out here on our *terrasse*—sheltering ourselves on the same day, at the same hour, from the sun's rays—we think of him painting Italian scenes by the light of his gas "sun-burner," and wish he would come out to Algiers. "Surely," we would say to him, "it is something gained, if we can, ever so little, harmonise the realities of life with our ideal world—if we can, without remark, dress ourselves more as we dress our models, and so live, that one step from the studio to the street shall not be the abomination of desolation."

The Break of Day.

Let us turn again to Nature and to Light, and transport the reader to a little white house, overlooking a beautiful city, on the North African shore, where summer is perpetual and indoor life the exception; and draw a picture for him which *should* be fascinating and which certainly is true.

Sunrise, December 10.—The mysterious, indefinable charm of the first break of day, is an old and favourite theme in all countries and climates, and one on which perhaps little that is new can be said. In the East it is always striking, but in Algiers it seems peculiarly so; for sleeping, or more often lying awake, with the clear crisp night air upon our faces, it comes to our couch in the dreamiest way imaginable—instead of being clothed (as poets express it) with the veil of night, a mantle seems rather to be spread over us in the morning; there is perfect quiet at this hour, and we seem to be under a spell not to disturb the stillness—the dawn whispers to us so

T

softly and soothingly that we are powerless to do ought but watch or sleep.

The break of day is perhaps first announced to us by a faint stream of light across the courtyard, or the dim shadow of a marble pillar on the wall. In a few minutes, we hear the distinct barking of a dog, a slight rustle in the pigeon-house above, or a solitary cry from a minaret which tells us that the city is awaking. We rouse ourselves and steal out quietly on to the upper terrace to see a sight of sights—one of those things that books tell us, rightly or wrongly, is alone worth coming from England to see.

The canopy of stars, that had encompassed us so closely during the night, as if to shut in the courtyard overhead, seems lifted again, and the stars themselves are disappearing fast in the grey expanse of sky; and as we endeavour to trace them, looking intently seaward, towards the North and East, we can just discern an horizon line and faint shadows of the "sleeping giants," that we know to be not far off. Soon—in about the same time that it takes to write these lines—they begin to take form and outline one by one, a tinge of delicate pearly pink is seen at intervals through their shadows, and before any nearer objects have come into view, the whole coast line and the mountains of Kabylia, stretching far to the eastward, are flushed with rosy light, opposed to a veil of twilight grey which still hangs over the city.

Another minute or two, and our shadows are thrown sharply on a glowing wall, towers and domes come distinctly into view, house-tops innumerable range themselves in close array at our feet, and we, who but a few minutes ago seemed to be standing as it were alone upon the top of a high mountain, are suddenly and closely beleaguered. A city of flat white roofs, towers, and cupolas, relieved here and there by coloured awnings, green shutters, and

A MOORISH HOME.

Face p. 274.

dark doorways, and by little courtyards blooming with orange and citron trees—intersected with innumerable winding ways (which look like streams forcing their way through a chalk cliff)—has all grown up before our eyes; and beyond it, seaward—a harbour and a fleet of little vessels with their white sails, are seen shining in the sun.

Then come the hundred sounds of a waking city, mingling and increasing every moment; and the flat roofs (some so close that we can step upon them) are soon alive with those quaint white figures we meet in the streets, passing to and fro, from roof to roof, apparently without restraint or fear. There are numbers of children peeping out from odd corners and loopholes, and women with them, some dressed much less scrupulously than we see them in the market-place, and some, to tell the truth, entirely without the white robes aforesaid. A few, a very few, are already winding their way through the streets to the nearest mosque, but the majority are collected in groups in conversation, enjoying the sweet sea-breeze, which comes laden with the perfume of orange-trees, and a peculiar delicious scent as of violets.

The pigeons on the roof-tops now plume their gilded wings and soar—not upward but downward, far away into space; they scarcely break the silence in the air, or spread their wings as they speed along.

Oh, what a flight above the azure sea!

"Quis dabat mihi pennas sicut columbæ;"

* * * *

the very action of flying seems repose to them.

It is still barely sunrise on this soft December morning, the day's labour has scarcely begun, the calm is so perfect that existence alone seems a delight, and the Eastern aroma (if we may so express it) that pervades the air might almost lull us to sleep again, but Allah wills it otherwise.

Suddenly—with terrible impulse and shrill accent impossible to describe—a hurricane of women's voices succeeds the calm. Is it treachery? Is it scandal? Has Hassan proved faithless, or has Fatima fled? Oh, the screeching and yelling that succeeded to the quiet beauty of the morning! Oh, the rushing about of veiled (now all closely veiled) figures on house-tops! Oh, the weeping and wailing, and literal, terrible, gnashing of teeth! "Tell it not upon the house-tops" (shall we ever forget it being told on the house-tops?) "let not a whole city know thy misdeeds," is written in the Koran, "it is better for the faithful to come to prayers"! oh, how the tempest raged until the sun was up and the city was alive again, and its sounds helped to drown the clamour!

Let us come down, for our Arab boy now claps his hands in sign, that (on a little low table or tray, six inches from the ground) coffee and pipes are provided for the unbelievers; and like the Calendar in Eastern Story, he proceeds to tell us the cause of the tumult—a trinket taken from one wife and given to another!

Oh, Islam! that a lost bracelet or a jealous wife should make the earth tremble so!

ARABS AND MOORS.

OF the various studies to be made in Algiers, there are none at the same time so quaint and characteristic as the Moors in their own homes, seated at their own doors or benches at work, or at the numerous cafés and bazaars; and nothing seems to harmonise so well in these Moorish streets as the groups of natives (both Moors and Jews) with their bright costumes, and wares for sale. Colour and contrast of colour, seem to be considered, or *felt*, everywhere. It is scarcely too much to say that no two Orientals will walk down a street side by side, unless the colours of their costume harmonise or blend together (they seem to know it instinctively), and then there is generally some quiet contrasting tone for a background, and a sky of deep, deep blue. A negress with a dark blue veil over her head sells oranges or citrons; an Arab boy with a red fez and white turban, carries purple fruit in a basket of leaves; and so on. The reader may think this fanciful, but it is truer than he imagines; let him come and see. It was not easy to sketch in the open street on account of the curiosity it excited, a crowd sometimes collecting until it became almost impossible to breathe. The usual plan was to go to the cafés and divans, and by degrees to make friends with the Moors.

WAITING.

THERE was one café, in a street that we have been to so often, that it is as familiar to us as any in the western world; and where by dint of a little tact and a small outlay of tobacco, we managed to make ourselves quite at home, and were permitted to work away all day, comparatively unmolested. It was a narrow and steep overhanging street, crowded at all times with Moors, on one side embroidering or pretending to sell goods of various kinds; on the opposite side there was a café, not four feet distant, where a row of about eighteen others sat and smoked, and contemplated their brethren at work. The street was full of traffic, being an important thoroughfare from the lower to the upper town, and there were perpetually passing up and down, droves of laden donkeys; men with burdens carried on poles between them; vendors of fruit, bread, and live fowls (carried by their legs, heads downwards), and crowds of people of every denomination.

In a little corner out of sight, where we were certainly rather closely packed, we used to install ourselves continually and sketch the people passing to and fro. The Moors in the café used to sit beside us all day and watch, and *wait;* they gave us a grave silent salutation when we took our places, and another when we left, but we never got much further with our unknown neighbours. If we can imagine a coterie in a small political club, where the open discussion of politics is, with one consent, tabooed for fear of a disturbance, and where the most frolicsome of its members play at chess for relaxation, we shall get some notion of the state of absolute decorum which existed in our little *café maure.*

It was very quaint. The memory of the grave quiet faces of these most polite Moorish gentlemen, looking so smooth and clean in their white bournouses, seated solemnly doing nothing, haunts us to this day. Years elapsed between the first and last visit to our favourite street, yet there they were when we came again, still doing nothing; and opposite to them, the merchants who do no trade, also sitting in their accustomed places, surrounded with the same old wares. There was the same old negro in a dark corner making coffee, and handing it to the same customer, sitting in the same place, in the same dream.

There is both art and mystery in "doing nothing" well which these men achieve in their peculiar lives; here they sit for years together, silently waiting, without a trace of boredom on their faces, and without exhibiting a gesture of impatience. They—the "gentlemen" in the café on the right hand—have saved up money enough to keep life together, they have for ever renounced work, and can look on with complacency at their poorer brethren. They have their traditions, their faith, their romance of life, and the deeply-rooted belief, that if they fear God and Mahomet, and sit here long enough, they will one day be sent for to Spain, to re-people the houses where their fathers dwelt. This corner is the one *par excellence*, where the Moors sit and wait. There is the "wall of wailing" at Jerusalem; there is the "street of waiting" in Algiers, where the Moors sit clothed in white, dreaming of heaven—with an aspect of more than content, in a state of dreamy delight achieved, apparently, more by habit of mind than any opiates—the realisation of "*keyf.*"

A CLOTHES AUCTION.

NOT far from this street, but still in the Moorish quarter, we may witness a much more animated scene, and obtain in some respects a still better study of character and costume—at a clothes auction in the neighbourhood of the principal bazaar. If we go in the afternoon, we shall probably find a crowd collected in a courtyard, round a number of Jews who are selling clothes, silk, and stuffs, and so intent are they all on the business that is going forward, that we are able to take up a good position to watch the proceedings. We arrived one day at this spot, just as a terrible scuffle or wrangle was going forward, between ten or a dozen old men (surrounded by at least a hundred spectators) about the quality or ownership of some garment. The merits of the discussion were of little interest to us and probably of little importance to anybody, but the result was in its way as interesting a spectacle as ever greeted the eye and ear.

This old garment had magical powers, and was a treasure to *us* at least. It attracted the old and young, the wise and foolish, the excited combatant and the calm and dignified spectator; it collected them all in a large square courtyard with plain whitewashed walls and Moorish arcades. On one side a palm tree drooped its gigantic leaves, and cast broad shadows on the ground, which in some places was almost of the brightness of orange; on the other side, half in sunlight, half in shadow, a heavy awning was spread over a raised daïs or stage, and through its tatters and through the deep arcades, the sky appeared in patches of the deepest blue—blue of a depth and brilliancy that few painters succeed in depicting. It gave in a wider and truer sense, just that quality to our picture—if we may be excused a little technicality and a familiar illustration—that a broad red sash thrown across the bed of a sleeping child in Millais' picture in the Royal Academy Exhibition of 1867, gave to his composition, as many readers may remember. But we cannot take our eyes from the principal group, or do much more than watch the crowd in its changing phases. To give any idea of the uproar, the "row" we ought to call it, would be to weary the reader with a polyglot of words and sentences, some not too choice, and many too shrill and fiercely accentuated; but to picture the general aspect in a few words is worth a trial, although to do this we must join the throng and fight our way to the front. Where have we seen the like? We have seen such upturned faces in pictures of the early days of the Reformation by Henry Leys; we have seen such passion in *Shylock*, such despair in *Lear;* such grave and imposing-looking men with "reverend beards" in many pictures by the old masters; but seldom such concentration of emotion (if we may so express it), and unity of purpose, in one group. Do our figure-painters want a subject, with variety of colour, character and movement in one canvas? They need not go to the bazaars of Constantinople, or to the markets of the East. Let them follow us here crushing close to the platform, our faces nearly on a level with the boards. Look at the colours, at the folds of their cloaks, bournouses and yachmahs—purple, deep red, and spotless white, all crushed together—with their rich transparent shadows, as the sun streams across them, reflected on the walls. The heavy awning throws a curious glow over the figures, and sometimes almost conceals their features with a dazzle of reflected light. Look at the legs of these eager traders, as they struggle and fight and stand on tiptoe, to catch a glimpse of some new thing exposed for sale; look at them well—the lean, the shambling, the vigorous, the bare bronze (bronzed with sun and grime), the dark hose, the purple silk and the white cotton, the latter the special affection of the dandy Jew. What a medley, but what character here—the group from knee to ankle forms a picture alone. And thus they crowd together for half-an-hour, whilst all ordinary business seems suspended.

Nothing could be done with such a clatter, not to mention the heat. Oh, how the Arab gutturals, the impossible consonants (quite impossible to unpractised European lips) were interjected and hurled, so to speak, to and fro! How much was said to no purpose, how incoherent it all seemed, and how we wished for a few vowels to cool the air! In half-an-hour a calm has set in and the steady business of the day is allowed to go forward; we may now smoke a pipe in peace, and from a quiet corner watch the proceedings almost unobserved, asking a question or two suggested by the foregoing scene. Is expression really worth anything? Is the exhibition of passion much more than acting? Shall grey beards and flowing robes carry dignity with them any more, if a haggle about old clothes can produce it in five minutes?

And so we sit and watch for hours, wondering at the apparently endless variety of the patterns, and colours of the fabrics exposed for sale; and perhaps we doze, perhaps we dream. Is it the effect of the hachshish? Is it the strong coffee? Are we, indeed, dreaming, or is the auction a sham? Surely that pretty bright handkerchief —now held up and eagerly scanned by bleared old eyes— now rumpled and drawn sharply between haggard fingers —is an old friend, and has no business in a sale like this? Where have we seen it before? Yes—there is no mistaking the pattern, we have seen it in Spain. It was bound turbanwise round the head of a woman who performed in the bull ring at Seville, on the occasion of a particularly high and rollicking festival of the "Catholic Church"; it was handed out of a diligence window one dark night on the Sierra Morena, when a mule had broken its leg, and the only method of getting it along was to tie the injured limb to the girth, and let the animal hop on three legs for the rest of the way. It found its way into the Tyrol, worn as a sash; it was in the market-place at Bastia in Corsica, in the hands of a maiden selling fruit; it flaunted at Marseilles, drying in the wind on a ship's spar; and the last time we saw it, if our memory serves us well, it was carefully taken from a drawer in a little shop, "*Au Dey d'Alger*," in the Rue de Rivoli in Paris, and offered (by that greatest of humbugs, Mustapha), as the latest Algerian thing in neckties, which he asked fifteen francs for, and would gladly part with for two.

It was a pattern we knew by heart, that we meet with in all parts of the world, thanks to the universality of Manchester cottons. But the pattern was simple and good, nothing but an arrangement of red, white and black stripes on a maize ground, and therein lay its success. It had its origin in the first principles of decoration, it transgressed no law or canon of taste, it was easily and cheaply made (as all the best patterns are), and so it travelled round the world, and the imitation work came to be sold in, perhaps, the very bazaar whence the pattern first came, and its originators squabbled over it as something unique.

But we can hardly regret the repetition of these Moorish patterns, for they are useful in such a variety of ways. Wind one of the handkerchiefs in and out amongst dark tresses, and see what richness it gives; make a turban of it for a negress's head; tie it nattily under the chin of a little Parisienne, and *hey presto!* she is pretty; make a sash of it, or throw it loosely on the ground, and the effect is graceful and charming to the eye. In some Japanese and Chinese silks we may meet with more brilliant combinations; but the Moors seem to excel all other nations in their skilful juxtaposition of colours. We have seen a Moorish designer hard at work, with a box of butterflies' wings for his school of design, and the hint might be taken at home.

THE ARAB QUARTER.

LET us leave the Moors and their beautiful fabrics for a while, and glance at the Arab quarter of the town. We may see Arabs by-and-by in the plains and in their tents, in their traditionary aspect; but here we come in contact with a somewhat renegade and disreputable race, who hang on the outskirts of civilisation. Many of them have come from the neighbouring villages and from their camps across the plains of the Sahel; and have set up a market of their own, where they are in full activity, trading with each other and with the Frank. This market-place is a sort of commercial neutral ground, where both Arabs and Kabyles meet the French in the strictest amity, and cheat them if they can. Here they may be seen by hundreds—some buying and selling, some fighting and not unfrequently cursing one another heartily; others seated close together in rows upon the ground, like so many white loaves ready for baking. Calm they are, and almost dignified in appearance, when sitting smoking in conclave; but take them individually, these trading men, who have had years of intercourse with their French conquerors, and they disappoint us altogether. They are no longer true followers of the Prophet, although they are a great obstruction to traffic, by spreading carpets on the ground in the middle of the road, and prostrating themselves towards Mahomet and the sun. Trade—paltry, mean, and cowardly as it so often makes men—has done the Arab irreparable harm: it has taught him to believe in counterfeits and little swindles as a legitimate mode of life, to pass bad money, and to cringe to a conqueror because he could make money thereby. He could not do these things in the old days, with his face to the sun.

The Arab is generally pictured to us in his tent or with his tribe, calm, dignified and brave, and perhaps we may meet with him thus on the other side of the Sahel, but here in Algiers he is a metamorphosed creature. The camels that crouch upon the ground, and scream and bite at passers-by, are more dignified and consistent in their ill-tempered generation than these "Sons of the Prophet," these "Lights of Truth." And they have actually caught European tricks. What shall we say when two Arabs meet in the street, and after a few words interchanged, pass away from each other with a quickened, jaunty step, like two "city men," who have lost time, and must make it up by a spurt! Shall we respect our noble Arab any more when we see him walking abroad with a stereotyped, plausible smile upon his face, and every action indicating an eye to the main chance? It may seem a stretch of fancy, but even the bournous itself, with its classic outline and flowing folds, loses half its dignity and picturesqueness on these men.

A step lower, of which there are too many examples in the crowd, and there is a sadder metamorphose yet—the patriarch turned scamp—one who has left his family and his tribe to seek his fortune. Look at him, with his ragged bournous, his dirt and his cringing ways, and contrast his life now, with what he has voluntarily abandoned. Oh! how civilisation has lowered him in his own eyes, how his courage has turned to bravado, and his tact to cunning; how even natural affection has languished, and family ties are but threads of the lightest tissue! He has failed in his endeavour to trade, he has disobeyed the Koran, and is an outcast and unclean—one of the waifs and strays of cities!

As we wend our way homeward, as John Bunyan says, "thinking of these things," we see two tall white figures go down to the water-side, like the monks in Millais' picture of "A Dream of the Past." They stand on the bank in the evening light, their reflections repeated in the water. It is the hour of prayer; what are they doing? They are fishing with a modern rod and line, and their little floats are painted with the tricolour!

OUR MODELS.

FROM the roof-tops of our own and the neighbouring houses we have altogether many opportunities of sketching, and making studies from life. By degrees, by fits and starts, and by most uncertain means (such as attracting curiosity, making little presents, etc.) we manage to scrape up a distant talking acquaintance with some of the veiled, mysterious creatures we have spoken of, and in short, to become almost "neighbourly."

But we never get much nearer than speaking distance, conversing from one roof to another with a narrow street like a river flowing between us ; and only once or twice during our winter sojourn, did we succeed in enticing a veiled houri to venture on our terrace and shake hands with the "Frank." If we could manage to hold a young lady in conversation, and exhibit sufficient admiration of her to induce her, ever so slightly, to unveil whilst we made a hasty sketch, it was about all that we could fairly succeed in accomplishing, and "the game was hardly worth the candle"; it took, perhaps, an hour to ensnare our bird, and in ten minutes or less, she would be again on the wing. Veiled beauties are interesting (sometimes much more interesting for being veiled); but it does not serve our artistic purposes much to see two splendid black eyes and a few white robes.

However, models we must have, although the profession is almost unknown in Algiers. At Naples we have only to go down to the sea-shore, at Rome to the steps of St. Peter's, and we find "subjects" enough, who will come for the asking; but here, where there is so much distinctive costume and variety of race, French artists seem to make little use of their opportunities.

It takes some days before we can hear of any one who will be willing to sit, for double the usual remuneration. But they come at last, and when it gets abroad that the Franks have money and "mean business," we have a number of applicants, some of whom are not very desirable, and none particularly attractive. We select "Fatima" first, because she is the youngest and has the best costume, and also because she comes with her father and appears tractable. She is engaged at two francs an hour, which she considers poor pay.

How shall we give the reader an idea of this little creature, when she comes next morning and coils herself up amongst the cushions in the corner of our room, like a young panther in the Jardin des Plantes? Her costume, when she throws off her haïk (and with it a tradition of the Mahommedan faith, that forbids her to show her face to an unbeliever) is a rich loose crimson jacket embroidered with gold, a thin white bodice, loose silk trousers reaching to the knee and fastened round the waist by a magnificent sash of various colours; red morocco slippers, a profusion of rings on her little fingers, and bracelets and anklets of gold filigree work. Through her waving black hair are twined strings of coins and the folds of a silk handkerchief, the hair falling at the back in plaits below the waist.

She is not beautiful, she is scarcely interesting in expression, and she is decidedly unsteady. She seems to have no more power of keeping herself in one position or of remaining in one part of the room, or even of being quiet, than a humming-top. The whole thing is an unutterable bore to her, for she does not even reap the reward —her father or husband, or male attendant, always taking the money.

She is *petite*, constitutionally phlegmatic, and as fat as her parents can manage to make her; she has small hands and feet, large rolling eyes—the latter made to appear artificially large by the application of henna or antimony black; her attitudes are not ungraceful, but there is a want of character about her, and an utter abandonment to the situation, peculiar to all her race. In short her movements are more suggestive of a little caged animal that had better be petted and caressed, or kept at a safe distance, according to her humour. She does one thing, she smokes incessantly and makes us cigarettes with a skill and rapidity which are wonderful.

Her age is thirteen, and she has been married six months; her ideas appear to be limited to three or four; and her pleasures, poor creature, are equally circumscribed. She had scarcely ever left her father's house, and had never spoken to a man until her marriage. No wonder we, in spite of a little Arabic on which we prided ourselves, could not make much way; no wonder that we came very rapidly to the conclusion that the houris of the Arabian Nights must have been dull creatures, and their "Entertainments" rather a failure, if there were no diviner fire than this.

We get on but indifferently with our studies with this young lady, and to tell the truth, not too well in Faṭima's good graces. Our opportunities are not great, our command of Arabic is limited, and indeed, we do not feel particularly inspired. We cannot tell her many love stories, or sing songs set to a "*tom-tom*"; we can, indeed, offer "backshish" in the shape of tobacco and sweatmeats, or some trifling European ornament or trinket; but it is clear that she would prefer a greater amount of familiarity, and more demonstrative tokens of esteem. However, she came several times, and we succeeded in obtaining some valuable studies of colour, and "bits," memoranda only; but very useful, from being taken down almost unconsciously, in such a luminous key, and with a variety of reflected light and pure shadow tone, that we find unapproachable in after work.

As for sketches of character, we obtained very few of Mauresques; our subjects were, as a rule, much too restless, and we had one or two "scenes" before we parted. On one unfortunate occasion our model insisted upon examining our work before leaving, and the scorn and contempt with which it was regarded was anything but flattering. It nearly caused a breach between us, for, as she observed, it was not only contrary to her creed to have her likeness taken, but it would be perdition to be thus represented amongst the Franks.[1] We promised to be as careful of this portrait as if it were the original, and, in fact, said anything to be polite and soothing.

On another occasion, we had been working on rather more quietly than usual for half-an-hour, and were really getting a satisfactory study of a new position, when, without apparent cause or warning of any kind, the strange, pale, passionless face, which stared like a wooden marionette, suddenly suffused with crimson, the great

[1] For fear of the "evil eye." There is a strong belief amongst Mahommedans that portraits are part of their identity; and that the original will suffer if the portrait receive any indignity.

OUR MODEL.

eyes filled with tears, the whole frame throbbed convulsively, and the little creature fell into such a passion of crying that we were fain to put by our work and question ourselves whether we had been cruel or unkind. But it was nothing: the cup of boredom had been filled to the brim, all other artifices had failed her to obtain relief from restraint, and so this apparently lethargic little being, who had, it seemed, both passion and grief at command, opened the flood-gates upon us, and of course gained her end. There was no more work that day, and she got off with a double allowance of bonbons, and something like a reconciliation. She gave us her little white hand at parting—the fingers and thumbs crowded with rings, and the nails stained black with henna—but the action meant nothing; we dare not press it, it was too soft and frail, and the rings would have cut her fingers, we could only hand it tenderly back again, and bid our " model " farewell.

We got on better afterwards with a Moorish Jewess who, for a " consideration," unearthed her property, including a tiara of gold and jewels, and a bodice of silver embroidery worked on crimson velvet; we purposely reverse the position and speak of the embroidery first, because the velvet was almost hidden. She came slouching in one morning, closely wrapped in a dirty shawl, her black hair all dishevelled and half covering her handsome face, her feet bare and her general appearance so much more suggestive of one of the " finest pisantry in the world," that we began to think that this must be one of our failures. But when her mother had arranged the tiara in her hair, when the curtain was drawn aside and the full splendour of the Jewish costume was displayed—when, in short, the dignity and grace of a queen were before us, we felt amply rewarded.

The Jewish dress differs from the Mauresque entirely;

it is European in shape, with high waist and flowing robes without sleeves, a square-cut bodice, often of the same material as the robe itself, and a profusion of gold ornaments, armlets, necklaces, and rings. A pair of tiny velvet slippers (also embroidered) on tiny feet, complete the costume, which varies in colour, but is generally of crimson or dark velvet.

As a "model," although almost her first appearance in that character, this Jewish woman was very valuable, and we had little trouble after the first interview, in making her understand our wishes. But we had to pay more than in England; there were many drawbacks, and of course much waste of time. On some holydays, and on all Jewish festivals, she did not make her appearance, and seemed to think nothing of it when some feast that lasted a week left us stranded with half-done work.

Without being learned in *costumes des dames*, we believe, we may say, that the shape and cut of some of these dresses, and the patterns of the embroidery (old as they are) might be copied with advantage by Parisian modistes; the more we study these old patterns, the more we cannot cease to regret that the *Deæ ex machinâ*, the arbiters of fashion in the city where Fashion is Queen, have not managed to infuse into the costume of our time more character and purity of design—conditions not inconsistent with splendour, and affording scope for any amount of extravagance.

We are led irresistibly into this digression, if it be a digression, because the statuesque figure before us displays so many lines of grace and beauty that have the additional charm of novelty. We know, for instance, that the pattern of this embroidery is unique, that the artificer of that curiously twined chain of gold has been dead perhaps for ages, that the rings on her fingers and the coins suspended from her hair are many of them real art treasures.[1]

The result of our studies, as far as regards Moorish women, we must admit to have been, after all, rather limited and unsatisfactory. We never once lighted upon a Moorish face that moved us much by its beauty, for the reason that it nearly always lacked expression; anything like emotion seemed inharmonious and out of place, and to disturb the uniformity of its lines. Even those dark lustrous eyes, when lighted by passion, had more of the tiger in them, than the tragedy queen.

The perfection of beauty, according to the Moorish ideal, seems to depend principally upon symmetry of feature, and is nothing without roundness of limb and a certain flabbiness of texture. It is an ideal of repose, not to say of dulness and insipidity; a heavy type of beauty of which we obtain some idea in the illustration before us, of a young girl, about thirteen years old, of one of the tribes from the interior. The drawing (on p. 291,) by a Frenchman, pretends to no particular artistic excellence, but it attempts to render, and we think succeeds in rendering, the style of a Mahommedan beauty in bridal array; one who is about to fulfil her destiny, and who appears to have as little animation or intelligence as the Prophet ordained for her, being perfectly fitted (according to the Koran) to fill her place in this world or in the next.

Thus decked with her brightest jewels and adorned with a crown of gold, she waits to meet her lord, to be his "light of the harem," his "sun and moon." What if we, with our refined æsthetic tastes, what if disinterested spectators, vote her altogether the dullest and most

---

[1] The "jewels" turned out to be paste on close inspection, but the gold filigree work, and the other ornaments, were old, and some very valuable and rare.

A PORTRAIT.

Face p. 295.

uninteresting of beings? what if she seem to us more like some young animal, magnificently harnessed, waiting to be trotted out to the highest bidder? She shakes the coins and beads on her head sometimes, with a slight impatient gesture, and takes chocolate from her little sister, and is petted and pacified just as we should soothe and pacify an impatient steed ; there is clearly no other way to treat her, it is the will of Allah that she should be so debased !

One day we had up a tinker, an old brown grizzled Maltese, who with his implements of trade, his patchwork garments and his dirt, had a tone about him, like a figure from one of the old Dutch Masters. He sat down in the corner of our courtyard against a marble pillar, and made himself quite at home ; he worked with his feet as well as his hands at his grinding, he chattered, he sang, and altogether made such a clatter that we shall not be likely to forget him. This gentleman, and the old negro that lived upon our doorstep, (sketched opposite) were almost the only subjects that we succeeded in inducing to come within indoors ; our other life studies were made under less favourable circumstances.

From the roof of our own house, it is true, we obtained a variety of sketches, not (as might be supposed from pictures with which we are all familiar) of young ladies attired as scantily as the nymphs at the *Théâtre du Chatelet*, standing in pensive attitudes on their house-tops, but generally of groups of veiled women—old, ugly, haggard, shrill of voice, and sometimes rather fierce of aspect, performing various household duties on the rooftops, including the beating of carpets and of children, the carrying of waterpots and the saying of prayers.

A chapter on "Models" would not be complete without some mention of the camels, of which there are numbers to be found in the Arab quarter of the town.

Some of them are splendid creatures, and as different from any exotic specimens that we can see in this country as an acclimatised palm tree from its wild growth.

Some one tells us that these Algerian "ships of the desert" have not the same sailing qualities, nor the same breadth of beam, as those at Cairo. But (if true) we should have to go to Cairo to study them, so let us be content. It would be interesting to see one or two of

our popular artists, who paint camels and desert scenes without ever having been to the East, just sit down here quietly for one day and paint a camel's head; not flinching from the work, but mastering the wonderful texture and shagginess of his thick coat or mane, its massive beauty, and its infinite gradations of colour. Such a sitter no portrait painter ever had in England. Feed him up first, get a boy to keep the flies from him, and he will sit almost immovably through the day. He will put on a sad expression in the morning, which will not change; he will give no trouble whatever, he will but sit still and croak.

Do we seem to exaggerate the value of such studies? We cannot exaggerate, if we take into full account the vigorous quality which we impart into our work. And we cannot, perhaps, better illustrate our argument in favour of drawing from, what we should call, *natural* models, than by comparing the merits of two of the most popular pictures of our time, viz.:—Frith's "*Derby Day*," and Rosa Bonheur's "*Horse Fair.*" The former pleasing the eye by its cleverness and prettiness; the latter impressing the spectator by its power, and its truthful rendering of animal life.

The difference between the two painters is, probably, one, more of education than of natural gifts. But whilst the style of the former is grafted on a fashion, the latter is founded on a rock—the result of a close study of nature, chastened by classic feeling, and a remembrance it may be of the friezes of the Parthenon.

The Bouzareah.

It would be passing over the most enjoyable part of life in North Africa, if we omitted all mention of those delightful days, spent on the hill-sides of Mustapha, on the heights of the Bouzareah, and indeed everywhere in the neighbourhood of Algiers, sketching in winter time in the open air.

Odours of orange-groves, the aromatic scent of cedars, the sweet breath of wild-flowers, roses, honeysuckles, and violets, should pervade this page; something should be done, which no words can accomplish, to give the true impression of the scene, to picture the luxuriant growth of vegetation (radiant in a sunshine which to a northerner is unknown), and to realise in any method of description, the sense of calm enjoyment of living this pure life in a climate neither too hot nor too cold, neither too enervating nor too exciting; of watching the serene days decline into sunsets that light up the Kabyle Hills with crests of gold, and end in sudden twilights that spread a weird unearthly light across the silver sea.

There is plenty to interest us here, if it is only in sketching the wild palmettos, or in watching the half-wild Arabs who camp in the neighbourhood, and build mud huts which they affect to call cafés, and where we can, if we please, obtain rest and shelter from the mid-day sun, and a considerable amount of "stuffiness," for one sou. But there is no need to trouble them, as there are plenty of shady valleys and cactus-hedges to keep off the sun's rays; the only disturbers of the peace are the dogs that guard the Arab encampments, and have to be diligently kept off with stones.

Perhaps the best spots for quiet work are the precincts of the Marabouts' tombs, where one can study unobserved behind some old wall and return quietly to the same spot, day after day. And here, as one experience of sketching from Nature, let us allude to the theory (laid down pretty confidently by those who have never reduced it to practice) that one great advantage of this climate is, that you may work at the same sketch from day to day, and continue it where you left off! You can do nothing of the kind. If your drawing is worth anything, it will at least have recorded something of the varying phases of light and shade, that really alter every hour.

Let us take an example. About six feet from us, at eight o'clock in the morning, the sheer white wall of a Moslem tomb is glowing with a white heat, and across it are cast the shadows of three aloe leaves, which at a little distance, have the contrasted effect of the blackness of night.[1] Approach a little nearer and examine the real colour of these photographic leaf-lines, shade off (with the hand) as much as possible of the wall, the sky, and the reflected light from surrounding leaves, and these dark shadows become a delicate pearl-grey, deepening into mauve, or partaking sometimes of the tints of the rich earth below them. They will be deeper yet before noon, and pale again, and uncertain and fantastic in shape, before sundown. If we sketch these shadows only each hour, as they pass from left to right upon the wall (laying down a different wash for the ground each time) and place them side by side in our note-book, we shall have made some discoveries in light and transparent shadow tone, which will be very valuable in after time. No two days or two hours are under precisely the same atmospheric conditions; the gradations and changes are extraordinary, and would scarcely be believed in by any one who had not watched them. Thus, although a colour-sketch cannot be continued to any good purpose when once left off, an infinite and overwhelming variety of work can be obtained in one day, in the space of a few yards, by the side of some old well or Marabout's tomb.

Our favourite rendezvous was a little Arab cemetery about six miles from Algiers, on the heights westward in the direction of Sidi Ferruch, near a little village called the "Bouzareah." This spot combined a wondrous view both of sea and land, with a foreground of beauty not easy to depict. It was a half-deserted cemetery with tombs of Marabout priests over which the palm trees waved, and

---

[1] Under some conditions of the atmosphere we have obtained more perfect outlines of the leaves of the aloe, with their curiously indented edges and spear-points, *from their shadows,* rather than from the leaves themselves.

little gravestones here and there surmounted with crescents. Sheltered from the sun's rays, hidden from the sight of passers-by, surrounded with a profusion of aloes, palms, cacti, and a variety of shrubs and flowers, peeping out between the palmettos that spread their leaves like fans upon the ground—it combined everything that an artist could desire.

Here we worked, sitting close to one of the tombs for its shade, with the hush of the breeze, the distant sighing sound of the sea, the flutter of leaves, bees and butterflies, and one other sound that intermingled with strange monotony close to our ears, which puzzled us sorely to account for at first. It turned out to be a snore; the custodian of one of the tombs was sleeping inside with his fathers, little dreaming of our proximity. We struck up an acquaintance with him, after a few days of coyness on his part, and finally made him a friend. For a few sous a day he acted as outpost for us, to keep off Arab boys and any other intruders; and before we left, was induced to sit and be included in a sketch. He did not like it, but he sat it out and had his portrait taken like any Christian dog; he took money for his sin, and finally, by way of expiation, let us hope, drank up our palette water at the end of the day!

If there is one spot in all Algeria most dear to a Mussulman's heart, most sacred to a Marabout's memory, it must surely be this peaceful garden of aloes and palms, where flowers ever grow, where the sun shines from the moment of its rising until it sinks beneath the western sea; where, if anywhere on this earth, the faithful will be the first to know of the Prophet's coming, and where they will always be ready to meet him. But if it be dear to a Mussulman heart it is also dear to a Christian's, for it has taught us more in a few weeks than we can unlearn in years. We cannot sit here day by day without learning several truths more forcibly than by any teaching of our schools; taking in, as it were, the mysteries of light and shade, and the various phases of atmosphere effect taking them all to heart, so that they influence work for years to come.

Is it mere heresy in art, or is it a brighter light dawning upon us here, that seems to say, that we have learned and achieved more, in studying the glowing limbs of an Arab child as it plays amongst these wild palmettos—because we worked with a background of such sea and sky as we never saw in any picture of the "Finding of Moses"; and because in the painting of the child, we had not perforce to learn any "master's" trick of colour, nor to follow conventional lines? And do we not, amongst other things, learn to distinguish between the true and conventional rendering of the form, colour and character, of palm trees, aloes and cacti?

First of the palm.[1] Do we not soon discover how much more of beauty, of suggested strength, of grace, lightness and variety of colour and texture, there is in this one stem, that we vainly try to depict in a wood engraving, than we had previously any conception of; and how opposed to facts are the conventional methods of drawing palm trees (often with a straight stem

---

[1] The palm-stem we have sketched is of a different variety and less formal in character than those generally seen in the East.

and uniform leaves looking like a feather broom on a straight stick), which we may find in almost any illustrated book representing Eastern scenes, from Constantinople to the Sea of Galilee.

Take, for instance, as a proof of variety in colour and grandeur of aspect, a group of palm trees that have stood guard over the Mahommedan tombs for perhaps a hundred years; stained with time, and shattered with their fierce battle with the storms that sweep over the promontory with terrible force. Look at the beauty of their lines, at the glorious colour of their young leaves, and the deep orange of those they have shed, like the plumage of some gigantic bird; one of their number has fallen from age, and lies crossways on the ground, half-concealed in the long grass and shrubs, and it has lain there undisturbed for years. To paint the sun setting on these glowing stems, and to catch the shadows of their sharp-pointed leaves, as they are traced at one period of the day on the white walls of the tombs, is worth long waiting to be able to note down; and to hit the right tint to depict such shadows truly, is an exciting triumph.

Second, of the aloe; and here we make as great a discovery as with the palm. Have we not been taught (in paintings) from youth upwards, that the aloe puts forth its blue riband-like leaves in uniform fashion, like so many starched pennants, which painters often express with one or two strokes of the brush; and are we not told by botanists that it flowers but once in a hundred years?

Look at that aloe hedgerow a little distance from us, that stretches across the country, like a long blue rippling wave on a calm sea, and which, as we approach it, seems thrown up fantastically and irregularly by breakers to a height of six or eight feet, and which (like the sea), on a nearer view changes its opaque cold blue tint, to a rich

AN ALOE HEDGE.

Face p. 302.

transparent green and gold. Approach them closely, walk under their colossal leaves, avoid their sharp spear-points and touch their soft pulpy stems. What wonderful variety there is in their forms, what transparent beauties of colour, what eccentric shadows they cast upon each other, and with what a grand spiral sweep some of the young shoots rear upwards! So tender and pliable are they, that in some positions a child might snap their leaves, and yet so wonderful is the distribution of strength, that they would resist at spear-point the approach of a lion, and almost turn a charge of cavalry. If we snap off the point of one of the leaves it is a needle, and a thread clings to it which we may peel off down the stem a yard long—needle and thread — nature-pointed, nature-threaded! Should not artists see these things? Should not poets read of them?

Of the cactus, which also grows in wild profusion, we could say almost as much as of the palms and aloes, but it might seem like repetition. Suffice it, that our studies of their separate leaves were the minutest and most rewarding labour ever achieved, and that until we had painted the cactus and the palmetto growing together, we had never understood the meaning of "tropical vegetation."

Many other subjects we obtain at the Bouzareah; simple perhaps, and apparently not worth recording, but of immense value to a student of Nature. Is it nothing, for instance, for a painter to have springing up before him in this clear atmosphere, delicate stems of grass, six feet high, falling over in spray of golden leaves against a background of blue sea; darting upward, sheer, bright, and transparent from a bank covered with the prickly pear, that looks by contrast, like the rock-work from which a fountain springs? Is it nothing to see amongst all this wondrous overgrowth of gigantic leaves, and amongst the tender creepers and the flowers, the curious knotted and twisted stem of the vine, trailing serpent-like on the ground, its surface worn smooth with time? Is it nothing for an artist to learn practically, what "white heat" means?

It is well worth coming to North Africa in winter, if, only to see the flowers, but of these we cannot trust ourselves to speak—they *must* be seen and painted.

It is difficult to tear ourselves away from this spot, and especially tempting to dwell upon these details, because they have seldom been treated of before; but perhaps the question may occur to some—are such subjects as we have depicted worth painting, or, indeed, of any prolonged or separate study? Let us endeavour to answer it by another question. Are the waves worth painting, by themselves? Has it not occurred to one or two artists (not to many, we admit) that the waves of the sea have never yet been adequately painted, because it is generally considered necessary to introduce something else into the composition, be it only a rope, a spar, or a distant ship? Has it not been discovered (though only of late years) that there is scope for imagination and poetry, and all the elements of a great and enthralling picture, in the drawing of waves alone; and should there not be, if nobly treated, interest enough in a group of colossal vegetation in a brilliant atmosphere, without the usual conventional adjuncts of figures and buildings?

So far, whilst sketching at the Bouzareah, we have spoken only of the foreground; but we have been all the time in the presence of the most wonderful panorama of sea and land, and have watched so many changing aspects from these heights, that we might fill a chapter in describing them alone.

The view northward over the Mediterranean, westward towards Sidi Ferruch, southward across the plains to the Atlas, eastward towards Algiers and the mountains of

Kabylia beyond; each point so distant from the other that, according to the wind or time of day, it partook of quite distinct aspects, fill up so many pictures in the mind's eye that a book might be written, called "The Bouzareah" (beautiful view), as seen under the different phases of sunshine and storm.

It has often been objected to by artists that these Eastern scenes have "no atmosphere," and no subtle gradation of middle distance; that there is not enough repose about them, in short that they lack mystery and are wanting in the poetry of cloudland. But there are clouds. We have seen, for the last few mornings (looking through the arched windows of the great aloe-leaves) little companies of small white clouds, casting clearly-defined shadows across the distant sea, and breaking up the horizon line with their soft white folds—reappearing and disappearing by some mysterious law, but seldom culminating in rain.

Yes, there are clouds. Look this time far away towards the horizon line across the bay, and watch that rolling sea which looks like foam, that rises higher and higher as we watch it, darkening the sky, and soon enveloping everything in a kind of sea fog, through which the sun gleams dimly red, whilst the white walls of the tombs appear cold and grey against a leaden sky. See it all pass away again across the plain of the Mitidja, and disappear in the shadows of the mountains.

There is a hush in the breeze and all is bright again, but a storm is coming. Take shelter, if you have courage, *inside* one of the Marabouts' tombs (there is plenty of space), whilst a tempest rages that should wake the dead before Mahomet's coming. Sit and wait in there, whilst one or two strong gusts of wind pass over, and then all is still again; and so dark that we can see nothing inside

X

A STORM AT THE BOUZAREAH

but the light of a pipe in one corner. We get impatient, thinking that it is passing off.

But it comes at last. It breaks over the tombs, and tears through the plantation, with a tremendous surging sound, putting to flight the Arabs on guard, who wrap their bournouses about them and hurry off to the village, with the cry of "Allah il Allah;" leaving the care of the tombs to the palms, that have stood guard over them so long. Oh, how they fight and struggle in the wind! how they creak, and moan, and strike against one another, like human creatures in the thick of battle! How they rally side by side, and wrestle with the wind—crashing down suddenly against the walls of the tomb, and scattering their leaves over us; then rallying again, and fighting the storm with human energy and persistence! It is a fearful sight—the rain falling in masses, but nearly horizontally, and with such density that we can see but a few yards from our place of shelter—and it is a fearful sound, to hear the palm trees shriek in the wind.

There was one part of the scene we could not describe, one which no other than Dante's pen, or Doré's pencil, could give any idea of; we could not depict the confused muttering sound and grinding clatter (if we may call it so), that the battered and wounded aloes made amongst themselves, like maimed and dying combatants trodden under foot. Many scenes in Nature have been compared to a battle-field; we have seen sheaves of corn blown about by the wind, looking exactly like the tents of a routed host; but this scene was beyond parallel—the hideous contortion, the melancholy aspect of destruction, the disfigured limbs in hopeless wreck, the weird, and ghastly forms that writhed and groaned aloud, as the storm made havoc with them.

And they made havoc with each other. What would

the reader say, if he saw the wounds inflicted by some of the young leaves on the parent stems—how they pierce and transfix, and sometimes *saw* into each other, with their sharp serrated edges, as they sway backwards and forwards in the wind. He would say perhaps that no sea monster or devil-fish, could seem more horrible, and we wish him no wilder vision than to be near them at night, when disturbed by the wind.

We have scarcely alluded to the palmetto leaves and branches that filled the air, to the sound of rushing water, to the distant roar of the sea, nor to many other aspects of the storm. It lasted, not much more than an hour, but the water covered the floor of our little temple before the rain subsided, and the ground a few feet off where we had sat was completely under water. Everything was steaming with vapour, but the land was refreshed, and the dark earth was richer than we had seen it for months—there would be no dust in Algiers until to-morrow.

On the Mountains.

THE beautiful mountain scenery, south of Medeah, on the lesser Atlas, led us to spend some time in sketching and in exploring the country. In spite of its wildness and solitariness we could wander about with perfect security, under protection of the French outposts. The crisp keen air at this altitude tempted us on and on. The mountain-ranges to the south were like an undulating sea, divided from us by lesser hills and little plains, with here and there valleys, green and cultivated; but the prevailing character of the scenery was rocky and barren. The great beauty was in the clouds that collected in this region at intervals, spreading a grateful shade and casting wonderful shadows on the rocks. The rain would fall heavily through them sometimes for three or four minutes, like summer showers, and the little dried-up torrent beds would trickle for a while; the Arabs would collect a few drops, and then all would be gone—the clouds, the rivulets, and every sign of moisture on the ground—and the mountains would stand out sharp and clear against the sky, with that curious, pinky hue, so well portrayed in the background of Lewis's picture of "A Camp on Mount Sinai."

Here we could pitch our tent in the deepest solitude, and romance as much as we pleased without fear of interruption. The only variation to the almost death-like silence that prevailed, would be the distant cry of a jackal, which disturbed us for a moment, or the moaning of the wind in some far-off valley, for the air seemed never still on these heights. A stray monkey or two, would come and furtively peep at our proceedings, but would be off again in an instant, and there were no birds; indeed, since we left Blidah we had scarcely heard their voices. The few Arab tribes that cultivated the valleys, seldom came near us; so that we sometimes heard no voices but our own from morning till night.

One day proved an exception. We had been making a drawing of the prospect due south, in order to get the effect of the sun's rays upon a sandy plateau that stretched between us and the next range of mountains; it was little more than a study of colour and effect, for there was not much to break the monotony of the subject—a sand-plain bounded by barren rocks. We had nearly finished our work, when two dark specks appeared suddenly on the sky-line, and quickly descending the rocks, began to cross the plain towards us. With our telescope, we soon made out that they were horsemen at full gallop, and we could tell this, not by the figures themselves, but by the long shadows that the afternoon sun cast from them upon the plain. In a few minutes they rode up to our tent. They were not, as our porters had insisted, some Arabs on a reconnoitring expedition, but two American gentlemen on hired horses from Algiers, who were scampering about the country without any guide or escort.

There was an end to all romance about desert scenes and being "alone with Nature"; we could not get rid of the western world, we were tourists and nothing more!

But in the solitude of these mountain wanderings, we had an opportunity of seeing one phase of Arab life which was almost worth the journey.

We had started early one morning from Blidah, but not so early, that in deference to the wishes of some of our companions, we had first attended service in a chapel, dedicated to "Our Lady of Succour." We went into the little building, which, like some rare exotic, was flourishing alone, surrounded by the most discordant elements—situated hard by a mosque and close to some noisy Arab dwellings. Service was being performed in the usual manner, the priests were bowing before a tinsel cross, and and praying (in a language of their own) to a coloured print of "Our Lady," in a gilt frame. There were the customary chauntings, the swinging of censers, the creaking of chairs, the interchanging of glances, and the paying of sous. Sins were confessed through a hole in the wall, and holy water was administered to the faithful, with a brush. Everything was conducted with perfect decorum, and was (as it seemed to an eye-witness) the most materialistic expression of devotion it were possible to devise.

Before the evening of the same day, we make a halt amongst the mountains. A few yards from us we see in the evening light a promontory; upon it some figures, motionless, and nearly the same colour as the rocks—Arabs watching the setting sun. The twilight has faded so rapidly into darkness that we can see no objects distinctly, excepting this promontory, on which the sun still shines through some unseen valley and lights up the figures as they kneel in prayer.

It was not the first nor the last time, that we had witnessed the Arabs at prayer, and had studied with a painter's eye their attitudes of devotion, the religious fervour in their faces, and their perfect *abandon*. The charm of the scene was in its primitive aspect, and in the absence of all the accessories, which Europeans are taught from their youth up, to connect in some way, with every act of public worship. Regarding the scene from a purely artistic point of view, we can imagine no more fitting subject for a painter than this group of Arabs at their devotions—Nature their temple, its altar the setting sun, their faces towards Mecca, their hearts towards the Prophet, their every attitude breathing devotion and faith.

THE FORT-NAPOLEON KABYLIA.

THE curtain fell upon the Kabyle War at the time of our first visit, and detachments of troops were at once told off to build a fort about two days' journey on horseback from Algiers. All around, on every promontory and hill, the little white tents were scattered thickly, and the sound of the bugle and the sight of the red képis of the soldiers, prevailed everywhere. The long war with the Kabyles, the mountain tribes, was practically over, and civilians came up from Algiers—some to see, some to trade—and quite a little colony sprung up. And here, on one of the heights shown in the sketch, we establish ourselves again. Whilst the Kabyle villages still smoulder in the distance, and revenge is deep in the hearts of the insurgent tribes, "one peaceful English tent" is pitched upon the heights of Beni-Raten, and its occupants devote themselves to the uneventful pursuit of studying mountain beauty. The view from this elevation is superb—north, south, east and west, there is a wondrous landscape, but northward especially—where far above the purple hills, higher than all but a few snowy peaks, there stretches a horizontal line of blue, that seems almost in the clouds. Nothing gives such a sense of height and distance, as these peeps of the Mediterranean, and nothing contrasts more effectively, than snowy peaks in sunlight against the blue sea.

All this we are able to study, in perfect security and with very little interruption; sketching first one mountain-side clothed with a mass of verdure; another, rocky, barren, and wild; one day an olive-grove, another a deserted Kabyle village, and so on, with an infinite variety which would only be wearisome in detail. It is generally admitted (and we should be unwilling to contest the point), that English landscape is unrivalled in variety of cloud effects, and that it is chiefly *form* and *colour* that we study with advantage in tropical climates. But directly we ascend the mountains, we lose that still, serene atmosphere that has been called the "monotony of blue." We read often of African sun, but very seldom of African clouds and wind. To-day we are surrounded by clouds *below* us, which come and gather round the mountain-peaks and remain until evening. Sometimes just before sunset, the curtain will be lifted for a moment, and the hill-sides will

be in a blaze of gold ; again the clouds come round, and do not disperse till nightfall, and when the mountains are once more revealed, the moon is up, and they are of a silver hue.

The air is soft on these half-clouded days, in spite of our height above the sea; and the showers that fall at intervals, turn the soft soil in the valleys into a hot-bed, as we should call it in England. The weather was nearly always fine, and we generally found a little military tent (lent to us by one of the Staff) sufficient protection and shelter, even on this exposed situation.

But we are not likely to forget the winds that lived in the valleys, and came up to where our tents were pitched—

sometimes one at a time, sometimes from three or four points of the compass together. It is a common phrase, to speak of "scattering to the four winds"; but here the four winds came and met near our little camp, and sometimes made terrible havoc. They came suddenly one day and took up a tent, and flung it at a man and killed him; another time they came sighing gently, as if a light breeze were all we need prepare for, and in five minutes we found ourselves in the thick of a fight for our possessions, if not for our lives. And with the wind there came sometimes such sheets of rain, that turned the paths into watercourses, and carried shrubs and trees down into the valley; all this happening whilst the sea was calm in the distance, and the sun was shining fiercely on the plains. These were rough days, to be expected in late autumn and early spring, but not to be missed for a little personal discomfort, for Algeria has not been seen without its storms.

Before leaving Kabylia, let us, from our note-book, just picture the rather incongruous elements of which our little society is made up. There has been a general movement lately, amongst the conquered tribes, who are beginning to re-establish themselves in their old quarters (but under French rule), which brings together for the night about a hundred Kabyles, with their wives and children.

Around the camp this evening there are groups of men and women standing, that bring forcibly to the mind, those prints of the early patriarchs from which we are apt to take our first and, perhaps, most vivid, impressions of Eastern life; and we cannot wonder at French artists attempting to illustrate Scriptural scenes from incidents in Algeria. There are Jacob and Joseph, as one might imagine them, to the life; Ruth in the fields, and Rachel by the well; and there is a patriarch coming down the mountain, with a light about his head as the sun's last rays burst upon him, that Herbert might well have seen, when he was painting Moses with the tables of the law. The effect is accidental, but it is perfect in an artistic sense, from the solemnity of the man, the attitude of the crowd of followers, the background of mountains which are partially lit up by gleams of sunset, and the sharp shadows cast by the throng.

This man may have been a warrior chief, or the head of a tribe; he was certainly the head of a large family, who pressed round him to anticipate his wants and do him honour. His children seemed to be everywhere about him; they were his furniture, they warmed his tent and kept out the wind, they begged for him, prayed for him, and generally helped him on his way. In the Koran there is a saying of similar purport to the words "happy is the man that hath his quiver full of them"—this one had his quiver full of them, indeed, and whether he had ever done much to deserve the blessing, he certainly enjoyed it to the full. From a picturesque point of view he was a type of beauty, strength, and dignified repose—what we might fitly call a "study," as he sat waiting, whilst the women prepared his evening meal; but whether from a moral point of view he quite deserved all the respect and deference that was paid to him, is another question. As a picture, as we said before, he was magnificent, and there was a regal air with which he disposed the folds of his bournous, which we, clad in the costume of advanced civilisation, could not but admire and envy. He had the advantage of us in every way. He had a splendid arm, and we could *see* it; the fine contour, and colour, of his head and neck were surrounded by white folds, but not concealed. His head was not surmounted with a battered "wide-awake," his neck was not bandaged as if it were wounded, his feet were not mis-shapen clumps of leather,

A WARRIOR AT PRAYERS.

his robes—but we have no heart to go further into detail. There is a "well-dressed" French gentleman standing near this figure, and there is not about him one graceful fold, one good suggestive line, one tint of colour grateful to the eye, or one redeeming feature in his (by contrast) hideous *tout ensemble*. These are everyday truths, but they strike us sometimes with a sort of surprise; we have discovered no new thing in costume, and nothing worth telling; but the sudden and humiliating contrast gives our artistic sensibilities a shock and fills us with despair.

A little way removed there is a warrior on horseback at prayers, his hands outstretched, his face turned towards the sun. It is as grand a picture as the last, but it does not bear examination. He came and sat down afterwards, to smoke, close to our tent, and we regret to say that he was extremely dirty, and in his habits, rather cruel. There were red drops upon the ground where his horse had stood, and his spur was a terrible instrument to contemplate; in the enthusiasm of a noble nature he had ridden his delicate locomotive too hard, and had, apparently, sometimes forgotten to give it a feed. It was a beautiful, black Arab steed, but it wanted grooming sadly; its feet were cracked and spread from neglect, and its whole appearance betokened rough usage. Perhaps this was an exceptional case, perhaps not; but to the scandal of those whose romantic picture of the Arab in his tent with his children and his steed, are amongst the most cherished associations, we are bound to confess that we have seen as much cruelty as kindness, bestowed by the Arabs and Kabyles, on their horses, and incline to the opinion that they are, as a rule, anything but tender and loving to their four-footed friends.

The Kabyles came round our tents in the morning before leaving, and the last we saw of our model patriarch, was flying before an enraged *vivandière*, who pursued him down the hill with a dish-cloth. He had been prowling about since dawn, and had forgotten the distinction between "meum" and "tuum."

Another day, there is a flutter in our little camp, for "the mail" has come in, in the person of an active young orderly of Zouaves, who, leaving the bulk of his charge to come round by the road, has anticipated the regular delivery by some hours, scaling the heights with the agility of a cat, and appearing suddenly in our midst. If he had sprung out of the earth he could not have startled us much more, and if he had brought a message that all the troops were to leave Africa to-morrow, he could scarcely have been more welcome. And what has he brought to satisfy the crowd of anxious faces that assemble round the hut, dignified by the decoration of a pasteboard eagle and the inscription *"Bureau de Poste."*

Some of the letters were amusing, one was from a boot-maker in Paris to his dear, long-lost customer on the Kabyle hills. He "felt that he was going to die," and prayed *"M'sieu le Lieutenant"* to order a good supply of boots for fear of any sudden accident, "no one else could make such boots for Monsieur." And so on, including subjects of about equal importance, with the latest Parisian gossip, and intelligence of a new piece at the "Variétés." One other letter we may mention, that came up by the same post, to one other member of that little band, perched like eagles on the heights; it was also unimportant and from home, and the burden of it was this—"BROAD-TOUCH" had stretched ten feet of canvas for a painting of one rolling wave, and "INTERSTICE" had studied the texture of a nut-shell until his eyes were dim.

Conclusion.

IF the foregoing sketches have seemed to some readers a thought too slight and discursive, and to be wanting in details of places, it is because, perhaps, they have reflected a little too naturally, the habit of a painter's mind, and have followed out the principle of outdoor sketching, which is to "hit off" as accurately as possible, the various points of interest that come under observation, and, in doing so, to give *colour* rather than detail.

But for this, perhaps, most readers will be thankful, and for two reasons. First, because it is a fact, that English people as a rule, care little or nothing for Algeria as a colony—that they never have cared, and probably never will. Second, because, in spite of the assertion of a late writer, that "Algeria is a country virtually unknown to Englishmen," we believe that the English public has been literally inundated with books of travel and statistics on this subject.

It is only in its picturesque aspect, and as a winter residence for delicate people, that Algiers will ever claim much interest for English people. Algeria has, however, one special attraction, in which it stands almost alone, viz., that here (within four days' journey from England) we may see the two great tides of civilization—primitive and modern—the East and the West—meet and mingle without limit and without confusion. There is no violent collision and no decided fusion; but the general result is peaceful, and we are enabled to contemplate it at leisure; and have such intimate and quiet intercourse with the Oriental, as is nowhere else to be met with, we believe, in the world. In fine, for artists, Algiers seems perfect; a cheap place of residence with few " distractions," without many taxes or cares; with extraordinary opportunities for the study of Nature in her grandest aspects, and of character, costume, and architecture of a good old type. And what they really gain by working here is not easily written down, nor to be explained to others; nor is it all at once discovered by themselves. It has not been dinned into their ears by rote, or by rule, but rather inhaled, and (if we may so express it) taken in with the atmosphere they breathe. If they have not produced anything great or noble, they have at least infused more light and nature into their work, and have done something to counteract the tendency to mannerism that is the curse of modern schools.

But not only to artists and amateurs—to those fortunate people whose time and means are as much at their own disposal as the genii of Aladdin's lamp; to those who can get "ordered abroad" at the season when it is most pleasant to go; to those who live at high pressure for half a year, and need a change—not so much, perhaps from winter's gloom as from "clouds that linger on the mind's horizon"; to all who seek a new sensation, we would say —pay a visit to the "city of pirates," the "diamond set in emeralds" on the African shore.

Cheap Edition, Demy 8vo. Cloth, 5s.

RANDOLPH CALDECOTT

A Personal Memoir.

By HENRY BLACKBURN.

With One Hundred and Seventy-Two Illustrations.

London: SAMPSON LOW, MARSTON, & COMPANY, Limited,
ST. DUNSTAN'S HOUSE, FETTER LANE, LONDON, E.C.
1892.

A few Copies remaining of the Original Edition, Royal 8vo. Cloth Gilt, 14s.

OPINIONS OF THE PRESS.

"In the late Randolph Caldecott we have lost a humorous designer of rare distinction and originality. . . . In other men you detect certain traditional habits of race, inherited defects; just as Goldsmith tells us that the family of the Blenkinsops could never look straight before them, nor the Hugginsons blow out a candle. Mr. Caldecott betrayed no hint of his artistic progenitors, and if he imitated no one he was equally difficult to imitate. His success 'in the line of children' prompted many rivals but no equals, and their efforts only serve to show how uncapturable was his spirit of fun and frolic, how intangible his delicate and winning gift of grace."—*Saturday Review.*

"We do not hesitate to give a high place amongst Christmas books to the memoir of Randolph Caldecott. It is written by a friend and fellow-labourer, one who knew the artist well; written most sympathetically and adorned with a copious and representative collection of drawings."—*Spectator.*

"Caldecott had in him the makings of an artist in the stricter sense. The drawings, paintings, and reliefs which he exhibited at Burlington House and elsewhere failed to make much impression through the timidity of their technique; but they had sterling artistic qualities nevertheless. In Mr. Blackburn's book two or three of his reliefs are reproduced, and we are enabled to see how excellent they are in arrangement of mass and rhythm of line. "Going to Cover" and "A Horse Fair in Brittany" would make beautiful friezes, so far as their length would go."—*St. James' Gazette.*

"Mr. Blackburn's sympathetic book exhibits his friend and fellow-labourer in a most attractive light. . . . He had qualities which not more than four or five English artists could approach."—*New York Tribune.*

"Mr. Henry Blackburn, the art critic, so widely known as the editor and originator of the "Academy Notes," has written this personal memoir with the object of giving some information as to the early work of this artist. Randolph Caldecott's Picture Books are known all over the world, they have been widely discussed and criticised, and they form undoubtedly the best monument to his memory; but certainly the material here collected will aid in forming a better estimate of Caldecott as an artist. To all those who love art and the narration of a singularly pure and successful career in it, Mr. Blackburn's memoir will be as 'welcome as the flowers in May.'"—*Sydney Morning Herald.*

"Mr. Henry Blackburn's 'Randolph Caldecott' is a very charming book. It tells the story of the artist's early life, his fondness for art, and his many experiments in modelling, decorative work and the like. The illustrations are produced with remarkable success."—*Graphic.*

"By all means set high upon your list this book, which is not only a biography but an autobiography, in right of its illustrations; and in right also of the many genial and humorous letters of the artist it contains."—*Truth.*

"This is a delightful volume."—*Pall Mall Gazette.*

www.ingramcontent.com/pod-product-compliance
Lightning Source LLC
Chambersburg PA
CBHW030423300426
44112CB00009B/830